THE
JOYFUL CHILD

THE
JOYFUL CHILD

A
SOURCEBOOK
OF ACTIVITIES
AND IDEAS
FOR
RELEASING
CHILDREN'S
NATURAL JOY

by
Peggy Jenkins, Ph.D.

ASLAN PUBLISHING

Published by
Aslan Publishing
3356 Coffey Lane
Santa Rosa, CA 95403
(707) 542-5400

The author wishes to thank the following publishers:

Harvest House Publishers, Inc., for permission to reprint text from *Daily Power Thoughts,* copyright © [n.d.] by Robert H. Schuller.

Foundation for Inner Peace for permission to reprint text from *A Course in Miracles,* copyright ©1975 by Foundation for Inner Peace.

Impact Publishers, Inc., P.O. Box 1094, San Luis Obispo, CA 93406, for permission to reproduce text from *Playfair: Everybody's Guide to Noncompetitive Play,* copyright ©1980 by Mat Weinstein and Joel Goodman. Further reproduction prohibited.

First Edition published by Dodd, Mead & Company, Inc.
Second Edition published by Harvest House Publishers, Inc.

Library of Congress Cataloging-in-Publication Data:

Jenkins, Peggy Davidson
The joyful child: a sourcebook of activities and ideas for releasing children's natural joy by Peggy Jenkins.—3rd ed.
p. cm.
Includes bibliographical references and index.
ISBN 0-944031-66-8

1. Children—Religious life. 2. Creative activities and seat work.
3. Joy—Religious aspects. I. Title.
BL625.5.J46 1996649'.51
QBI96-20153

Copyright © 1996 Peggy Jenkins

Cover Illustration by Theresa Smith
Set in Linotron 202 Trump Mediaeval.
Printed in the USA
Third Edition

To our teachers of Joy—
the children
And to the Joyful Child
within each of us—
longing to be released.

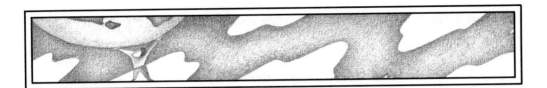

Contents

Part Two: Activities to Release Children's Natural Joy

ACKNOWLEDGMENTS

I first give all-inclusive thanks to God and the higher beings whose help I so often called upon and so lovingly received.

I thank both Arnold Patent and Torkom Saraydarian for the inspiration of their thoughts on joy. Arnold's espousal of universal principles was a major impetus for this book.

I extend appreciation to Sathya Sai Baba for his Education in Human Values Program. Its five teaching methods provided a valuable framework for the activities in the book.

Heartfelt thanks go to friend Alice Rice, who acted as a midwife for *The Joyful Child*. Alice was with me throughout the long birthing process—supporting me, encouraging my ideas, contributing a wealth of material, editing and proofreading my chapters. She was a wonderful gift from the Universe.

I owe a debt of gratitude to my son, Ric Davison Griffin, for taking over all the household responsibilities when my husband of the time was hospitalized during the final months of the book's preparation. Ric's emotional support, level-headed suggestions, and word-processing help were invaluable.

The book would not be nearly so readable if it were not for the meticulous editing of Jeffrey Lockridge. Accolades to Lee Britt for her editing help also.

I am forever grateful to Mary Kennan for her vote of confidence and her marvelous encouragement.

My warm thanks to Dr. Robert Muller and to Dr. Marjorie Timms for their valuable contributions to this work.

It took writing this book for me to realize how much I am loved and supported. So many friends called to encourage me and to let me know they were sending love and light. My appreciation goes to them and to all who gave energy to the book in this way. Such unseen help was as valuable as any visible help I received.

ABOUT THE BOOK

This book is not just for the children in your life. It is also for you. As you learn to guide your children's discovery of joy, your awareness will expand and you will grow more in touch with your own inner joy.

The Joyful Child is both a source and a resource book. Between its covers is a wealth of ideas and activities. In addition, it is liberally sprinkled with quotations and references to lead you to a wide variety of excellent resources.

I have not tried to say everything about the subject of releasing children's inner joy, but rather to point the way to your own inner knowing and discovery.

The book is divided into three parts. Part I sets the stage for the activities in Parts II and III and should be studied first. It provides the philosophical framework, which you will transmit to your children below their level of awareness (as explained in Chapter 3).

Consider how you treat new ideas. As you encounter the new ideas in this book, choose the approach that will give you the best possible results. See whether Dr. Schuller's thoughts on this subject align with yours:

> Often we hear the question: How do you treat people? A far more important question is: How do you treat ideas?
>
> > Treat them tenderly . . .
> > > They can be killed quickly.
> > Treat them gently . . .
> > > They can be bruised in infancy.
> > Treat them respectfully . . .
> > > They could be the most valuable thing that ever came into your life.
> > Treat them protectively . . .
> > > Don't let them get away.

> Treat them nutritionally . . .
>> Feed them and feed them well.
> Treat them antiseptically . . .
>> Don't let them get infected with the
>> germs of negative thoughts.
> Treat them responsibly!
>> Respond! Act! Do something with them![1]

As you may imagine, treating ideas in these ways will help you treat the people in your life equally well. Ideas that you don't accept or grasp can be placed on your mental shelf or back burner to be considered later. If they are truthful, they will re-emerge and become part of your thinking.

I wish you a joyful journey as you reflect on and respond to the views in the chapters that follow.*

---

*When referring to children in the singular, I have alternated gender, rather than using he/she, him/her, and so forth.

PART I

Philosophies and Ideas to Release Natural Joy

Life itself cannot give you joy
Unless you really will it.
Life just gives you time and space—
It's up to you to fill it.
CHINESE PROVERB

A Look at Joy

Joy is the most infallible sign of the Presence of God.
TEILHARD DE CHARDIN

The closer you come to your core, the greater is your joy.
TORKOM SARAYDARIAN

Spirit is pure JOY and you are spiritual in nature.
JACK BOLAND

Joy is you *at the deepest level, and your joy is one with
the infinite timeless joy of the unbound universe.*
ROBERT ELLWOOD

*The only obstacle to releasing joy is the unwillingness to
express love for someone or something.*
ARNOLD PATENT

Joy is not the absence of suffering. It is the presence of God.
ROBERT SCHULLER

The time to acknowledge joy has come. Joy, as an expression of love, is a healing energy much needed by humanity and the planet at this time. It is my reason for writing this book. I would like everyone to learn to discover and release the joy within. All the ideas and activities presented in the book have that intent. Consider them as stepping-stones in strengthening our children's natural joy and in renewing our own.

Joy has been called the greatest attainment in life. To discover joy is to return to a state of oneness with the Universe. Pure joy is the true nature of God and is therefore our birthright as children of God. The more joyful we are, the closer we are to God and the more in harmony with all life.

Since joy is our birthright, its source is internal, not external. It comes from within, from that intangible area called our soul. Society teaches our children that joy is only a greater degree of happiness and that both come from such things as a chocolate fudge sundae, a favorite TV program, a new car, or a visit to Disneyland. Like most people, I was raised with this common misconception, but I have come to see joy and happiness in a new light and to appreciate their important differences.

Happiness has its seat in the emotions. It is a reaction of the personality and occurs when the personality experiences conditions that satisfy its emotional nature. Thus, having a chocolate fudge sundae or winning a prize may produce happiness or pleasure, but not joy. Joy is a quality of the soul. It is realized in the mind, according to the sages, when personality and soul are in harmony.

Author Saraydarian explains joy as an electrical and fiery substance which radiates out from our core, which "flows through the nerve channels, muscles, bones, and bloodstream as electricity flows through wires," and which we will measure someday, as we now measure electricity.[1]

Unconditional love is our essence and joy is its expression. Joy is the presence of love for self and for others, a state of gratitude and compassion, an awareness of being connected to our higher self and of being one with everything. "There is no real and true joy if that joy is not imbued with love. Love cannot exist without joy."[2]

Joy is untouched by circumstances, whereas happiness is affected by what goes on around us. Joy grows in spite of conditions. Happiness does not. One can be in joy while unhappy. For instance, one can have pain or distress but feel the pure joy of "being," the awareness of Universal Love. When my husband was critically ill in the hospital I felt despair (at the level of my personality), yet also a joyous trust in the Universe (at the level of my soul). Many have felt joy well up amid drudgery, in a hospital bed, or even in a prison cell.

Saraydarian says it so well: "Joy is not the absence of hindrances, problems, and difficulties. On the contrary, joy is the flash springing out of each victory earned by the inner man through these obstacles. Joy grows in battle, in conflict, in service, in sacrifice."[3]

Joy is there awaiting our recognition and nurturance. Many of us, however, are skillful at rejecting joy. This stems from low self-esteem and cultural conditioning. As we align ourselves at deeper levels with the universal principles outlined in Chapter 2, we will expand the joy within ourselves and our children.

In *Bus 9 to Paradise*, Leo Buscaglia reports that for the ancient Egyptians joy was a sacred responsibility. They believed that upon their death the god Osiris would ask them two questions: "Did you bring joy?" and "Did you find joy?" Those who answered yes could continue their journey into the afterlife. Leo suggests that, now as then, these questions are the vital ones we should continually ask ourselves.[4]

I am reminded of the emphasis that Mother Teresa puts on joy. Her novices are told that in order for them to do their work they must discover the joy within themselves. She insists that they stay only if they can do their work joyfully.

Benefits of Joy

What are some of the significant benefits of joy? Why is it important? I quote a favorite excerpt on joy, from the book *Conversations with JC:*

> Joy is high energy. Joy, as an expression of God, is the source of all energy, all power. Aligning yourself with joy, choosing to fill your consciousness with joy, establishes within you a power that removes negative perception. You think joy is for your entertainment. I say to you, acknowledging and accepting the power of joy allows you to express so abundantly and in ways that are beyond your awareness now. Living in, expressing, and sharing joy is your wealth, your power, your vitality. . . . Staying in the high joy vibration is maintaining an awareness of joy no matter what conditions you perceive. Joy springs forth from within, No one makes you joyous; you choose joyousness. Choose it now.[5]

Joy is the gateway to higher levels of energy and to our higher development. We are called upon at this time to raise our energies, to expand our awareness. Joy and inner peace can help us do this.

Illness, financial hardship, unemployment, and family difficulties may seem to keep us from experiencing joy but, with a changed perspective, joy can be present through all of these. Understanding universal principles can help us gain this new perspective. We can choose to live in joy regardless of our outer circumstances. And living in joy will bring improvement to these outer circumstances.

Joy has long been recognized as an important factor in the restoration of health. Proverbs 17:22 tells us: "A cheerful heart is a good medicine, but a downcast spirit dries up the bones." Most people know how Norman Cousins healed himself from a life-threatening illness through joy and laughter. Many others are discovering that when they choose joy *first*, all that they need unfolds and increases: healing, prosperity, harmony, companionship, and inspiration.

When our mind is ordered, balanced, and confident, it works with maximum efficiency. When we are joyful, our powers and capabilities blossom. Joy sharpens our intellect and strengthens our memory so that we may better shape what lies outside us. We flow with the Universe, we see the purposefulness in all things, and we are at peace with life. Just as the physical body is nourished by food and drink, the soul is nourished by joy.

Saraydarian describes other benefits of joy in his *Joy and Healing:*

☆ The energy of joy expands our consciousness and our understanding.

☆ Joy makes our mind clear and our heart sensitive.

☆ Joy burns away impurities in our physical, emotional, and mental systems. It disperses worries, anxieties, grief, greed, irritation, and other negative emotions.

☆ Each moment of joy stays within our nature as a reservoir of energy for future use.

☆ Joy regenerates our whole physical, emotional, and mental systems.

☆ Joy expands the field of our magnetism and opens us to receive impressions, inspiration, and transforming energies from Above. Such contact profoundly enriches our creative abilities and lifts us to higher vibrational planes. Future, higher evolution will belong to those who live in joy, who share joy, and who spread joy.[6]

Choosing Joy

Releasing joy, remembering joy, choosing joy is what this book is all about. The Bible makes many references to choosing joy. Here are some well-known examples:

> Make a joyful noise unto God.
>
> Eat thy bread with joy.
>
> The joy of the Lord is your strength.
>
> This is the day which the Lord has made; let us rejoice and be glad in it.

And Jesus Christ said, "These things have I spoken unto you, that my joy might remain in you, and that your joy might be full."

Poet Don Blanding chooses a more graphic joy. In *Joy Is an Inside Job*, he writes:

> Finger the word "Joy" with your thoughts. Feel the tingle of its dynamic infectious energy. It is a force as real as electricity. Toss the word "Joy" around in your mind to know its buoyant lift. Chew the word "Joy" like a nourishing morsel, for the vitamins of well-being resultant from assimilating its stimulation. It is a force. Turn the word "Joy" like a lozenge on your tongue. Taste its spiced syllables. During the enjoyment of Joy we are transformed, literally.[7]

To those who say, "You can't just turn on Joy like a light," he responds: "You do not doubt, when you turn the switch, that the light will radiate from the light globe, because you know of the great dynamos. Have equal or greater reliance on the inexhaustible power of the Presence of Creative God and you will never doubt your Joy-Supply."

To release Joy we must know that at every moment we can express joy, if we choose. And we come to know that nothing is ever worth separating ourselves from joy, from others, from God.

There are two vibrational streams around us. We can choose the lower one of struggling and "efforting" or the higher one of joy. Joy is our natural state of being. It is what we are when we act in accordance with what is natural and truthful in us.

Some people object to feeling or expressing joy in the face of such conditions as war, crime, child abuse, drug addiction, and hunger. Is it right to feel joy when our brothers and sisters are suffering? The best way we can serve the world is to be in touch with our inner joy—the Spirit within us. When we are connected to this inner teacher, we know exactly what we must do. When we act from our center of joy, we serve humankind in the highest way possible.

We choose joy when we feel good about ourselves even though another puts us down. We expand our capacity for joy when we recognize the need for love in those who criticize us; when we let go of our self-doubt and self-criticism; when we *accept* new ideas, things, and people; when we let go of all expectations. The list could go on and on.

Arnold Patent, a seminar leader whose focus is on universal principles, reminds us that joy is always there within us and that the only obstacle to releasing it is our unwillingness to express love for someone or something.[8] This unwillingness usually takes the form of judgment. When we lay all judgment aside, peace and joy result. Letting go of what is blocking our flow of love allows us to express the joy that is truly our inheritance. Expressing our joy also frees those around us to open up to their inner joy, thus increasing the flow of harmony in the universe. Our commitment to expanding joy keeps it coming back to us.

The young child is often a beautiful example of joy. Around joyful children we feel the unconditional love that is at the root of all joy. We sense the deep peace within them that bubbles forth as joy. But what happens to children between kindergarten and ninth grade? What dampens their joy and enthusiasm as they move up the grades? Children become conditioned out of their natural state of joy by the messages they receive, messages that say it is not okay to be joyful because life is hard and full of troubles, scarcity, and limitations. As parents and teachers, how can we nurture our children's birthright, the natural joy of early childhood, so that it grows stronger instead of weaker with age? What life principles will lead children toward this goal? These questions are addressed in the next chapter.

Joy is life realizing what its parent,
the universe, God, if you wish, is, was always,
and shall ever be—joy.
ROBERT ELLWOOD

Foundations of Joy

et's look at three of the pillars that form the foundation for joy: self-esteem, human values, and universal principles. When these pillars are in place, we are able to discover and release the joy within.

Self-esteem

> *The greatest evil that can befall man is that he*
> *should come to think ill of himself.*
>
> GOETHE

We want our children to express the Joy of the Spirit—the gift of God within. But they can't if they don't like themselves. If they think of themselves as losers, if they suffer from low self-esteem, they will block their innate joy. You'll hear them saying things like "I'm dumb." "Stupid me." "I can't do it." "It isn't fair." "It's hopeless." "Why am I always the one picked on?" "I'm just a klutz." "He made me do it." "I'm lousy at everything." (For the classic symptoms of low self-esteem I refer you to L. S. Barksdale's excellent book, *Building Self-Esteem.*[1]) Low self-esteem is learned, and anything learned can be *un*learned.

Sound self-esteem is a feeling of self-worth, of self-respect, of being lovable. It is the greatest gift we can give our children. We help shape their future by our unconditional love and acceptance. We feel their joy when we hear them say, "I feel great." "I know I can ace that test." "I'm in charge of my future." "This is my choice and I'll take responsibility." "I'm going for it."

It is important to differentiate *self-esteem* (how we *feel* about ourselves), from *self-concept* (how we *think* about ourselves) and *self-image* (how we *picture* ourselves). Some authors use these words interchangeably, but I consider their differences important. When there is a conflict between our thoughts and our feelings, our feelings tend to dominate. They carry much more force. You can feel very angry and still think to yourself, "This isn't worth being angry about." Which usually wins out—the feeling or the thought?

Self-image and self-concept are often tied to our actions; but for sound self-esteem we must feel lovable *despite* our actions. We usually have many self-images and self-concepts corresponding to the areas of our lives, but only one overall gut-level feeling about our worth and lovability. For instance, we may have an image of ourselves as tennis player, dancer, speaker, gardener, artist, teacher, parent; and we may perform these roles well, not so well, or badly. None of these self-images or self-concepts has anything to do with our overall self-esteem. We can do well at all of the above and have low self-esteem, or we can fail miserably at many of them and have high self-esteem. Self-esteem has nothing to do with either image or performance.

A child must be able to fail at a skill or a test and know that it doesn't affect his identity, his worthiness. Bill misses the final shot that would win the game for his team. If he has low self-esteem, he thinks, "I'm a loser, I'm worthless, I might as well quit." If he has high self-esteem, he knows his self-worth is not dependent upon what he does, so he is willing to try again.

There is always somebody who can do better than we can, so if our self-respect is based on our performance, we are in big trouble.

The feeling of unworthiness that blocks our joy is most often buried deep in our subconscious, put there through subliminal messages. Most of our negative feelings about ourselves were fed into us when we were below the age of seven and; therefore, in a natural hypnogogic state—an alpha or theta brain wave level, where hypnosis takes place. Thoughts and feelings that go in at that level become strongly programmed. Overheard criticisms, put-downs, misinterpretations of parental anger or scoldings can all chip away at the child's self-worth and leave him feeling joyless and worthless.

Do our children get stuck in a feeling of unworthiness because of our thoughtless words? We can change that by becoming more aware and by choosing different words. Whether we call it supportive self-talk, affirmation, or auto-suggestion does not matter. What matters is that we become aware of the indelible impression our words and *thoughts* can make. This will be discussed further in Chapters 3 and 6.

Some parents and teachers use esteem-building statements with their children while the children are sleeping. This way they speak directly to the receptive subconscious mind and bypass the conscious mind, which can reject what it hears. Children may subject their subconscious to negative programming by dozing in front of the TV, by falling asleep with the radio on, and by waking up to either one. We can teach them, instead, to program themselves positively—to listen to tapes of self-esteem affirmations or to do supportive self-talk at the beginning and end of the day.

Many teachers and parents who have children say self-esteem affirmations report amazing results. I know of a kindergarten teacher who had her children say, "I like myself," three times each morning as they arrived in the classroom. Before long, disruptive behavior had fallen off and one child was telling another, "I like you now because I like me." Older children have made great strides with affirmations such as, "I am lovable and capable" or "I love and accept myself just as I am." Through constant repetition, these statements make an impression on the subconscious mind and eventually affect the feelings. A child's feelings about herself could be the single most telling factor in determining her level of joy. (For more on self-esteem affirmations see Chapter 6.)

"WHO AM I?"

Self-esteem affirmations are based on an understanding of our true identity. Are our children caught up in what Alan Watts calls "the conspiracy against knowing who you are"? Do they know that they are an eternal and precious part of the Source, a unique individualization of the perfection and wholeness of the Creator? Do they know that their very existence proves their worth and importance? And that no one is more or less worthy, more or less important than they are?

Do our children know that they are much more than their body, or their awareness, or their actions? The body is only a vehicle that helps us function on the earth plane, much as a car is a vehicle that gets us around. We can lose many parts of our body and not be diminished in our true identity, which is Divine Energy.

Our awareness comes from our total life experience and is limited, even though it keeps expanding. Therefore, it does not reflect our true perfection as an expression of the Source. However, we are always doing the best our awareness permits at any given point in time. Our motivation comes out of our awareness. It is a mistake to think, after the fact, that we could have or should have done better. We do the best we can at any moment, but a moment later we may have a different awareness.

Our actions reflect our true selves even less than our awareness does. Actions are what we do, not what we are. Ganz and Harmon explain it this way: "When you are told that you are good when you act good, and that you are bad when you act bad, you often accept the false concept that you are what you do. The hidden message that then goes into your mental computer is: 'If I act bad, I am bad; if I act good, I am good,' and 'I don't deserve to feel good when I act bad or when I make a mistake.' "[2]

In a school that I know of, some of the first-graders had begun physically hurting other children. The teacher had them role-play as animals. When one animal would "hurt" another, the "victim" would reply, "I love (or like) you, but I don't like what you're doing." Then the children started to say this to the ones who had actually hurt them. There was a dramatic change in behavior as children began to separate themselves from their actions.

L. S. Barksdale, a prominent researcher on self-esteem, suggests that we constantly affirm: "I accept myself totally and unconditionally as a unique and precious being, ever responsible for my own life, ever doing the best my current awareness permits, ever growing in wisdom and love."[3] You might consider putting this on a cassette tape and on 3 × 5 cards to review many times a day.

It is important to work on our own self-esteem because low self-esteem is *contagious*. Our children catch it from us. Whether teachers or parents, we must make it our personal priority to develop a high level of self-esteem. Total and unconditional acceptance of another is only possible when we can totally and unconditionally accept ourselves. Only when we have high self-esteem, in the deepest levels of our being, can we nurture it in the children whose lives we are molding. To paraphrase author J. C. Pearce, we heal our children by healing their models—ourselves. (For more on self-esteem, see Chapter 3.)

> No printed word, nor spoken plea
> Can teach young minds what men should be.
> Not all the books on all the shelves—
> But what the teachers are themselves.
>
> ANONYMOUS

All people, children included, have a deep need to know: Who am I? Where did I come from? Why am I here? Where am I going? We must help our children answer these unspoken questions. Childhood is the "preparatory age" for our mission—for what we came here to do. As parents and teachers, we help the child cope with the physical and psychic needs of earthly life. "But this should not be done in such a way as to produce a complete forgetfulness of whence we came, and whither we shall return, and the reason for our presence here."[4]

I believe it is important to remind each child often that she is a child of God. When children come to know that Mother/Father God is their true parent, it brings them great joy. The temporary losses, separations, and misunderstandings of life are not as traumatic.

Remind children also that they come from the Spirit World and will return there. Be on the alert for stories and descriptions of other planes of existence. As to why they are here, answer according to their understanding and to yours: to learn, to love unconditionally, to expand their awareness, to be truly helpful, to make the world a better place to live, or to be joyous are some of the answers you might give.
Here is a favorite quote of mine from Sathya Sai Baba:

> Know full well the task for which you have earned this human
> frame, with all its potentialities and possibilities.
>   It is to grow in love,
>   expand that love,
>   practice love,

strengthen love,
and finally become Love, and merge in
the Illimitable Love which is God.[5]

And another from him: "Man loves, because he is Love. He seeks Joy, for he is Joy. He thirsts for God for he is composed of God and he cannot exist without Him."

Values

The fate of men and nations
is determined by the values
which govern their decisions.

In a cross-cultural study of moral development, Harvard professor Lawrence Kohlberg found a common progression. Children in every culture moved through the same stages of moral development one stage at a time and always in the same order.

Children cannot understand moral reasoning more than one stage beyond their own. Kohlberg says that a child is drawn to reasoning one stage above his level because it resolves more problems, but that development to the next higher stage occurs only when there is conflict, when the child's outlook is not adequate to cope with a given moral situation. Faced with disequilibrium, the child searches for better and more adequate reasons.

I believe that basic values education corresponds to the conventional stages of moral development, where the goal is maintenance of the existing social order. Children need a sense of structure before they can move on to the principled stage, where people begin to act in accordance with ideals that transcend existing social conventions. This stage is explored in the section "Universal Principles." The rate at which people go through the stages of moral reasoning varies greatly and may be accelerated by the higher energies coming to the planet at this time. Transpersonal studies may determine that these are stages of soul development and not restricted to one lifetime.

Values education, often called character education, is a practical means of learning to choose the ways of living that are most conducive to inner joy and lasting contentment. It seems to be a first step for children as they evolve toward an understanding of universal principles. Juvenile delinquency, teenage pregnancy, substance abuse, and other social problems of the young make the need for such education apparent. Many observers feel that the very survival of our society, and of the world, depends upon a widespread renewal of commitment to an active moral life. Parents and educators are realizing the importance of returning to a curriculum that includes ethics and responsibility to our fellow humans.

According to a recent Gallup poll, Americans in overwhelming numbers say that they want schools to do two things. First, to teach children to read, speak, think, write, and count correctly; and second, to help children develop reliable standards of right and wrong that will guide them through life.

Former Secretary of Education William J. Bennett said in a speech, "If we want our children to possess the traits of character we most admire, we need to teach them what those traits are."[6] He went on to say, ". . . By exposing our children to good character and inviting its imitation, we will help them develop it for themselves. . . . We must have teachers and principals who not only state the difference between right and wrong, but who make an effort to live that difference in front of students."

Parents and educators are feeling the need for a plan of education that includes a life-building, character-making assimilation of ideas—a curriculum designed to help children practice values essential to civilization.

There are a number of such character-education programs available. A recent model that I favor because it is comprehensive, simple in design, and costs nothing to adapt is called Education in Human Values (EHV). Originated by Sri Sathya Sai Baba, chancellor of a university in India and founder of a network of schools there, the EHV Program has been adapted by educators to the cultures of many countries, including America.[7]

EHV finds that "through the philosophical, ethical, and legal literature of the world's cultural traditions runs a common thread of universal human values." The program identifies five basic values: TRUTH, RIGHT ACTION, PEACE, LOVE, AND NONVIOLENCE, and within each of these, a comprehensive list of sub-values. Included are the highest values of the world's great civilizations. Taken together, they provide "a developmental vision of our human potential." Thus, "the pursuit of TRUTH will lead to RIGHT ACTION; RIGHT ACTION promotes PEACE; PEACE enables LOVE to flow; and LOVE expands into NONVIOLENCE."

Let's take a look at what is meant by each of these values according to the EHV Program.

1. LOVE is the supreme value in life. It is not an emotional energy but an energy essence that radiates from each of us like light and warmth from the sun. It shows us the interrelationship of the basic values: LOVE as thought expresses itself in TRUTH; LOVE as action, in RIGHT ACTION; LOVE as feeling, in PEACE; and LOVE as understanding, in NONVIOLENCE (harmlessness).

The flow of Love is opened through developing self-respect and self-confidence. Aspects of Love are compassion, devotion, caring, joy, forgiveness, goodwill, trust, acceptance, sharing, generosity, patience, and understanding. Love in children is kindled by *our* modeling love.

2. TRUTH: Human beings are endowed with two marvelous faculties that can be developed in children to bring them closer to the realization of Truth: memory and intuition.

Memory is our ability to retain and recall information and knowledge at the right time. At the bedrock of the layers of memory is Truth. We can help children improve their memory through quotations, songs, and storytelling. Intuition is the wisdom of the heart. Often called the sixth sense or divine knowing, it is our power of insight and lies behind all sparks of genius. Intuition and creativity are facilitated by the mental calm acquired through meditation or listening within. (See Chapter 5.)

Some aspects of Truth are knowing, discrimination, honesty, optimism, quest for knowledge, self-knowledge, spirit of inquiry, and synthesis.

3. RIGHT ACTION. Truth in action is right action. According to the EHV Program, right action directs positive thought into purposeful and rewarding activities. It can be taught by the practice of such skills as the following: cooperation, responsibility, honesty, leadership, efficient use of time, speech and energy, listening, following directions, concentration on the task at hand, care of books and materials, punctuality, and personal hygiene.

Through the development of these skills, "children realize their potential to contribute to their own well-being and to the well-being of others."

4. PEACE is emotional equilibrium. It is our deep reservoir of inherent calm. This tranquil state, when temporarily hidden, may be found again through the disciplines that cultivate freedom from restlessness and stress. We need to offer children the means to withstand the pressures opposing inner peace, so that their inborn calm may sustain them even in adverse circumstances. Sitting in silence for a minute or two is a form of meditation recommended for young children.

Emotional balance is also acquired through self-esteem, friendliness, humility, honesty, fair play, sharing with others, respecting the right of ownership, and respecting the rights of teachers. The development of these qualities results in the elimination of such tendencies as possessiveness, greed, pride, jealousy, hatred, and anger—all stumbling blocks in the path of peace.

Aspects of Peace are contentment, inner silence, patience, reflection, satisfaction, self-acceptance, self-control, self-respect, understanding, and optimism.

5. NONVIOLENCE cultivates the child's respect for life and the elements of nature. It speaks to the essential oneness and unity of all creation. The root meaning of nonviolence is to be unhurtful to others by being benevolent. It is *harmlessness* in thought, action, and emotional reaction. It is consideration of others expressed in caring and helpful acts, a concern for equality, justice, and a sense of solidarity. It teaches constructive ways of resolving conflicts.

Children can come to realize that their thoughts, words, and actions all have an effect on the people around them. The more control they have over these expressions of their personality, the more they can help create a peaceful world.

The sub-values of Nonviolence are either psychological, such as compassion, concern for all life, cooperation, and good manners, or social, such as brotherhood, citizenship, social justice, equality, service to others, and appreciation of other cultures and religions.

To teach these values *directly*, the EHV Program suggests five methods that I have incorporated into the activities section of this book (Part II): silent sitting or tuning in, singing songs, learning quotations, listening to storytelling, and participating in group or creative activities.

Values education sets the scene for a tranquility that allows children to explore their inner selves and discover their joy. With these five standards for behavior, children can learn to ask themselves, as they count on the fingers of their hand: Is it loving? Is it truthful? Is it harmless? Is it right action? Does it bring peace?

Universal Principles

> *The outer education is concern for humanity.*
> *The inner education is oneness with humanity.*
> *If there is no concern, there can be no oneness.*
> *But if there is oneness, then concern is*
> *automatically there.*
>
> SRI CHINMOY

One could compare the "outer education" to values education and the "inner education" to universal principles.

The inner-directed stage of development is more complex and creative, and requires a higher level of understanding. Such an understanding has nothing to do with our physical age. At this stage we must often toss out earlier ways of looking at the world.

Universal principles are truths that have been revealed by the mystics of the ages, confirmed by the philosophers, and proven true by the scientists in the laboratory of life. These principles are immutable—they do not change with time or place or situation or person. They cannot be bent. They are forever. We can find great comfort and security in the universality of these principles, which show us the interrelationship of all things.

I have often felt deprived that as a child I was unaware of the existence of mental and spiritual laws. It brought me so much joy when I discovered them, and I kept thinking how much more important they are to *all* children than the three R's.

Children deserve to know that such truths exist, even if they are not yet ready to work with them. Knowing that the Universe is not happenstance—that it can be trusted at all times—helps children claim their birthright of joy.

Let's approach the universal principles through a look at energy. All is energy. There is nothing that is not energy. It is the essence of the Universe. Unformed, invisible energy is always flowing into the human mind. It enters the mind pure and flows out of the mind formed with the pattern of thoughts that are in the mind.

Energy flows in circular spirals; what goes out comes back. It brings back to us what we have thought, felt, or pictured. This has been called the Law of Attraction.

This energy is so powerful that it will return to us abundance, health, and great joy, if that is the dominant pattern in our mind and feeling. By the same token, if our consciousness is permeated with thoughts of lack, fear, dis-ease, and unhappiness, then these are what will flow back into our lives.

As co-creators with the Source, we are the directors of the undifferentiated energy flowing through us. This energy is ours to use as a means to make our thoughts and feelings manifest or take form. It is our choice and responsibility to attain full mastery over it and to direct it into the highest forms that we can conceive. This would include such qualities as unconditional love, trust, compassion, acceptance, serenity, harmlessness, and joy.

The key is our consciousness. The more we align our consciousness with universal principles, the more available this energy will be to us. The more we open ourselves to its flow through us, the more we open ourselves to abundance, health, and creativity. And the greater our self-mastery, the greater our joy.

The following universal principles or cosmic laws can help us use our energy in ways that will enhance our innate joy. By their nature, the principles tend to overlap. Many are just another way of explaining the most fundamental law, the Law of Cause and Effect.

Countless books have been written about these principles, so in a single chapter like this, I won't try to explain each one fully or even to mention them all. My approach to them was inspired by many teachers, most recently by Arnold Patent. Arnold has done an outstanding job of identifying, listing, and capsulizing twenty-four universal principles; sharing them has become his life's work.

THE LAW OF PERFECTION. The One Presence and One Power in the Universe is impartial Love, and it expresses its wholeness and perfection through Universal Laws. We, as human beings, are inherently whole and perfect expressions of Perfect Love, our Creator. By beholding that perfection in ourselves and others, we bring it forth. We have free will, however, and can use it either to see clearly what is whole and pure in ourselves and our children or, by distorting our vision, to see something false. The principle to keep in mind is that whatever we view as less than perfect is an illusion. There is Divine Perfection (an immaculate concept) behind every manifest form.

Polly Berends, author of *Whole Child, Whole Parent*, clarifies this by saying, "A clear picture of the perfect child in the parent's consciousness, which sees all imperfection as irrelevant to the child's true being, allows the child to develop truthfully with the speediest and most effortless falling away of all irrelevant behavior."[8]

I have in my file a beautiful example of someone choosing to live by the principle of perfection. It is a copy of a letter that I have found very inspirational over the years. I have no idea who the author is but feel certain she would not mind sharing it.

> I want to write you about my eyes. Whereas I was blind, now I see. It has been a great thing to get away from New York; away from myself. I have learned to demonstrate—and I am going to tell you what the wonderful secret is, for it is wonderful.
> Now, it is this: not to see or hear or repeat any kind of imperfection. It is seeing, hearing, and repeating good, and good only,

at all times, under all circumstances, in spite of everything that appears to the contrary.

I make the resolution every morning when I first open my eyes, and review it every hour of the day. I see perfection, a perfect cause and perfect effect, perfect God and perfect man, and refuse to make any kind of exception—I refuse to admit the slightest imperfection in myself, in my friends, in my so-called enemies, in my affairs, in the affairs of the world.

I take my stand for the perfection of God, and everything and everybody He has made. I look upon the world with God's eyes and see it as He sees it. I refuse to see in any other way.

I stop a dozen times a day to renew the resolve and to make sure that I am not repeating error, giving way to fear and criticism. I watch my thoughts even about people—the lame, the old, the unlovely (to sense) that I pass—and the stray animals. I have taken my stand for the perfection of all things, and I will not, I absolutely will not, release the perfect standard.

The result has been simply marvelous, slow but marvelous. I am working again, not the way I used to work, but working. No more do I need glasses. They have become unnecessary.

The outward conditions are pictures of our inward thinking. To change the picture, one must change the thoughts that produce the picture.

This woman knew how to "let thine eye be single." She saw, not the world's many imperfections, but the single perfection behind them—the Perfection of the Universe. Her case may seem extreme to you, but she has certainly shown us that this illusory world will change in response to a change in our consciousness.

The principle of the spiritual perfection of the Universe is embodied in all the following principles. Some find it hard to reconcile values and principles, especially when it comes to seeing the perfection or purposefulness in everything. Sooner or later, we come to know that truth forever changes with our perspective.

Here is a simple explanation that most children can understand. Consider a bowl of sand. It looks gray, but consists of black and white particles. A tiny microbe in the midst of that sand would see only black and white mountains. A human being would see only a bowl of gray sand. A giant as big as the Earth would not even see the bowl of sand at all. Each entity correctly sees the truth at a *different* level—the level he's functioning from.

THE LAW OF ONENESS OR UNITY. Another fundamental truth is that, at the higher energy levels, we are one with everyone and everything on the planet. In this Oneness we are aware of our individuality, but cannot tell where we leave off and another begins. We are all within the Mind of Infinite Intelligence and, consequently, we all share the One Universal Mind.

Because our minds are joined, not separate, our thoughts and prayers can directly affect others. Because our minds are joined, consciousness can be transmitted without a word. An example is the "hundredth monkey" story, which is related in the next chapter. Because our minds are joined within the One Mind, new inventions and discoveries can come forth in many places at the same time.

In Chapter 14 of *Magical Child*, Joseph Pearce gives an excellent example, among many, of our oneness or unity. Researcher Dr. Charles Tart placed two people in separate isolation chambers a considerable distance apart. One person was connected to a polygraph, which recorded brain wave activity; the other person received shocks. The polygraph reading showed significant leaps at the precise instants the person in the other isolation chamber was shocked.[9]

Kinship With All Life is filled with amazing examples of our connectedness with other life forms.[10]

We can choose to focus on our separateness from others or to accept and feel our connectedness with all beings. The latter leads to joyfulness and peacefulness. As we expand our consciousness, we naturally bridge the gap of separation.

There is a corollary here that I keep in my awareness every day: "What is the highest and best for one is the highest and best for all." In my business dealings, family, and friendships, I work continually at applying this principle, remembering that my interests and the interests of others are truly not separate, but one. It has been a real challenge at times.

THE LAW OF CAUSE AND EFFECT. This is the most familiar and fundamental universal principle. In the East it is called karma, and in the Bible, "As ye sow, so shall ye reap." It says that every thought, feeling, or action has a corresponding result. This law enables us to create and guide our own destiny. We can take our life out of the area of "coincidence" into the area of choice. The whole of human life is cause and effect. There is no such thing as chance. That means that there are no accidents in the Universe and there are no victims, either. We are the creators of circumstances.

Emerson tells us: "Within yourself lies the cause of whatever enters your life." What we experience is either what we have agreed to experience or what we believe. "You get what you expect" is the way some people say it. Our expectations are often subconscious beliefs—they have been buried deep within us for ages—but we can find out what they are by looking at what we have. Remember what was said earlier about undifferentiated energy flowing into our mind? We attract the circumstances that are in alignment with the energy signals we emit. The good news is that we can bring joyous events and people into our lives by filling our minds with joyous thoughts right now.

Our joy is also enhanced as we realize this is not a world of happenstance. Nothing can come into experience uninvited. We are the "chooser" and if we have inadvertently created an experience not to our liking, we can diminish its effect on us by choosing a positive mental attitude toward it.

The Law of Cause and Effect is a wonderful teacher for us if we stay fully aware of how we "cause," and therefore create every minute of our lives. A corollary is the

Law of Magnetic Attraction, which says that whatever thoughts, feelings, and habits we entertain will attract others of like quality. In other words, "like attracts like"; fear attracts fear; love attracts love. Sometimes this is easier to remember than cause and effect when we are monitoring our thoughts and feelings.

THE LAW OF RECIPROCITY. Akin to the Law of Cause and Effect, this is also known as the LAW OF GIVING AND RECEIVING. Through it, we see that giving and receiving are the same. We give only to ourselves because we are all one. Giving leads to receiving, which leads to giving, and so on. We can give and receive joyfully, knowing that as we give we receive, and as we receive we give. Our receiving often comes from an unexpected source and always in the way most needed. Holding on to what we have only blocks the flow to us. The more we give, the more will come to us.

THE LAW OF ATTENTION. This can be stated in several ways: Where our attention goes, energy flows; what we focus on expands; what gets our attention gets us; thoughts held in mind produce after their kind. Or simply, energy follows thought.

A helpful way of approaching this principle is to think about what you want, not about what you don't want. Too often we put all our attention on the problem—we worry about it, we talk about it, we picture it—and then we wonder why it gets bigger instead of smaller, or wonder why, even when we manage finally to solve it, similar problems appear.

What we focus on expands, so if we focus on lack, doubt, jealousy, anger, self-pity, and such, we'll bring more of these into our experience. This is especially true if feeling accompanies thought, for feeling is the power behind manifestation. Consider thought as male and feeling as female. When the two are fully aligned, there is a mystical marriage and the result is manifestation. When our thoughts and our feelings agree that we are deserving of joy, we open the door to joy in our lives.

The principle of focusing on what we want to expand is an easy one to teach children and to learn from them. There are some object lessons around this idea in my book, *A Child of God*.[11] I also refer you to "The Magnifying Game" on page 70 of *Models of Love*.[12] It tells the story of how Mother Mary might have taught little Jesus to choose carefully what he gave his attention to. She teaches that whatever we give our attention, we give power, and so helps little Jesus to give power to the world of the Spirit, and not to the world of appearances.

A wonderful imagination stretcher for all of us is to look beyond what our five senses tell us and to see the Divine Essence in everyone and everything. This week we might practice seeing the lovable child in everyone, including ourselves.

ALIGNMENT WITH THE HIGHEST IDEALS. If we focus on our highest ideals, we will draw to ourselves energy of the highest vibrations. We will become aligned with all who are thinking that way. Conversely, if we indulge in low-level thinking, such as bigotry or jealousy, we unconsciously open ourselves to energy of the lower vibrations.

Our life is our laboratory in which to practice the best we know. We can encourage our children (and ourselves) to do everything for the highest purpose. For instance, if a child has an after-school job, he can see it simply as a means to earn money and gain work experience, or he can also see it as an opportunity to practice such universal principles as nonjudgmental cooperation, trust, compassion, and unconditional acceptance.

Start children early with thinking about the purpose for each activity. This will help them to focus on the highest ideal. It may be a daily purpose that constantly changes. Help them to reach for an ideal that has meaning for them, rather than a daily "to do" list. One child said her purpose for school that day was "to feel joyful by loving myself and others." When there are choices to be made, a child has a much easier time of it if he can see which choice aligns best with his purpose.

To align ourselves with the highest ideal, Arnold Patent suggest that we do an Ideal Day Exercise before we get out of bed. We do this by getting in touch with the joy we want to feel and then projecting it into the day's activities.[13]

In order to manifest the joy and perfection that is the truth of our child's being, we need to focus on it. Our primary job as parents and teachers is not to do things for our children—but to hold in our minds their perfection, their wholeness, their goodness, their joy. As Berends puts it, "The biggest task of parenthood is in thought."[14] What you know, feel, or see for your child, she can experience.

THE UNIVERSE IS AN UNFAILING SUPPORT SYSTEM. Ours is truly a benevolent universe when we choose to be in harmony with it. The Universe totally and unconditionally loves, protects, nourishes and supports us.

Our challenge is to let go and trust that this is true. Trust is the cornerstone of love. The more we trust the magnificent support we have from the Universe, the more we can open up to the love in and around us.

In *Magical Child*, Pearce points out how anxiety cripples intelligence. Much of a child's anxiety is absorbed from his parent. The more we, as parents, trust our Universe as an unfailing support system, the less anxious we, and therefore our children, will be. Someone once said that to trust the Universe is to know that all the rules are fair and that there will be wonderful surprises.

Keep in mind that your children may be aware of a level of support that you are unaware of—often in the form of invisible friends or guardian angels. Validate them by acknowledging their unseen world. Most of us know of children who were made fun of for having such friends and who then closed off that part of their awareness.

Another useful ability that young children learn to screen out is the seeing of auras. Pearce says in *Magical Child* that when a child reports seeing something her parent can't see, and has no grasp of, the parent is usually disturbed. This negativity is immediately apparent to the child, who can see the parent's aura change to red. Many such children admit that they don't see colors anymore because "it caused too much trouble."

When we focus on the ideal—on the *essence* of what we want, not the particulars

—our will is in harmony with the Universe and we get maximum support from it. Its power comes to our aid. The sub-principle is "The Universe Handles The Details," when we are truly aligned with our highest thoughts and feelings. It seems that the Higher Self goes out in all directions and draws to us the people, events, and circumstances that create what we want. This happens beyond the level of the mind.

Every day I see examples of the Universe handling the details of my life and that of my friends. Whenever I feel the need to meditate, it fascinates me how my busy phone will stay quiet. When the inspiration for this book came through, the Universe began sending all sorts of support: a publisher, an abundance of reference books and ideas, a word processor, a computer class nearby, friends willing to critique my writing. Have you noticed how information comes to you when you most need it? So often just the right book or "teacher" appears on our Path at the perfect moment.

The other day a friend of mine who teaches joyously called to tell me how the Universe had just handled the details in her life. The minute it became clear to her that she wanted to reduce her teaching load, the ideal teacher stepped forward to help—someone who had the skills, the same philosophy, and who very much wanted the extra work. Details are just one way we are supported when we are in alignment with the Universe.

INTUITION—OUR CONNECTION TO INFINITE INTELLIGENCE. To keep aligned with the highest thoughts and feelings regarding our children, or anyone, we can practice listening within. As we listen to our Higher Self, rather than to our personality or ego-self, we will feel the needless struggles and exertions in our life—our "efforting" —fall away. Listening to our intuition is a way of letting go and letting the Universe handle the details. An important aspect of listening is listening to our body. Our Higher Mind sends us physical signals to warn us when we are out of alignment with the universal principles.

UNCONDITIONAL ACCEPTANCE. To be unconditionally accepting of ourselves and others means letting go of value judgments. Our judgments come from not seeing the inner person, the real self. "Every time you judge," writes Bartholomew in *I Come as a Brother*, "understand what you are doing. You are stepping on somebody's neck in order to stand up that much higher, not in the world's estimation, but in your own."[15]

Some say that 90 percent of our mental activity revolves around grievances, grudges, and value judgments, many of which we aren't even aware of. They are ingrained habits, modeled by our culture and stemming from low self-esteem. Researchers in Ames, Iowa, observing parents and preschoolers at home, report that the parents used fourteen negative comments for every positive one, and that two- and three-year-old preschoolers received an average of 432 negative comments per day. Another study shows that teachers offer students three negative comments for every positive one. This is all the more significant when we consider that youngsters let in the negative more easily than the positive, and that those with low self-esteem may block out the positive altogether because "that's not me."

"Judgment stands as an obstacle to self-love," we read in *Living With Joy*. "By rejecting other people through your judgments, you have set up a message in your subconscious that you are only going to accept yourself under certain conditions. This leads to an inner dialogue of self-criticism."[16]

A Course in Miracles asks us to recognize that "judgment in the usual sense is impossible. In order to judge anything rightly, one would have to be fully aware of an inconceivably wide range of things; past, present and to come."[17]

Value judgment and compassion cannot exist together, states Bartholomew, because once you understand that a person can act no differently, you cannot judge him. He goes on to say that, due to the stronger energy available now, judgment is the killer of our consciousness in this particular decade.[18] Energy either expands or it contracts. Judgment causes it to contract and stop moving through us. This blockage can cause many difficulties. The axiom "what you resist, persists" may be appropriate here.

To release the energies blocked by judgment, it is necessary to forgive ourselves and everyone else. Forgiveness is not for the other person but for us—to free up our energy. Forgiveness really means the release of criticism and value judgment. It means giving up any desire for revenge. It starts with our willingness to see things differently, but that doesn't mean we have to *like* the other person's behavior. With unconditional acceptance, we know that each person is always doing the best he can, though perhaps not the best he knows. He is doing the only thing he can do to resolve a need.

As the Law of Cause and Effect states, we cause our own experience; at one level we have asked for the lessons received, and so has the other person. Each of us must choose between being "right" or being joyful.

ABUNDANCE IS OUR NATURAL STATE. And so is joy—and yet we tend to block both. The Law of Abundance gives us a beautiful opportunity to practice aligning with the highest thought and feeling. Remember that feeling is the secret of creating and what we focus on expands, so all we need do is to practice feeling abundant. Abundance takes many forms—friends, health, shelter, a fulfilling job, help and time when we need them most, vacations, creative ideas, just to name a few.

It is never too early to help children recognize the abundance in their lives—energy, toys, clothes, food, books, trips, pets, friends, allowance—and give daily thanks for it. Expressing gratitude is a beautiful way of focusing our energy on the things we would like to increase.

Children tend to be in tune with the Law of Abundance. It is usually the adult consciousness that blocks the natural flow of both joy and abundance in their lives. Let's teach them never to look to the material world for their abundance, but to look to the invisible energy surrounding them. The visible always comes from the invisible, via our thoughts and feelings.

Now Is All There Is. Troubling themselves over the past and the future—which, after all, do not exist—has cost both children and adults a lot of joy. Young children are so much happier than adults because they don't care about the past, and they don't try to control the future.

When we teach them to guard against anything that might happen, or to judge themselves by what *has* happened, we rob them of the Now, the only time there is to experience joy. There is no moment with more potential for peace and joy than the one at hand. "All life is in this day. Help your children stay in it."[19] Try to spend some hours with your children when you do not speak about anything that has to do with the past or future. Let them know that when they are facing a difficulty, they must be totally in the Now in order to tune into the guidance that is available to them.

Means and Ends Are the Same. Whatever means we select to achieve a result determines that result. "Let us perfect the means; the end will take care of itself," says Swami Vivekananda. He explains: "The realization of the ideal is the effect. The means are the cause: attention to the means, therefore, is the great secret of life."[20]

If a joyful life is the end we desire, we get it by discovering our inner essence, by experiencing joy, and not by efforting, straining, expressing anger or impatience. To achieve a peaceful family or classroom, we must think peace, and act peacefully, moment by moment.

How often do we think that our lofty end justifies an unworthy means? A warm, accepting, nonjudgmental child does not become that way through constant criticism. For a child to like herself, she must receive approval, not ridicule. If a child is to learn confidence, he must be encouraged.

To enhance your children's joy, nourish them with your joy. Encourage them to bring joy to all their activities.

The Mirror Principle. Others mirror back to us what is within us—in our consciousness. Or, to put it another way, how we perceive the world is a mirror of what is inside our minds. We attract people and events to show us part of our consciousness that we need to see more clearly.

Polly Berends speaks eloquently on this:

> We can look at the child as a sort of hand mirror in which we can perceive and improve our mental image of ourselves and life. . . . Our children are not images of ourselves but of our thoughts about ourselves. The image itself cannot be faulted or corrected, nor can we even fault or correct ourselves as causes of the image. In this mirror we do not see either our true selves or the true self of the child, but only the reflections of our beliefs about ourselves and about reality. So we must not view

what we see with fear or guilt or blame or any thought that gives reality to the image. . . . To try to correct the child is like putting a lipstick smile on the reflection of an unhappy face in the mirror. To correct or try to change ourselves is like putting a lipstick smile on the unhappy face itself. Both actions are absurd; only the knowledge of something truly happy can transform the face and the face's reflection with a genuine smile.[21]

To help maintain our inner joy and peace, we can use a hand mirror to remind us that what we experience is our state of mind projected outward . . . fear, doubt, confusion, lack—or love, peace, order, abundance.

The Mirror Principle is an ingenious device for revealing what we need to work on. It does not mean that if we meet a thief, we are one. It means we have a judgment against thievery, and it is that judgment we need to look at. We can serve others best by clearing our own mirror of consciousness so that they'll see nothing but their Divine Self. Unconditional love is the way. Any mirror that shows us other than love is not reflecting the truth of our being.

THE LAW OF LOVE. The love we are speaking of is Universal Love—*agape* love. It is the power that holds the Universe together, that allows us to know our oneness with everyone and everything. Love is total trust in the Universe. Love fears nothing.

We are constantly choosing to come from love or from fear. Dr. Jampolsky in *Love Is Letting Go of Fear* reminds us that our basic emotions are love and fear and that fear is really an illusion we've created with our free will.[22] It is not a part of the Creator, which is pure Love. Whenever we make ego-based choices, we are coming from fear. Anything we do, think, or feel that is not truly loving stems from fear. Pain can be a reminder that we are acting fearfully—and unlovingly—to ourselves or others. Without fear, the body would not hurt.

Let's keep asking ourselves if our thoughts, our deeds, our feelings are rooted in love or in fear. How much more peace and joy our children will feel when we speak to them, not from our fearful egos—not in rigid rules and orders and judgments— but rather from love.

To remind myself to keep looking through the lens of love, I took an old pair of glasses and taped the word "love" on one lens and "fear" on the other. I placed these where I was sure to see them every time I passed by.

Most of the previous principles have to do with choosing between fear and love. For instance, living in the Now instead of the past or future can eliminate a lot of fear. Knowing that to give is to receive and that abundance is our natural state diminishes fear of lack or scarcity. We expand our love as we relinquish value judging, and practice forgiving ourselves and others.

As it says in I John 4:18, "There is no fear in love, but perfect love casts out fear." What we put our attention on expands—so all we need do is choose perfect love, minute by minute.

The big Lie about Life
is that there is something to
fear.
The big Truth about Life
is that fear is an
illusion.
Let's get hooked on the big Truth.
RUSTY BERKUS, *Life is a Gift*[23]

In closing, universal principles tell us how our spiritual world operates. They are the natural culmination of human values, which lead up to them. Values education is a necessary stage in our human development. With standards to live by, children gain an inner peace that promotes the expansion of their consciousness. In time, they leave the stage of standards and duality and pass on to a higher one, when they accept the oneness and perfection of everyone and everything in our universe.

You can teach these truths in informal situations—getting dressed, riding in the car, taking a walk, at mealtime, during meal preparation and cleanup time. You might choose a principle or value to focus on each week with your children. Contemplating or meditating on your choice can give you some ideas of how to approach it at the child's level of understanding. Help children understand how guilt, anger, hurt, and confusion fade away, how every aspect of their lives becomes more joyous, when they learn to work in harmony with universal truths and principles.

There is nothing either good or bad
but thinking makes it so.
SHAKESPEARE

Who Is Teaching Whom and How?

GUIDELINES FOR PARENTS AND TEACHERS

CHILD OF LIGHT

Child of Light, I Bless You!
I think of you, I pray for you,
not in terms of what I think
  you need,
or what I think you should do or
  be or express.
I lift up my thoughts about you.
I catch a new vision of you.
I see you as a child of light.
I see you guided and directed by an
inward Spirit that leads you
  unerringly

into the path that is right for you.
I see you strong and whole;
I see you blessed and prosperous;
I see you courageous and confident;
I see you capable and successful.
I see you free from limitation
  or bondage of any kind.
I see you as the spiritually perfect
  being you truly are.
Child of light, I bless you!

AUTHOR UNKNOWN

The above blessing embodies the highest purpose parents and teachers could desire—to see children as perfect, unique, spiritual beings. This is unconditional love. Being a model of such impartial love is the greatest gift we can give children.

Children are very aware when love is present and when it is not. What we feel in our heart is what we really teach—not what we tell the child or make the child do, nor even, contrary to popular opinion, what we ourselves do. Research shows that the young child "imprints" our unexpressed thoughts and feelings: he learns to think and feel what *we* think and feel, what we do on the *inside*.

Transmission of Consciousness

The condition of our consciousness registers directly in the child's consciousness and it is accordingly translated into well-being or distress.

POLLY BERENDS

We now know that 95% of the child's learning process goes on automatically, through unconscious imprinting to the models available. This information, based on many research papers, was presented by J. C. Pearce to the Council for Excellence Through Self-Esteem and the Joyful Child Symposium.[1]

Pearce reported that, on average, only 5% of the young child's mind is available to us for conscious manipulation through verbal training. All our demands, instructions, and orders to modify the child's behavior address only 5% of his learning process. Our unexpressed thoughts and feelings teach his other 95%—*below* the level of consciousness. By age two, our children reflect back to us our hidden faults: they have imprinted who we *really* are and not who we *say* we are; Pearce noted that children are driven to follow their models at all costs.

He also shared a most appropriate quote from his meditation teacher, Swami Chivalasananda:

> Until that which you think, that which you feel, and that which you act and speak are a single integrated whole, not only are you at war with yourself, robbing yourself of your own energies, you fragment and split every child you come across automatically.

To me, this is what Berends means when she says that, sooner or later, children begin to take on the parents' errors in the form of their own mistaken beliefs. I applaud her thought that correction has to be made in the consciousness of the parent, and that it's really a kind of condemnation and trespassing to think that it is the child who must be fixed.[2]

There is a true story from a 1903 book on New Thought that illustrates this so beautifully that I'm going to quote it in its entirety. The story actually took place before the turn of the century, so you can see that these are not newfangled ideas. Brain researchers may only be catching up with what metaphysicians have long realized.

> Knowing that I was interested in all New Thought teaching, the father in this story came one day to see me, "to talk things

over," as he said. He plunged at once into the middle of his subject. He was a middle-aged man, well-dressed, well-kept, and a businessman to his fingertips.

"Now," he said, "I don't look like a crank, do I? You wouldn't pick me out of a crowd as being anything but what I look, a plain, everyday man of business, would you?"

I assured him he might set his mind at rest on that score.

"Well, I thought I would ask you point blank," he said, "because something has happened in our family which I call a miracle! No, I won't say that either. I mean that the effects seem miraculous. That's the same thing with a difference. Now, let me tell you about it. Perhaps it will be an old story to you, but I tell you it's made a difference in our home—a big difference!

"We have an only child, a little girl, ten years old. She's happy and healthy, a bright child, and quick. Up to about a year ago what we went through with that young one you would never believe! You wouldn't believe me if I told you the things she did. It looked to me like obsession, as the spiritualists call it. She would get into frenzies of rage, stamp, bite, kick, smash things—anything and everything.

"We scolded her, coaxed her, whipped her, shut her up in her room, starved her—yes, I'm ashamed to say, we sent her supperless to bed many times—did everything we could think of—*all no good, no good, time wasted.* Just to give you an idea of the kind of things she did, here's an instance I remember: her mother had dressed her one day in a new suit of clothes, new shoes, all complete, and when she was ready to go out for a walk, what do you suppose the little rascal did? Ran up to the bathroom and locked herself in; turned on the water in the bath tub and rolled in it; spoiled everything she had on; and got a spanking for it! Well, that's only one instance in a thousand. Nothing we could do had any effect on her.

"One day my wife said to me, 'You are always talking about New Thought and the wonderful things it does for you in business, why shouldn't we try New Thought on Mabel?' 'That's different,' I said. 'Mabel is too young to understand and she wouldn't listen to talks about "All is good" anyway.' 'No,' my wife said, 'but you could put things in such a way that she *would* listen. You could praise her to me in her hearing, and I could echo what you say, and in that way we might undo some of the harm we have done!' I was astonished. 'Harm!' I said, 'What harm have we done? Haven't we given up our comfort and peace for this ungrateful little wretch? Doesn't she spoil all your happiness? Has she ever shown you any gratitude for all the love you waste on her?'

"But my wife cut me off short. 'That's just where we are wrong,' she said. 'You have put it all into words for me, and it's as clear as day. We are doing the child great harm. Every manifestation of temper she shows is something we have worked to bring about. We have made the child what she is, and now we must undo it if we can. You must help me. You must do most of the training at first, because she will notice more the things you say. You know, she is more afraid of you than she is of me.' That was a pretty hard thing for a father to hear, you know, because I have always loved the child and tried to do the best I could for her, but it was true.

"So we concocted our plot, if you like to call it so, and resolved to put it into effect forthwith. I had been doing most of the *talking* about New Thought in that family, but when it came down to the point of *applying* New Thought in the case of our own daughter I had to let my wife map out the plan and I followed directions. We had a good chance to begin that evening. At dinner Mabel upset the salt on the table when she thought I was not looking, and when I reproved her for it she burst into such a howl of sobbing that she had to be carried kicking and fighting out of the room. My wife looked at me in a very exasperating way as if I had made a mess of things, and said, 'You missed a good opportunity there!' 'You wouldn't have me praise her for upsetting the salt out of pure mischief, would you?' I said. 'No, but you don't understand,' she said. '*We* made her mischievous. *We* must get the mischief out of her head. We must overlook all her faults for the present and insist, insist always upon her goodness!'

"Well, I don't want to weary you by telling you how many times I had to bite my tongue to keep still. It seemed as if that youngster just romped in devilments of all kinds for the next two weeks, but every day when I came home I would pick her up in my arms and say, 'Oh! I've got the best and sweetest little girl in the whole world. There isn't any girl I know as good as my Mabel!' And my wife would say, 'She has been so sweet all day. She never gives me any anxiety now. I'm just as proud of her as I can be!' So that was the way we talked to each other about Mabel, and we took good care that she heard it all, too. I felt like giving up the game, though. We seemed to be making so little headway, and really it was like telling a lot of lies right straight along. But my wife generally has her own way about things, and she said she could see a difference in the child. 'You don't see it,' she said, 'because you are not with her, but I have watched her closely and I can see she is trying to do better.' The next day when I came home my wife met me in the hall; her face was radiant. 'It is all right,' she said, 'I'll tell you all about it later.' That evening Mabel climbed up on my knee of her own accord and put her arms about my neck. 'I'm going to be what you said I was,' she whispered, 'the best girl in all the world.' And that's what she is today. Her bad temper is all gone; she is anxious to help us; she is happy; she is like sunshine about the place. That's the way it happened."[3]

The lesson seems obvious. We teach children more by what our consciousness transmits than by any other way. Space makes no difference. A child a thousand miles away still lives in our consciousness through our fixed ideas of him or her. Many stories of thought transmission attest to this. It works because what is truly believed of others we awaken within them. The vibration transmitted by the belief persists until it awakens a corresponding vibration in the other person.

The sages advise us never to accept as true of others what we would not want to be true of ourselves. To awaken a state within another, we must first awaken it in our own consciousness. This is why there is wisdom in the Golden Rule. In the West we say, "Do unto others as you would have them do unto you," but I prefer the Eastern version: "Do *not* do unto another that which you would not have done unto you." More will be said on the Golden Rule in Chapter 4.

Another interesting story about how a young child imprints the consciousness in his environment is told in *Magical Child*. An Eskimo shaman took his five-year-old son, Ootek, and left him with a wolf pack for twenty-four hours. The cubs played with him, roly-poly, the entire time. As a result of his experience, Ootek learned what all the wolf calls meant. He could now tell his tribe what the wolves were saying: where to find a herd of caribou or locate visitors several hours away from camp.[4]

Probably the best-known story of the transmission of consciousness is *The Hundredth Monkey*[5]. It shows us that when enough of us are aware of something, all of us become aware of it.

The Japanese monkey, *Macacaa fuscata*, has been observed in the wild for over thirty years. In 1952, on the island of Koshima, scientists were providing the monkeys with sweet potatoes dropped in the sand. The monkeys liked the taste of the raw sweet potatoes, but found the sand unpleasant. An eighteen-month-old female found she could solve the problem by washing the potatoes in a nearby stream. She taught this trick to her mother. Her playmates also learned and taught their mothers, too. The scientists watched the spread of this cultural innovation.

Between 1952 and 1958, all the young monkeys learned to wash the sandy sweet potatoes. The only adults who learned to do this were those who imitated their children; the others kept eating dirty sweet potatoes. Then something startling occurred in the autumn of 1958. When the sun rose one morning, there were a certain number of Koshima monkeys who had learned to wash their potatoes—let's say the number was ninety-nine. Later that morning the hundredth monkey learned. Then it happened! By that evening, almost all the monkeys were washing sweet potatoes. The added energy of the hundredth monkey somehow created a consciousness breakthrough.

Most surprising of all, the scientists observed that the habit of washing sweet potatoes then spontaneously jumped across the sea—to colonies of monkeys on other islands and to the mainland troop of monkeys at Takasakiyama. It seems that when a certain critical number of us achieves an awareness, this new awareness may be communicated from mind to mind.

Children As Our Teachers

Just as these Japanese monkeys were taught by their children, so we are taught by our children. In fact, it has been suggested that our children are really here as our teachers and not vice versa. When we reverse roles and see them as here to teach us about life, we allow ourselves to experience much growth.

Dr. Ron Smotherman says, "You can learn more from a child about those things that mean the most to you in life than from any professor, psychologist, or theologian." How do they teach us? "Children teach by being, not by being full of information," he says.[6] One way their "beingness" teaches us is through mirroring. I have explained how our inner thoughts and feelings are imprinted on children below their level of awareness. Through imprinting, they become perfect mirrors of our state of consciousness. The young child will reflect our internal state. When we are at peace, the child is at peace. When we are anxious, the child is anxious, and starts acting out. Berends likens our children's behavior to a windsock indicating the directions of our true feelings.

In *The Children's Material*, we are advised: "Watch each student who comes before you closely. He is an expression of yourself which you have not allowed yourself to recognize. This is his purpose for being there, just as your presence is an opportunity for him to see aspects of himself reflected in you."[7]

Honest parents and teachers will look within and learn much about themselves, and about the lessons they are here to learn from the children. Giving unconditional love is a basic lesson for all of us, and the child is willing to put us through a lot to help us see how conditional our love may be. If we are giving to get in some way, the child knows it. The child's heart and soul longs for the parent's love, not for the material gifts so often offered in lieu of it.

Having a "teacher" in our home can awaken great joy if we are willing to see our child in this way. This requires looking beyond physical age and size, which have nothing to do with the soul's age. Although we may be bigger in body, our children can be spiritually wiser. One reason for this is that young children are not yet disconnected from their spiritual source through societal conditioning. Another is that many children are "old souls," who are returning to assist both humanity and earth, as we move into the New Age.

As parents and teachers, we are well-advised not to let our pride get in the way when we discover in these children an awareness and ability beyond our own. Many children are able to see and hear out-of-body beings and to exercise mind over matter. It is natural for children up to age seven to perceive things beyond the three-dimensional realm. Our responsibility is to acknowledge these natural abilities in both children and adults so that they are spared ridicule and rejection. If we are open, we will learn more from them than we teach them. Such learning requires us to become like little children—to be open and receptive to new ideas, and to the feelings of the heart.

When thinking of my children, I am always comforted by the immortal words of Kahlil Gibran on children:

> They come through you but not from you,
> And though they are with you, yet they belong not to you.
> You may give them your love but not your thoughts.
> For they have their own thoughts.
> You may house their bodies but not their souls,
> For their souls dwell in the house of tomorrow, which you
>   cannot visit, not even in your dreams.
> You may strive to be like them, but seek not to make them
>   like you.[8]

In reality, we are all brothers and sisters. We all have within us a spark of universal wholeness. Our children may be ancient friends. I often introduce my high school son as my teacher and I mean it most sincerely. One wonderful way he has taught me is to remind me when my awareness has slipped momentarily. For instance, I might say that something is making me angry and he'll remind me that I'm *choosing* anger. Lately, he has tuned into value judgments and catches me every time. I loved it the other day when I began to judge a situation and he asked, "What would Arnold Patent say about that, Mom?"

Often just his "being" will remind me of the universal principles when I most need reminding. I've learned much from his ability to stand back and not get caught up in the drama going on around him.

My daughter has been just as much my teacher in her own unique way. Since she arrived five years earlier than my son, and I was not as "aware" then, I did not always recognize her as a "teacher," even though I was learning from her daily. Asserting oneself, taking risks, being quick, efficient, and decisive are just a few of the things she has taught me. I have often felt that she is a wise old friend, come to support me by showing me another way of looking at the world. Often our children are here to teach us some very hard lessons, such as to love them unconditionally, no matter what they do.

A delightful little book that lets us see children as our spiritual mentors is *Learning From Children*. The author, Paul Welter, says, "The first step toward viewing children as master teachers is to get down to their eye level, or even a bit further down so that you can look up to them. The next step is to do something with them. As you do this, observe them closely and listen carefully to them. Finally, reflect on what you are learning about life from them."[9]

Welter discusses some of life's lessons that children teach us: having faith, trust, and hope; being honest and sensitive; expressing love; having a sense of wonder; being spontaneous; laughing, forgiving, creating, thinking; learning to play and sing.

How do children teach us? Welter suggest the following five ways:

☆ The child shocks or surprises the adult into considering a new truth.

☆ The child creates a peak emotional moment, which expands the inner vision of the adult, and the adult sees the world in a deeper, wider, richer way.

☆ The child entices the adult into playing, and the adult finds joy in a new way of life.

☆ The child serves as a model for the adult in some specific area, such as honesty, spontaneity, or the expression of love.

☆ The child loves the adult openly, and the adult learns what it feels like to be worthwhile.

Thoughts on Teaching

> *A child educates itself. The teacher spoils*
> *everything by thinking he is teaching.*
> SWAMI VIVEKANANDA

In his treatise on education Vivekananda says, "You cannot teach a child any more than you can grow a plant."[10] Plants and children develop according to their nature and all we do is help them go forward in their own natural way.

By their nature, plants know what nutrients they need to grow and develop. So it is with children, and what they need to be fed is love. Love is the "life-force" food they need above all else because love is what they are. It's everyone's true nature. Children need to know God has planted His love within them—within all of us— like the seed of a tree in the earth. Properly nurtured, the seed will grow into a tall and beautiful tree.

Because the Divine is planted like a seed within them, all knowledge and all power are also within them—within their soul. The true purpose of education, as its Latin root suggests, is bringing out the wholeness and perfection already there. This is the process of spiritual unfoldment. The true role of parent and teacher is to help children connect with what already lies within them—and bring it forth.

We can best serve our children by encouraging them to express the gifts they bring into this life and by teaching them what they *really* need to learn—not what we *think* they need.

Here is another thought on teaching: As you teach another you teach yourself. *The Children's Material*, the children's version of *A Course In Miracles*, states: "Learn well the concept you think you are teaching the child, for it is this very same lesson which you must learn also. Do not assume that because you are the 'teacher' you have learned the lessons. You would not be teaching them if this were so."[11] Therefore, we are advised to do our teaching well, for it is in this way we ourselves will learn. What we are teaching teaches us.

Teacher Preparation

Children need role models—the support of personal examples as models for behavior. This is why it's so important for the guiding adults to "walk the talk"—to "practice what they preach." Children need teachers who live peace, love, and joy from their inner core.

The stresses of daily living can create a tremendous gap between what we know to do and what we actually do. We often end up not modeling the best we know, and not showing the sensitivity and awareness that children need from us.

The answer lies in staying centered. Centering is an integration of mind and body that helps us develop a pool of inner stillness. Centering is coming back to our base of operation. It is calming ourselves and turning our vision inward. One way of getting centered is through meditation.

Teacher Michael Nitai Deranja says, "It has been my experience that regular, deep periods of meditation provide the most direct means of effective teacher preparation, even taking precedence over time spent on lesson plans or background preparation."[12] He points out four benefits of teacher meditation:

1. An increased awareness of student needs, such as sensitivity to their energy levels.
2. Discernment of the early stages of student frustration, when corrective action can be minimal.
3. Improved perception of student behavior, as meditation calms and clarifies the emotions and thoughts.
4. A deepened capacity for love and joy resulting in more loving relationships with children.

More important than any instruction is the love and creativity that emanates from teacher to children all day long if the teacher has centered early in the day. There are many ways people choose to turn their vision inward. Listening to music, visualizing, prayer chanting, and conscious breathing are some. Such centering allows the teacher to put the focus on the child, where it belongs, rather than on the lesson. Children know when what we're teaching is more important to us than they are.

*We teach what we are
and what others are to us.*
A COURSE IN MIRACLES

The Question of Praise

You may know that there is no such thing as constructive criticism, but did you know there is damage in praise?

Since praise is a tool so often used by parents and teachers, a word must be said about constructive versus destructive praise. Some forms of praise actually undermine the child's self-esteem.

This is true of *evaluative praise*, the most often used of the three types of praise. Evaluative praise makes a judgment. For example, "Excellent paper! What a good girl, that was a great job." Like a drug, it makes us feel good temporarily, but we get hooked on it. It generates a sense of dependency. Children may become so conditioned that they must receive this kind of praise in order to feel good. It teaches them to look to others for approval—for evidence of worth. Such children chase after approval, pestering adults for it because they haven't developed their own internal standards. "Do you like this, teacher?" "Is this good?"

Evaluative praise invalidates the child's inherent worth and implies that worth is proven through the approval of others. It identifies or locks them in with their actions. Children come to think they are what they do. Evaluative praise says one is good if one acts good, and one is bad if one makes a mistake. This identification with actions makes the child feel one's worth is proven by her achievements and conduct. It undermines self-esteem, since sound self-esteem is based on genuine love of self, and love of self requires unconditional acceptance of self. A child who equates personal worth with performance can never do well enough. There is always a higher standard or someone who can do better. This is a pathway to tension, stress, and misery.

There are other destructive aspects of evaluative praise. There is pressure in it —the child feels manipulated. And if only some children in the group are praised, others may feel very discouraged and inadequate. A child with low self-esteem is unable to accept praise because of feeling inferior; therefore looking on anyone who praises as either stupid or out to con for some advantage.

So what are the alternatives to evaluative praise? Simple recognition of a desirable act and appreciation of the benefits it brings. Children respond most favorably to this, for they sense they are being acknowledged as individuals instead of being evaluated on the basis of their actions. Such praise is called *descriptive praise* and *appreciative praise*. *Descriptive praise* describes instead of evaluates. It's a factual observation of an act that provides desirable benefits. Instead of "You did a good job washing the floor," descriptive praise says, "The floor is really spotless." *Appreciative praise* often follows descriptive praise: "I sure appreciate your help. Thanks."

As with all praise, comments should address what the child has done and *not* the being. She is not great for having painted a great picture. He is not good for having made his bed. The rule is to focus on the act and not the actor, on the deed and not the doer. The child is always "okay."

Descriptive and appreciative praise let the receiver interpret the message. It allows the receiver to think, "I'm a good worker," or "I'm a helpful person." It builds self-acceptance.

Take a moment to think before praising. Praise that most easily comes out of our mouths is evaluative or judgmental praise. "What a good boy you are." "That was an outstanding job." "You're so dependable." Such statements eventually damage self-esteem. Let's remember to describe and appreciate the desirable *actions*. This leaves the focus of evaluation where it belongs—inside the children themselves. Then self-worth is built, and not dependency. For more on this subject, see *Talk Sense to Yourself: The Language of Personal Power*.[13]

Television

In a chapter entitled "Who Is Teaching Whom and How" it would be remiss not to say a few words about television. TV is a parallel educational system that should be carefully examined.

The average American child has watched 6,000 hours of television before entering kindergarten at age five. The average American family watches more than six hours of television every day. Just what effect does this have on children and their state of joy?

TV affects the imagination and visual imagery. By projecting adult-created images, television stifles a child's imagination, the innate ability to create images, and thus cripples the ability to mature. Television fills the child's brain with a synthetic counterfeit of the images it is supposed to create on its own, according to researcher J. C. Pearce. The value of early childhood stories, with their metaphoric and symbolic characters, lies in stimulating and encouraging the child to form his own mental images. So it is with all verbal stories, whether read or listened to. Pearce tells of a child exclaiming that she enjoyed radio much more than TV "because the pictures are so much prettier."

TV has obliterated storytelling in most families—especially the important bedtime story. Stories play a valuable role in a child's development, as do imaginative play and daydreaming. TV interferes with all of these.

TV affects human relationships. It has supplanted valuable parent-child interaction. "The primary danger of the television screen," according to Urie Brofenbrenner, "lies not so much in the behavior it produces—although there is danger there—as in the behavior it prevents: the talks, the games, the family festivals, and the arguments through which much of the child's learning takes place and through which the character is formed."[14]

Many children are starved for love because TV makes it difficult for families to schedule time to express love in ways that are meaningful. A *Reader's Digest* poll indicates that the average American father spends less than 10 minutes a week of quality time with his children. However, he manages between 10 and 20 *hours* of TV watching.

The child not only has the TV-addicted parent as a model, but also accepts television characters as models for attitudes and behavior. Meaning, dignity, and worth are decided by comparing the self with the television characters.

Dr. Wayne Dyer has this to say about the effects of television:

> Continuous watching of television programs and commercials reinforces smart-alecky behavior (virtually all situation comedies use sarcasm and wisecracking as their basis for humor) and conveys the idea that being empty-headed and having a jiggly body is what women are all about, that pleasing others and achieving status are the primary purposes in life, and that happiness and success are external qualities that one purchases.[15]

A related issue is that television conditions children to see complex problems solved in 30 or 60 minutes. This creates a low tolerance for the frustrations of problem-solving in real life. Television provides no models for the patience and perseverance actually needed in relationship problems.

TV fosters violence through the images it promotes. Video images of violence are powerful motivators. A study by the American Academy of Pediatrics states that repeated exposure to TV violence can make children violent and accepting of real-life violence.

As it is, children think of violence as entertainment. TV has an inherent bias in favor of war, says Jerry Mander in the book *Four Arguments for the Elimination of Television*: "War is better television than peace. It is filled with highlights, contains action and resolution, and delivers a powerful emotion: fear. Peace is amorphous and broad. The emotions connected with it are subtle, personal and internal. These are far more difficult to televise."[16]

What we focus on expands. The constant attention given violence in the mass consciousness causes further violence to manifest.

TV affects the ability to concentrate and to read. Television's rapid pace causes children to be easily distracted, and impairs their ability to focus on the printed word. TV's short sequences discourage the continuity of analytical thought required in reading or in following any but the shortest and simplest speech.

TV hinders a child's spiritual development. The Vissells address this aspect of the subject especially well in their chapter on television in *Models of Love*.[17] Three key points:

1. TV pays scant attention to spiritual concerns, but instead draws the child almost fully into the material world.
2. When used to teach pre-reading skills and such, TV may over-stimulate the logical side of the child's mind, causing it to seek dominion over his intuition, his imagination, and the spiritual aspects of his being.

3. Although offered the child as "quiet time" by many well-meaning adults, TV may overwhelm rather than relax. Some quiet time is needed every day to process the events of the day, to resolve conflicts, and to reflect on "Who am I?"—if the child is to develop spiritually. But when the child watches TV, the Vissells go on to say, it fills the mind with other people's ideas and images, denying the freedom to discover alone. The child ends up frustrated, overloaded, and lacking in self-knowledge.

Watching television may have other adverse effects on our children, as well, but that need not blind us to its positive uses and possibilities. The real issue is not whether our children watch TV, but *how*. Television can be used to expand our children's awareness if we view it with them and discuss the values that are being portrayed. When we spot messages that we would not want in our children's subconscious, we teach them how to cancel them immediately, by overlaying them with a strong affirmation to the contrary. The subconscious operates on the last command given it. Help children know that they are complete and "okay" as they are. They don't need anything external to make them more complete. TV watching can be a time to help them rebel against the falsehoods the world considers as real. We can lead them from the false to the real.

The National PTA suggests that each TV have a card on top with the following words: WHO? WHAT? WHEN? WHERE? WHY? As children watch, adults ask questions, using one or more of these words. The child verbalizes what is seen, and the hypnotic effect of the TV is broken.

Thoreau said, "You cannot kill time without injuring eternity." We each have been given a precious twenty-four hours a day to use in the most constructive manner. If we teach our children to participate in life, to be active and involved, they will choose doing, over watching others do.

Attitude Guidelines

1. *As parents, we will have greater influence on our children if we become friends with them.* If we put friendship with our children first and parenting second, our relationship with them will be happier, healthier, more productive, and lasting. Whether or not we are good parents or the children accept our values, our relationship will endure if it is based on friendship. In the end, we will more strongly influence our children's values. And we will continue to have many more opportunities to learn from our "teachers."

If we want to be friends with a child, then we apply *all* the standards of friendship. We deal with the child as an equal, and are as open and honest as we are with any trusted friend. We show the same respect and consideration that we show our other friends. For instance, we generally don't make decisions for friends or do things they can do for themselves. Nor are we afraid to tell a friend that we don't have an answer or don't know how to handle a situation.

2. *As parents, we should remember that we can give our children what they need without sacrificing our own needs.* Children can be taught to understand and respect our needs, if we learn to put ourselves first, and not our children. The kinder and more loving we are to ourselves, the kinder and more loving we can be to our children. There is joy in being around parents who love and accept themselves. It rubs off on their kids, and they, in turn, are a joy to be around.

"If parents are doing what is right for them, if they are feeling joyful and happy, fulfilled and creative in their own life, then their child is receiving the greatest amount of energy possible from the parent."[18] The ideal of sacrifice is no longer appropriate. When we radiate joy, creativity, and fulfillment, those around us are also uplifted.

3. *As teachers, we should keep an attitude of openness about all information.* It is important that we not present today's knowledge as the final truth, or we will fail in our soul's task to help open up human consciousness.[19] Much new knowledge will be available in the coming days. We can tell our children that these are the ideas that people have believed until now about such and such, but that doesn't mean they are necessarily true, much less true for all times. We can encourage children to go within to see if these ideas are true, or we can ask, "What if there were more to know? What would it be?" Memories might come to mind.

Remind children that they are all "entities" fully knowing, but that right now they are involved in a game of *not* knowing. Ask them to step outside that game and to tell you the best way to handle the situation. What is the most helpful response? Allow for wisdom and you'll probably get it.

4. *Avoid reward and punishment.* Such behavior causes the child to identify with actions and feel "less than" when a mistake is made. Remember that the child is not the action and each is doing the best current awareness permits. We are all doing the best we can with what we know at the moment.

If a child's behavior is unsatisfactory, do not scold. Instead work on expanding awareness in the indicated area. Help to expose the pros and cons of a particular action, instead of threatening punishment. When we need to withhold privileges, make certain it is seen as a natural consequence of a choice made—not as a punishment. At such times, our children need to know that they are loved for their intrinsic worth as unique and precious beings—not for how they behave or what they achieve. Separate them from their performance. Never see them as failures. They may experience disappointments, but they won't feel they are failures until we teach them that by our reactions. Feeling like a failure is a learned response we can help eliminate from their lives.

5. *Children learn best from those they love.* They also learn more when they're having fun. There is a university professor in Arizona who teaches a scientific subject that requires remembering a lot of facts. He decided to test out the idea that

students would learn more if they were relaxed and having fun. Each day he surprised them with some form of fun or relaxation. Sometimes it would be the crazy outfit he was wearing. At other times he would have all the chairs removed and pillows on the floor. The result was that he was able to teach in three weeks what used to take six months!

6. *Look upon each child as a child of God.* If we have the privilege of serving even one of these children we are blessed. It is a privilege that many don't have.

We can serve children most effectively if we feel the presence of God living inside of them. Sri Chinmoy tells us that "the way to feel the presence of God inside your children is to feel His presence inside yourself first. Then it is easy to see the presence of God inside others. If you maintain your own divinity within yourself, then no matter whom you see, that person will be a projection of your own divinity."[20]

To paraphrase Dr. Louise Hart in *The Winning Family*, there is no one right way to parent or teach. Find the way that works for you. Learn to trust yourself. Learn to take good care of yourself, for you own sake and theirs. If parenting and teaching are not a joyful experience, look for new skills, new methods, and new strategies that will be effective in *your* situation.[21]

Why They Do What They Do

A LOOK AT BEHAVIOR AND LEARNING STYLES

"What a show-off! Why does she always have to be the center
   of attention?"
"He's so laid back! Why can't he make up his mind and do
   something?"
"Why does she have to ask so many questions? Who cares
   anyway?"
"He's always trying to control me! Why can't he let me do
   things *my* way?"

Children who make statements like these are usually encountering behavior styles that are different from theirs, and hence puzzling to them. Much joy is blocked when children don't understand why people behave as they do. Even more joy is blocked when the adults in their life don't understand or appreciate children's behavior and learning styles.

The Greek physician Hippocrates was among the first to identify four basic temperaments. German author and lecturer Rudolph Steiner has added much to the literature of human temperament, as has Swiss psychologist Carl Jung, with his theory of psychological types. Many others have made important contributions, and research continues. In January, 1987, *The New York Times* reported a long-term study at the University of Minnesota on 350 pairs of twins. It concluded that the genetic makeup of a child is a stronger influence on personality than environment. It pointed to the importance of treating each child according to his temperament, instead of trying to treat them all the same.

It seems that we come into this world with a basic temperament or behavior style (I use the terms interchangeably)—a characteristic and habitual manner of thinking, behaving, and reacting. Our behavior style reflects an inner need or drive to express ourselves in a certain way. Our temperament or style proves ultimately to be exactly right for our life purpose—our path of service and the lessons we must learn. Keirsey and Bates state it well when they say, "Nature will no more allow a child to come into this world temperamentally formless than she would allow a snowflake to be asymmetrical. Children are different from each other from the beginning, and no amount of preachment or 'conditioning,' or trauma for that matter, will diminish that difference."[1]

The more teachers and parents know about a child's behavior style, which is innate and need-driven, the more they'll be able to validate the child, thus building self-esteem and releasing joy. If "Why can't s/he be more like me?" is the unspoken plea, the child will feel the rejection behind it. With a "style" that aims to please, the child may deny the natural birth temperament, which is a strength, in favor of emulating others. In essence, a mask will be used, hiding the natural style and, thus, joy.

It gives children great joy to learn that there are basic behavior styles, each with its strengths and weaknesses, and that a weakness is only an overextension of a strength. Children discover that they have strengths—often for the first time in their life. Their new feeling of self-worth is unmistakable, a joy to see. They come to realize the futility of trying to copy a popular child whose natural behavior style is the opposite of theirs. With greater self-acceptance they are able to direct energy into more positive channels.

"Different Strokes for Different Folks"

Recently a sensitive teacher of gifted elementary school students asked her class what unit of study they would like to do next. To her surprise and delight, they came up with "getting along with different kinds of people." These students now understand why they do what they do, and why "different folks need different strokes."

An overview of the four basic behavior styles follows. For those who want more in-depth study, books and materials are suggested in the References and Resources section.

Here's an example of how various strengths are used in a typical situation. A Sunday school class was studying the story of David as a boy tending his father's sheep. They were given modeling clay and asked to make a figure of a shepherd boy.

Danny finished quickly and went on to fashion sheep, a sheep dog, and a wolf. No one would have known one animal from another if he hadn't told them.

Irene didn't finish—in fact, she never really got started. She was too busy entertaining the others.

Sam finished his project on time. It was a neat job, worthy of display.

Carole's work was exceptional. The folds of the shepherd's robe were done in detail but she was upset about not getting the curve of the crook he carried exactly right.

D I S C Children

Let's look at examples of these four very different types of children—**D, I, S, C** children. The letters stand for **D**ominant, **I**nfluencing, **S**upportive, and **C**onscientious, words which help identify the four basic behavior styles as described by some of today's behavioral scientists. You may be familiar with the terms used by Hippocrates—choleric (**D**ominant), sanguine (**I**nfluencing), phlegmatic (**S**upportive), melancholic (**C**onscientious). The **D** style has a need to direct others; the **I** style has a need to influence others; the **S** style needs to support or help others; and the conscientious **C** needs to do things the right way according to internal standards.

The ideal four-person team or committee will have one of each style. The **D** will generate ideas, the **I** will promote them, the **S** will follow through, and the **C** will watch the details and make sure everything is done right.

Keep in mind that temperament has nothing to do with character or morals. A person does certain things or reacts in certain ways, according to temperament, irrespective of upbringing, education, standards, or knowledge. Also keep in mind that no one shows signs of only one temperament, but usually has one or two that predominate.

D CHILDREN

Let's meet Danny and Dora Dominator. These are the "bold ones." They test the limits and appear fearless. They like action and challenge. The magic words are, "Think you can do it?" They have a short attention span for fine motor activities. Running, jumping, climbing, and action toys that go fast are more to their liking.

These children are natural directors and tend to dominate the group because of their leadership ability. They feel they have to lead in every situation because only they understand what is required and have the energy and insight. They are full of inner and outer activity, boisterous and impatient. As soon as they have thought of a plan, they want to put it into action, without allowing time for second thoughts.

Although good organizers, they have no patience for detail. They initiate things but then get others to do the work. They feel they can do ten things at once. Basically "loners," they dislike doing things by committee. Their "loner" status is often reinforced by rejection from children who are overwhelmed by their aggressive, risk-taking behavior. Without good communication and support from adults to help modify their behavior, **D** children become more and more alienated from a system where 80% of the others they meet are unlike them.

I CHILDREN

Now, let's meet Ivan and Irene Influencer. They can be recognized by their talkativeness and their need for attention and approval. They give all sorts of information, but their knowledge may be superficial or incorrect.

The **I** temperament is people-oriented and seldom does anything without others. The complaint, "There's nothing to do," usually means that there is no one to do it with. Irene's solitary hours are spent having her dolls talk to one another and relate as people. Talking is very important to **I** children, and families that don't have regular periods of talking may lose them to outside groups.

These children thrive on hugs, praise, and eye contact. They'll work for good grades to impress the teacher, or they may get only average ones because they're too busy socializing to study. They have a short attention span and will flit from one activity to another. "She's never still a minute" and "He's such a live wire" are frequent descriptions of Irene and Ivan. They are interested in whatever is new. They will promise anything and then forget it immediately. They are imaginative and have a lot of ideas that come and go. They notice everything and remember nothing.

As "act now—think later" children, their emotions are a combination of highs and lows. With their extreme optimism and enthusiasm about what people can or will do, they can easily be hurt. Adult guidance is needed to help **I** children set personal priorities and goals so that all their time is not taken up by trivialities or by others. They need much help in learning how to organize and follow through. They're without habits, living in the moment and adapting to the immediate situation.

These children like to give pleasure and so will do things as personal favors. They respond to love, not bullying. "Do it for me" is the magical phrase.

S CHILDREN

Sam and Sally Supporter are steady, reliable, and amiable. They are naturally calm and quiet. Their general attitude toward the world is "Leave me alone." This does not mean they are unfriendly. On the contrary, they are kind, thoughtful, and concerned about others. A natural reserve holds them back, but they are well-liked because they are easy to get along with and willing to accommodate others.

These steady **S** children are creatures of habit, and they keep to their habits. Security and routine are important to them: they want a regulated life with regulated hours and good square meals at set times. When there's to be a major change, they need to know about it far enough in advance to get mentally prepared. They fear change in the status quo and strive to keep things as they are.

Sally and Sam learn slowly but remember everything. They don't react quickly or give spontaneous answers, but the decisions they make are sensible. They are "think before they act" children, which is why adults find them "so easy to live with." They stick to a task until it is done and are remarkably consistent for their ages.

S children may need to be told to "get on with it." They can be pushed and ordered and, although they may grumble, they will obey. The challenge for adults working with them is not to take advantage of them. They need to be encouraged to stand up for their rights. Also, they need to learn to cope with anger or rejection from others when they say "no."

C CHILDREN

Carol and Chuck Conscientious are logical and analytical thinkers. They are able to judge the importance of things, and like to be given reasons for doing things, instead of being told, "Do it because I said do it." They are serious about life and want to produce quality work. This style, more than the others, is driven by its value system.

These children are perfectionists and don't do anything without a pretty good chance of success. Even though they are the most gifted, they have a poor self-image and entertain feelings of failure and incompetence. They set high goals for themselves, and when these are not reached, they can get very depressed. Because of their sensitive, artistic nature, it is easy for them to have their feelings hurt and to feel inferior. More than the other styles, the C needs an abundance of success.

This temperament tends to see the sad and gloomy side of life. Those who attempt to jolly them may be looked upon as frivolous. When their sympathies are aroused, C children will be most helpful and self-sacrificing. They identify with the suffering of other people. These children have the potential to be geniuses, but need much help and understanding so that they do not grow up to be pessimistic and self-pitying. The joy of the Spirit needs especially to be released in them.

C's are apt to ask searching questions: "Why can't we see God?" "Why do people act the way they do?" "Why did Grandpa have to die?" They have a great need to find out.

REMINDERS

Bear in mind that no person has a single behavior style. Most of us have a unique combination of the four, with one or two styles usually predominating. Also, please remember that a behavior style classification means only that we tend to use that behavior a lot. It is *not* who we are. We are never our behavior or our actions. This is an important principle of self-esteem. When we use the **D I S C** styles, we are labeling behavior only—not people. Most of us use labels all the time to describe people, usually uncharitable labels, because we don't understand the different temperaments and how a given temperament may respond to stress. When we gain that understanding, we tend not to label people anymore.

In speaking about behavior styles and their labels, Kathleen Butler says, "Labels can aid us to see further than we might see without them. The label can be a signal system to others about the way the person is likely to view the world. Labels should help us 'get on their wave length.'" However, in working with style labels, she asks us "to use labels as a departure point, not an ending point."[2]

And there is always the role of self-esteem to consider. With low self-esteem, our children use their natural strengths in a negative way—the leader becomes a bully; the gregarious person becomes fickle; the accurate person becomes nit-picky. Or they may create stress for themselves by adopting a behavior style that is not natural to them in order to please others. With sound self-esteem, our children will be comfortable with their natural style and use it to best advantage.

We want never to change a child's temperament, only to bring out the best in it. We do this by emphasizing strengths within the framework of values. Remember, the child's strengths are the abilities and talents chosen for this lifetime in order to accomplish soul's purpose—to learn her life's lessons. Understanding the child's inherent temperament can give both parent and child a glimpse into the child's life design. Acceptance of it can release much joy.

Children need to have their strengths pointed out to them, but they also need to be made aware of the strengths of others. In this way they may learn to harmonize their styles with the styles of others. Teach them about the four basic behavior styles and the spirit of the Golden Rule.

Spirit of the Golden Rule

The Golden Rule says, "Do unto others as you would have others do unto you." When we apply it literally and treat others as we want to be treated, we may alienate those with temperaments unlike our own. Better results could be obtained by teaching older children, "Treat others as they want you to treat them." But we need also to teach them about behavior styles, for without some understanding of behavior styles, they won't know *how* others want to be treated. Of course, all people want to be treated with fairness and love, but these words mean different things to different people.

Irene Influencer might think it's really entertaining, hence loving, to tell all the details of her vacation to a friend. But, if her friend happens to be the **D** style, which doesn't like detail and gets very impatient with long discussions, her account will come across as anything but loving. Or a **D**, who thrives on the unexpected and a frequent change of pace, might not understand why his **C** friend is upset over a late Friday afternoon invitation to go away for the weekend. **C**'s need time to think things through.

Sally Supporter hates surprise parties, so you can imagine how upset she was when Ivan Influencer thought that was the nicest thing he could do for her birthday.

To love your neighbor as you love yourself implies meeting the needs of the other person. Let's look at a couple of common areas where needs tend to conflict. One area is task vs. relationship. The pure **C** and **D** styles give higher priority to accomplishing the task at hand than to relating with others (unless that *is* the task, as they see it). **I**'s and **S**'s are more people-oriented and so give priority to relating with others. The implications are clear. An **I** trying to get along with a **C** could do well to stay focused on the task and to socialize later. On a committee, a controlling **D** who is sensitive to the needs of others would allow the **S**'s and **I**'s some time to relate before jumping into the task at hand.

Another area where the needs of the temperaments conflict is pace. In general, the **D**'s and **I**'s are fast-paced people who make quick decisions and take risks. They easily become impatient with the slow-moving and slow-thinking **C**'s and **S**'s, who like to think things through before making a decision. They need time to analyze, to count the costs. To be effective with our children we can adjust our pace to theirs, and we can also teach them about adjusting their pace to others', in the "Spirit of the Golden Rule."

These are just two areas where the styles are clearly different. The more your children know about the temperaments, the better they can be at treating others as they want to be treated, and the better they can adjust their own behavior style to harmonize the relationship.

However, if such adjustments are called for frequently, this can be stressful. For instance, a child who needs to analyze decisions would be stressed by continual prodding to make snap decisions. The **I** children, the natural verbalizers, would most certainly suffer in an environment where "children are to be seen and not heard." Or consider how hard it would be for the action-prone **D** to sit still for long periods and not be allowed the degree of control a **D** child so naturally seeks.

A LOOK AT FIVE AREAS

To further our understanding of these basic behavior styles, let's compare their differences in five areas: basic goal, influence on others, unique contribution to the group, overused behavior, and how to increase their effectiveness.

Area I. BASIC GOAL: Conscious or unconscious, the goal of the child's behavior pattern is to reach the place where the child feels "right with the world."

Four examples:

D Dora and Danny Dominator want to take charge—to control a situation, to face a new challenge. They are risk-takers, always willing to try, even if it means failing or exposing their limitations. These children are not concerned about being ridiculed. They dare to be different.

I   Ivan and Irene Influencer seek approval and popularity. To achieve these, they are willing to spend time with others. Homework and household tasks have to wait. They get involved in extracurricular activities for contacts and visibility. In competitive activities, their goal of popularity makes them good winners and good losers.

S   Sam and Sally Supporter need to help others and to keep things as they are. They wish to maintain the status quo because it is familiar, even though it may also be detrimental.

C   Carole and Chuck Conscientious strive to be correct, to avoid mistakes, particularly those that might antagonize others. These children like things in their proper places and set high standards for themselves.

Area II. INFLUENCE: Each temperament makes use of its particular strengths to influence others.

D   Danny and Dora rely on themselves to find answers. When Danny challenges his coach's decision, other children become aware of adult fallibility and begin to think for themselves. Dora dares to try a new hair style first.

I   Ivan and Irene influence others by praise and favors. "I wish I could draw as well as you!" "I will help you rake the lawn so we can go swimming sooner."

S   Sally and Sam influence others by their consistency of performance and their willingness to be accommodating. Friends can count on their ability to stick to a task and to adapt themselves to a diverse group of people.

C   Carole and Chuck influence others by their store of logical information and factual arguments. Their friends come to them when they need answers or explanations.

Area III. UNIQUE CONTRIBUTION TO THE GROUP: Those who have a clear idea of their abilities are better able to develop their sense of role and worth within the group.

D   Danny and Dora are of real value to any group because they avoid passing the buck and get other children off the hook. They seek new and innovative methods of problem solving.

I   Irene and Ivan are valuable to the group because of their gift for relieving tension. They do this by sharing how they are feeling and by volunteering first so that less confident children get a reprieve. They are the press agents for activities and the promoters of other children's skills.

S   Sam and Sally are easy to be around and maintain a steady pace that gets the work accomplished. Their value to the group lies in getting work done, and in bringing cohesiveness to the group.

C   Chuck and Carole bring value to the group not only by obtaining needed information, but also by defining, clarifying, analyzing, and testing it out. They work well on planning committees and with quality control.

Area IV. OVERUSED BEHAVIOR: The strengths of a behavioral pattern, when overused, become weaknesses. Adults can help children use their strengths appropriately.

D Children like Danny and Dora are self-confident. They tend to think their way is better than others'. But their self-confidence becomes overbearing when they boss others around to get their own way. For example, taking over other children's games—uninvited.

I Irene's and Ivan's desire to please others becomes a weakness when they over-praise. These children need help in giving praise that is deserved—not just saying what they think the other person wants to hear.

S Sam and Sally tend to overuse modesty and conservatism. They downplay the importance of their contributions so often that others finally believe them. They become stuck in the familiar and need to be pushed to try something new—for instance, something other than hamburgers when they go out.

C Carole and Chuck tend to over-concentrate on doing the "right" thing. They can become wet blankets because of this, spoiling everyone else's fun by being too conscientious.

Area V. HOW TO INCREASE EFFECTIVENESS: Offer suggestions that will help the child strengthen weaker areas and use stronger ones more productively.

D Danny and Dora, and others like them, are individualists who must live in an interdependent world. They can become more effective by learning patience and empathy through participation with others. Participation is easier for them if they are given the most challenging task in the group.

I Children like Ivan and Irene would increase their effectiveness if they learned to manage their time and balance their emotions. They need to develop a sense of urgency and must learn the consequences of dallying. Their tendency to see everything as either fantastic or terrible could be offset by learning to be more objective.

S Children with the behavioral style of Sam and Sally are more effective and happier when they receive sincere appreciation—not only for what they *do*, but for the kind of children they *are*. They need to learn to accept compliments and to make sure that they are not taken for granted. These children can also increase their effectiveness if they develop shortcuts instead of sticking to the early steps that are no longer necessary. Taking more risks would be appropriate for them.

C Chuck and Carole can feel happier and more effective if they gain confidence in themselves and a greater appreciation of others. They must learn to cope with conflict and to stick up for their rights. Also, they can learn to be more flexible and be willing to move ahead without every detail in place.

We're each a blend of all four of these behavior styles, which, in various combinations, make up a total of fifteen classic behavior patterns. These patterns can be determined by a scientifically validated educational tool called The Child's Profile, which is designed for ages 4–12.[3] There is also a teen profile, adult profile, and an interpretative guide for each of The Child's Profile patterns. In addition to the above areas, these guides discuss the basic fears and general disposition of each style; how each tends to judge others; and what each does under pressure.

Learning Styles and Stress

A wonderful way to help children discover their joy is to offer them instruction and activities that are compatible with their learning style.

Behavior styles can easily be translated into learning styles. The challenge of the adult is to create an atmosphere that will meet the needs of the child's temperament. Then the child will be self motivated.

If comfort motivates the **S** children, recognition the **I** children, authority the **D** children, and "getting it right" the **C** children, we clearly need "different buttons for different kids."

When parents or teachers do not take into consideration a child's learning style, they may encounter style-related stress. There are actually two kinds of style-related stress.[4] *Self-stressing* arises from inability to understand and to balance the various influences of one's style. This stressing is most severe when the child has two conflicting styles, such as **D/C** or **I/C** or **S/D**. Remember, we're not just one style. *Environmental stressing* occurs when the demands of the environment are mismatched to the behavior style of the child. The adult needs to consider the temperament of each child. What is a comfortable experience to one child may be most stressful to another. Such stress drains away children's energy and blocks the joy of achieving their potential.

Let's take a brief look at the four learning styles so as to better meet the child's needs. For a good working understanding of this subject, I invite you to delve into the literature. (See "References and Resources.")

THE DOMINANT LEARNING STYLE

D children, with the dominant learning style, need to exert influence, to have responsibility. Remember, the **D** temperament wants to be in charge. When **D** children are not motivated, ask yourself, "Do they have opportunities to voice their opinions or participate in decision making?" A degree of control or power is very motivating to children of this style. They thrive on opportunities to show their leadership.

Since **D**'s are risk-takers and challenge-seekers, unmotivated **D**'s may really be asking for more challenging work or opportunities. If a task is easy, **D**'s will not be interested. Let them know that it's difficult and that you don't know if they can handle it. Befriend them, challenge them, and solicit their help. Then you will have leaders, not bullies.

This style loves a change of pace and constant variety. **D** children are extremely impatient. Your instructions and explanations to them must be direct and brief, or you will lose them. They're task-oriented and want fast results. Since details are unimportant to them and they tend to rush through things, they will need help in appreciating the benefit of quality work. Help them also to see that the responsibilities they desire come from outstanding workmanship.

To function at their best, **D** students need physical involvement in their learning —a "hands-on" experience. They hunger for action and freedom and have trouble sitting still for long. The usual classroom approach to learning frustrates them, with its constant commands to "sit still," "do your homework," and "face the front of the room." Other classroom stressors for the pure **D** style are having to follow detailed directions, redo assignments, and work within a rigid time schedule or without the freedom to experiment.

The self-stressors for this learning style include a desire to try every new experience and to find every new approach to existing situations.

Because traditional teaching methods have little appeal to the **D**'s, they often drop out of school to go "where the action is."

THE INFLUENTIAL LEARNING STYLE

I children, with the influential learning style, tend to need recognition and approval from others—first from the adults in their lives, and later from their peers.

The greatest fear of **I** style children is rejection, so they become "nice" kids and seek to please parents and teachers. They are constantly checking the expression on others' faces. Love is the magic word—not punishment or criticism. Mentors must make themselves lovable to this child.

If these children are underachieving, you might ask, "Do they need more recognition, such as seeing their work exhibited or their names in print? Do rewards such as certificates, ribbons, trophies, stickers, or other visible acknowledgments seem to be especially motivating for them?" A personal note written on a composition can be a powerful motivator for this child, if the comments are positive. The **I** student needs to be recognized, known, and acknowledged by his teacher.

Since **I** children are socializers, the teacher who gives them an opportunity to work with groups will show them the social advantage of learning something together. However, **I** children may need assistance in planning their time carefully, since it can be lost in too much socializing.

I learners work well in a democratically run classroom and participate enthusiastically in group decisions. They learn from group discussions, from dramatic play, and from role-playing. They need to be personally involved with what they are learning. Some form of interpretive expression is important for them. They have a built-in desire to communicate in a personal way with others and thrive on two-way exchanges. **I** learners prefer cooperation to competition: even when they win they can suffer the pain of a loser because of their ability to identify with others.

Some of the environmental stressors for the **I** learner, as outlined by Butler, are having to do things sequentially, being separated from their friends as punishment, and having to carry their ideas and answers through to finished products.[5]

The ways **I** learners stress themselves include feeling inadequate when they displease important others, striving for high grades to gain praise and attention, having an overwhelming desire to be liked and accepted, being unable to control their feelings, and being easily hurt. They need our help to become more objective about themselves—and about others.

In summary, I quote Keirsey and Bates, who say this type of child "can be particularly responsive to teachers who are accepting and nourishing, who verbalize recognition of feelings, who individualize their instruction, who use lots of small group interaction, who genuinely respond to and accept the ideas of class members, and who avoid sarcasm and ridicule as a means of class control."[6]

THE SUPPORTIVE LEARNING STYLE

S children, with the supportive learning style, are "team people" because of their hunger for belonging—to the family group, the classroom group, the club group. They are motivated by the opportunity to be helpful and are the most loyal and dependable of the styles.

They fit into the traditional classroom better than any of the other temperaments. Most teachers have a lot of **S** in their own temperament and these children can understand them and relate to their methods. **S** students like workbooks and lessons presented sequentially, in increments that make sense. When they are underachieving, it may mean they are just asking that a task be more clearly explained to them, or that it be broken down into steps.

These students feel best associating with other children of varied interests. They aren't interested in objects or events, so they need to be stimulated by the interests of others to arouse the slumbering forces within.

They are also the best listeners of the four temperaments and have the ability to calm excited people. Therefore, they can help others gain a different perspective and settle their differences.

Loss of security is a primary fear of **S** students, so they resist change. A change of plans, a change of directions, or a change of teachers can throw them. Nor do they like long-term, independent projects or open-ended discussion groups.

Some other environmental stressors for **S**'s are incomplete or unclear directions, having to use new approaches when their own approach works well for them, unpredictable friends, messy rooms, and competition.

Self-stressors for them include an inability to manage their time, finish their projects on schedule, or organize their world the "right" way. In essence, this style creates stress by its need for order and predictability, and will profit from learning how to be more flexible.

THE CONSCIENTIOUS LEARNING STYLE

C children, with the conscientious learning style, are the most complex. They hunger for competency and have an endless list of "should know's." They revel in the world of thought and research, loving the intellectual challenge of discovering new ideas and new information. They look for whatever will enable them to understand, explain, predict, and control. They seek to structure their cognitive world according to definite rules and principles. **C** students prefer to acquire new knowledge, rather than waste their time writing about what they already know.

When they are underachieving, often they have given up reaching their own high standards. They figure if they give up, at least they won't fail. It's up to adults to help them reconsider their standards and establish priorities. The **C** students will benefit from taking a look at their choices and from realizing they cannot know *everything* and they haven't time to do everything *perfectly*.

As with the **I** style, learning how to manage time will be helpful to **C** children, but for very different reasons. They see so much to do that they become overwhelmed. They can easily feel overburdened. When **C**'s are underachieving, it is well to ask, "Do they need more time or fewer assignments to be satisfied with the quality of their work?"

It should also be asked, "Does the child need to know the rationale for the activity?" **C**'s are motivated when they can see a logical reason for an assignment, project, or rule.

The conscientious style has a fear of appearing inadequate—of making mistakes. These children worry a lot, thus hampering their progress. They have a built-in system of self-doubt and need the experience of frequent success to counteract it.

Like the **S** style children, **C**'s resist change and quick decisions. They want to know all the details and reasons. Unless you allow time for thoroughness, you could have a very de-motivated **C** on your hands.

These children are extremely sensitive to feelings—their own and others'. A harmonious environment is especially important to them; the lack of it can be discouraging.

Other environmental stressors, according to Butler, are teachers who insist on discovery learning, teachers and students who "fool around" in class, repetitive work, projects that require hands-on creations, too little time to study completely, and teachers who are not well-versed in their subject matter.[7]

Self-stressors for **C** learners include a tendency to equate grades with self-worth, a fear that they haven't studied long enough, and an inability to finish projects because they see the vast amount of knowledge still to be covered.

WHAT? WHO? HOW? WHY?

Related to their temperament, each style seems to have a favorite question:

> The **D** asks What? (What needs to be done? What's in it for me?)
>
> The **I** asks Who? (Who will do what? Who will I want to work with?)
>
> The **S** asks How? (How do I do this? How can I help?)
>
> The **C** asks Why? (Why are we doing this? Why is it necessary?)

LOOK – LISTEN – DO

There are visual, auditory, and kinesthetic learners. Some people learn best by looking at charts, slides, graphs, or written explanations, others by hearing the message, and still others by actually moving through it—by using their sense of touch. The last are the kinesthetic learners, and they learn by doing. Role-playing or acting-out situations helps them, or even writing out their assignments.

All three types can be found in all four behavioral styles. By careful observation, you can determine which way each child best absorbs information. Listen to the children's speech which uses visual words, "I see what you mean," "It looked that way to me"—and which uses auditory descriptors—"I hear you," "Sounds okay"—or feeling words—"How does it feel?" "It just doesn't feel right!" "I am not in touch with that."

As teachers or parents, we want to be sure that our learning preference doesn't limit the way that we teach. We need to speak on all three channels—auditory, visual, and kinesthetic. Talking on the channel best understood by a child can certainly release loads of joy.

IN CONCLUSION

Give your children the joy of knowing that we can all behave differently and still be okay. Teach them the strengths of the different temperaments and show them how an apparent weakness is just an overextension of a strength.

An ancient Chinese proverb says:

> Those who want to leave an impression
> for one year should plant corn.
> Those who want to make an impression
> for ten years should plant trees.
> Those who want to leave an impression
> for a hundred years should educate a human being.

When we understand behavior and learning styles, we are more likely to make a positive impression on our children's future. We will be preparing them for success, while enhancing their joy.

OUTLINE OF STYLES AND NEEDS

Adapted from Alice Rice, teacher of gifted children

By knowing a student's behavior style, you can help develop strengths and compensate for limitations.

A. The **D**ominant child needs:
   1. Opportunities for
      a. Change
      b. Leadership
      c. Freedom
      d. Accomplishment
   2. Support in
      a. Following through
      b. Finding challenges
   3. Adults who avoid
      a. Too much direction
      b. Win-lose tactics
      c. Personal criticism
B. The **I**nfluencing child needs:
   1. Opportunities for
      a. Prestige and recognition
      b. Interaction
      c. Enjoyment
   2. Support in
      a. Setting and meeting deadlines
      b. Finding new trends and ideas to promote
   3. Adults who avoid
      a. Rejection
      b. Negativism
      c. Arguments
      d. Public disapproval
C. The **S**upportive child needs:
   1. Opportunities for
      a. Ownership
      b. Sincerity
      c. Cooperation
      d. Predictability

2. Appreciation for
    a. Ensuring group achievement
    b. Improving current practices
    c. Helping personal growth of others
3. Adults who avoid
    a. Overloading
    b. Sudden change
    c. Competition

D. The **C**onscientious child needs:
1. Opportunities for
    a. Independent work
    b. Cognitive development
2. Support in
    a. Making realistic trade-offs
    b. Mapping out logical options
    c. Leading when risk is low
3. Adults who avoid
    a. Criticism of efforts
    b. Blunt or personal questions
    c. Incomplete or inaccurate directions
    d. Insisting on group activities

Behavior Style Summary

	D	I	S	C
	Dominant	**Influencing**	**Supportive**	**Conscientious**
BEHAVIOR STYLE	Dominant	Influencing	Supportive	Conscientious
TEMPERAMENT	Choleric	Sanguine	Phlegmatic	Melancholy
PRIORITY	The task: the results	Relationships: interacting	Maintaining relationships	The task: the process
PACE	Fast/Decisive	Fast/ Spontaneous	Slow/Easy	Slow/ Systematic
ACHIEVES ACCEPTANCE BY	Leadership Competition	Playfulness Stimulating environment	Conformity Loyalty	Correctness Thoroughness
FEARS	Loss of control Being taken advantage of	Fixed environment Loss of prestige	Loss of security Sudden change	Making mistakes Criticism of work or effort
GAINS SECURITY BY	Control	Flexibility	Close relationships	Preparation
SUPPORT THEIR	Goals	Ideas	Feelings	Thoughts
LIKES YOU TO BE	To the point	Stimulating	Pleasant	Precise
IRRITATED BY	Indecision Inefficiency	Routine boredom	Impatience Insensitivity	Surprises Inaccuracy
UNDER TENSION WILL	Dictate Assert	Attack, be sarcastic	Submit Comply	Withdraw Avoid
TO MOTIVATE GIVE	Power, authority Direct answers Instructions Challenging assignments Credit for achievements	Freedom to speak Recognition Opportunity to help	Structure Sincerity Explanations of how Traditional procedures	High standards Tactful instructions Explain why
WANTS	New/Varied activities To be first Power position Credit earned	To be convincing Social approval Favorable environment	Demonstrated sincerity Family approval Reassurance Appreciation	Limited exposure Quality Privacy Accuracy
DECISIONS ARE	Decisive	Spontaneous	Considered	Deliberate
WANTS TO MAINTAIN	Success	Status	Relationships	Credibility

Adapted from *Relationship Strategies Workbook*[8]

PART II

Activities to Release Children's Natural Joy

Feeling joy is a choice we make.
It's a natural choice when we're encouraged
with activities that connect us to our inner joy.

The Joy of Listening Within

Everyone eventually will join in this great
effort to follow his inner guide in all things.
Through listening, each one can tune in to his
own source of power and knowledge. To the extent
that we make the effort we will be rewarded. . . .

LEE COIT, *Listening*

Since the true source of joy lies within, the greatest gift we can give children is the time, the techniques, and the encouragement to go within.

Most of a child's day is heavily scheduled with input time and some output time, but seldom do we provide needed time out—quiet do-nothing time all alone, when the inner teacher can be heard. This can happen while lying on the grass, strolling through the woods, brushing a dog, or—in a formalized way—while meditating.

Listening Within or taking time out can make the rest of the child's time more effective and more productive. It's like throwing a ball. Only if we pull our arm back can we throw a ball very far. Indeed, the farther back we pull our arm, the farther we can throw. Life operates the same way. The deeper within we go, the more likely we are to tap our wellspring of energy, wisdom, and joy, and the greater our impact on the outer world. This can be further illustrated by having a child shoot an arrow from a bow or serve a tennis ball. Let the child experience the difference pulling back makes.

I use "Listening Within" to cover the spectrum from deep meditation to brief silent-sitting sessions. Quiet time, focusing, bio-feedback, centering, tuning-in, and guided imagery are other terms that are often used, although they are not synonymous.

THE STORMY SEA

As we turn within, we move to our center of peace and joy. Picture a stormy sea with high waves beating against a rocky cliff. A ship is tossed this way and that. Notice the quiet, the stillness at the bottom of the sea. The tossing waves tell us nothing of the undisturbed peacefulness below. It is only the surface of the sea that is involved in a storm.

The waves represent our outer life—full of activity and, sometimes, turbulence. In the depths of each person, just as in the depths of the sea, there is a point of stillness that we find when we "enter the silence." This is where we discover abiding peace and joy.

The analogy can be explained to children with pictures, or a film, or through guided imagery. Help them recognize that the "stuff" that is taking place in their lives is taking place only on the surface. By listening within they will discover the deep calm underneath. When they reach the depths of their sea, the waves of fear, doubt, guilt, and worry will not affect them—they will be centered in their stillness, where peace and joy abide.

Very young children know this naturally, and "entering the silence" is often done in the form of daydreaming or staring blankly. This is a natural meditative state—a biological rhythm that takes the child beyond the sensory world. You might notice when your child is in this state and encourage him to return to it on a regular basis.

Meditation

The art of meditation is Listening Within in its purest form. Learning to listen doesn't require meditation, but meditation can help. The word meditation comes from the Sanskrit, meaning "doing the wisdom," i.e., getting in touch with our inner wisdom.

Robert Ellwood beautifully describes meditation as "simply allowing the mind to take some time off to relax and just be itself." He says, "The great wonderful secret meditation holds is that when the mind is really stilled and really *is* itself—fully, without any holdbacks—it is identical with the deep joy at the heart of the universe. Meditation is stilling all that is not God and joy in the mind, so that the God-joy leaps through unimpeded."[1] Is this not what we want for ourselves and our children —this stillness in which joy can arise?

THE PURPOSE

The purpose of meditation is to commune with the Source of all Life, to experience the unity between what lies within and what lies without. Through uniting our lower mind with the Higher Mind, we recognize the Universal Center within as the source of true peace, joy, and inspiration. We can then allow that Presence to flow through us so that we might be of service to humanity.

BENEFITS

Joel Goldsmith in his classic, *The Art of Meditation*, cautions us: "Any meditation that has within itself a single trace of a desire to get something from God or to acquire something through God is no longer meditation."[2] Meditation is its *own* reward, and should not be entered into for any other reason.

Besides getting the meditator in touch with the fruits of the Spirit, such as joy, love, and peace, parents and teachers report many specific benefits for children. Some of the ways it has proven valuable:

☆ *Improved psychological health*. Children are calmer, less fearful, and happier with themselves. They are more aware of their feelings and better able to accept and express them.

☆ *Increased creative expression*. This is evidenced in artwork, speaking, and writing. (In Japan, highly skilled craftsmen have long meditated before starting an important piece of work, so as to better reach the inner source of creativity.)

☆ *Expanded sensitivity and awareness of all life*. Children become more tuned in to animals and plants and feel a greater oneness with others.

☆ *Activated intuition*. Meditation is one of the most effective ways of developing children's intuition—their direct connection to higher levels of awareness.

☆ *Enhanced creative problem solving*. Meditation helps children get in touch with all levels of their being. They have more personal resources to draw upon and get wonderful insights.

☆ *Increased ability to concentrate*. Children tend to be more alert and to have a greater attention span when involved in learning activities.

☆ *Greater relaxation*. Meditation alleviates stress and brings relaxation to the nervous system. Recent research shows that meditation just prior to studying or test taking may result in higher grades.

Group meditation also fosters many benefits: a sense of fellowship, empathy with others, a peaceful group vibration, deeper sharing, and a willingness to listen to others. The combined power of group meditation allows a greater influx of positive energies.

Meditation helps all kinds of children: hyperactive, retarded, disabled, emotionally disturbed, intellectually gifted, unexceptional as well as exceptional. But please *don't impose* meditation on your children or you may turn them against it forever. Instead, make it an adventure or a game. Set an example for them and watch for signs that they are ready. The results of Listening Within may not be apparent at first, but with sincere effort will show eventually. The following quotation from an anonymous source sums up, for me, the benefits of meditation. The symptoms of inner peace correspond beautifully to the ways I have described inner joy.

Symptoms of Inner Peace

Watch for signs of Peace. The hearts of a great many have already been exposed to it and it seems likely that we could find our society experiencing it in epidemic proportions. Some signs and symptoms of inner peace:

1. Tendency to think and act spontaneously, rather than from fear
2. An unmistakable ability to enjoy each moment
3. Loss of interest in judging other people
4. Loss of interest in judging self
5. Loss of interest in interpreting the actions of others
6. Loss of interest in conflict
7. Loss of ability to worry (a very serious symptom)
8. Frequent, overwhelming episodes of appreciation
9. Contented feelings of connectedness with others and with nature
10. Frequent attacks of smiling through the eyes and from the heart
11. Increasing tendency to let things happen rather than make them happen
12. Increasing susceptibility to Love extended by others as well as the uncontrollable urge to extend it.

If you have all or even most of the above symptoms, please be advised that your condition may be too far advanced to turn back. If you are exposed to anyone exhibiting several of these symptoms, remain exposed at your own risk. It is likely that this condition of Inner Peace is well into its infectious stage.

Children who have learned to listen within are the most likely to attain inner peace, with all of its wonderful benefits.

GETTING READY

There is great joy for children in knowing that they have an inner teacher to whom they can listen. In fact, the only true teacher is the teacher within. Therefore, one of our goals is to help them make the best possible contact with that teacher. The techniques and ideas that follow will be helpful, but bear in mind that the children need to be able to listen to their inner teacher in any and all situations. Let's be careful that they don't get so attached to any one technique or idea that they choose not to listen unless the circumstances are "ideal."

In preparing our children for meditation, we'll want to remember our role as a model. We can only teach what we practice within ourselves because, as was discussed in Chapter 3, our consciousness is transmitted. When we serve as a true model, the young child will feel safe in turning within.

SETTING THE STAGE

Preparing an environment conducive to meditation can aid the turning within process and can also be fun for the children. A special meditation rug or individual mats are helpful. Children in a classroom can be gathered without speaking by means of a prearranged signal. You can dim the lights, play soft music, light a candle, hit a gong, or ring a bell.

A candle close by reminds them at a subconscious level of their inner flame. Incense and dimmed lights help set a mood, as does softly played music. Soothing music aids in the relaxation process, while stately music is a powerful agent in the readjustment of consciousness. The subtle influence of music captures the subconscious mind. However, since the point of meditation is to reach the place of stillness, one needs to be judicious about the use of music. When inner peace is found, music can be a distraction. It is not conducive to true meditation.

Singing or chanting is also good preparation for meditation. Because it is also a breathing exercise, it focuses the mind. You or the children might make up simple chants or use one like *Oooohhhmmmmmmm*. Sometimes a spontaneous chant may burst forth, such as, "Thank you, thank you, thank you," over and over, in a singsong way.

Another aspect of setting the stage for meditation is to invoke the Light—to ask for the white light of protection around the body. Or you may want to have the children start with a prayer—such as "I am still and peaceful. I listen for the still small voice of God within me." Or it might be a prayer of forgiveness: it is always wise to let go of grievances or grudges before meditating.

Keep in mind that, if there is too much ceremony associated with meditation, some children will be unlikely to incorporate it into their daily schedule. Others will find the candle, the incense, the special music and place to sit a needed structure that allows them to turn within. Remember the behavior styles. Meditation is another place where "different folks need different strokes." Regardless of style, most children appreciate having a little nest that they can go to when they feel the need to be alone. In the classroom, it can be a little alcove or a carpeted refrigerator carton or a fifty-gallon fiberboard drum. Knowing who you are requires time alone.

CONTROL OF THE BODY

Preparing for formal meditation means controlling the body, the emotions, and the thoughts—in that order. For true meditation it is important to have a relaxed body and a straight spine. The life force moves up the spine, and a bent spine inhibits the flow. When the base of the spine and the head are in line, the life force can rise up through the body and facilitate concentration. Sitting on the floor with legs crossed helps to keep the spine straight, as does sitting in a straight-backed chair with feet flat on the floor. Lying flat on the back with knees raised, with the head and small of the back against the floor, is recommended, unless you are inclined to fall asleep in that position.

Keeping the body still helps still the mind. A quiet physical body enables Spirit to come into our thoughts. Children can learn to relax and still the body by repeating the following sequence: inhale, tense all the muscles (feet, legs, arms, hands, stomach, face, etc.), then relax them all at the same time as you exhale. Repeating the sequence three to six times should suffice for children. Or you might prefer progressive relaxation if a deeper state of relaxation is desired. Have them take one part of the body at a time, tense it and relax it. Starting with the toes, continue on to the ankles, calves, knees, thighs, hips, fingers, hands, arms, stomach, shoulders, head, face, eyes, and mind. Relaxation is essential to meditation: it enables one to forget the body.

Usually the hands are turned upward in the lap because that position relates to receiving. The important thing is to allow the body to be comfortable and, therefore, not a concern of the mind.

Encourage the children to focus their eyes on a point between the eyebrows and a little above, in the forehead. Holding an image there helps keep the attention focused on the "third eye." Uplifted eyes send energy to the brain and upper spine. A gummed sticker or paper reinforcer can be put on the forehead to help focus their attention, but caution them against straining their eyes. Tuning in is most effective when the eyes are closed. The sense of sight uses a lot of energy. Give children who are uncomfortable with their eyes closed the alternative of lowering them.

CONTROL OF THE EMOTIONS

Just as relaxing the body is valuable, relaxing the emotions is also important. Before meditation, it is wise to clear the mind of upsetting thoughts, to forgive and forget. Breathing exercises are an effective means of calming the emotions. Our breath, mind, and life force are tied together. When one is disturbed so are the others; when we control one we control the others.

As preparation for meditation, consider some deep breathing to draw energy currents into the brain. Have the children do belly breathing as opposed to chest breathing in order to draw more oxygen into the system. A popular exercise is to breathe in slowly to the count of 5, hold the breath for the count of 5, and exhale slowly to the count of 5. Holding the breath oxygenates the blood and promotes concentration, but some authorities feel it is ill advised for any child or adult who tends to hold things in. Those people need to place more emphasis on exhaling.

As the children breathe in, you might suggest that they are breathing in joy; and as they breathe out, that they are expelling sorrow. Or as they breathe in, they can feel that it is peace they're bringing into the body—and as they exhale, it is restlessness or irritation that is leaving it.

You can make the above breathing exercises as short as two or three cycles or the focus of an entire meditation.

Simply watching your breath is another form of meditation. You don't do anything but notice your breath coming in and out. You pick a place to focus on, such as the nostrils or chest, and observe your breath going in and out. When your mind wanders off, gently return it to awareness of your breathing.

CONTROL OF THE THOUGHTS

Concentration exercises are the most effective way to direct attention away from our habitual thought patterns. Concentration makes mental relaxation possible as it clears away obstacles. Concentration is usually considered the first stage of meditation and should be practiced a few minutes at the beginning of it. High achievement in any endeavor is the result of concentration, and this is especially so for meditation. It is said in the *Bhagavad Gita*, the holy book of India, that concentration precedes wisdom.

Focus the mind and hold it steadily upon an idea, object, symbol, scene, or sound for a definite time, such as one to five minutes for beginners. It is easiest to hold the mind on something that is concrete, not abstract, and that has personal interest or appeal. Children might choose something simple, such as a candle, a watch, a flower, a leaf, a pencil, a symbol on a piece of paper, a stone, or a piece of fruit.

Have the children think of themselves as magnets pulling the object of concentration toward them. You can demonstrate this idea with an actual magnet. If they are concentrating on a flower, for example, encourage them to get the feeling that nothing exists in the entire world but that flower and themselves. When thoughts enter their mind, they are to return their total focus to the flower.

You may remind them that correct body posture aids concentration. Sai Baba has said that if the body is in a straight position, the life force, which is between the 9th and 12th vertebrae, may rise up through the body and give the quality of intense concentration to the mind.

One mother of young children began their concentration training by giving them each a watch to be held in the hand. She said, "I want to teach you to drive your thoughts instead of letting them drive you. So, look at the face of the watch, and see how long a time you can keep your thoughts perfectly still. . . ." This was done in the spirit of challenge and adventure—not forced. The mother reported, "They found that they could hold their minds still while looking at the watch for a gradually increasing period of time. For a minute, a minute and a half, two, three minutes, gradually extending the time, while nerves and muscles were completely relaxed, until they could make their minds blank by concentrated effort for five minutes at once. When the attention wandered it was recalled by mental effort, and the mind made blank again. Those who have not so worked with themselves," she continued, "have no idea of the feeling of utter rest that comes with the successful accomplishment of this exercise. To me it ranks first in importance of all exercises in the mental training of the young. They take a great interest in it and it is never tiresome."[3]

This mother went on to say that eventually her children so learned to control their thoughts that they could sit in silence with her, "waiting in complete passivity for an hour of perfect repose." They found joy in the complete rest and relaxation, and in the self-mastery that comes from subjugation of an unruly mind. They are now able to direct their energy where they want it. Not being at the mercy of their thoughts, they are able to truly listen within.

Sri Chinmoy reminds us: "Concentration comes directly from the soul, from the soul's indomitable will power. . . . When the light of the soul has entered into the mind, it is extremely easy to concentrate on something for hours and hours. During this time there can be no thoughts or doubts or fears. No negative forces can enter into the mind if it is surcharged with the soul's light."[4]

Through stilling the body, emotions, and mind, one passes beyond awareness of the body, into an inner sanctuary—a wordless place of no thoughts. Here, there is a deep feeling of calmness, freedom, and joy.

Variations on Listening Within

> *Whenever and wherever you put yourself in touch*
> *with God, that is the state of meditation.*
>
> SAI BABA

Each person's soul has its own preferred way of meditating, so it is best to offer children a variety of methods and not insist they conform to your preference. In time, they will find the method of centering most suited to them. Encourage them to get in touch with whatever gives them the most inner peace and joy. Emphasize listening, rather than techniques.

Beside the meditations already presented, there are many other types of Listening Within exercises for children depending upon their age, temperament, and experience.

Here are just a few, plus some resources:

SILENT SITTING

The young child who is not able to sit should, of course, not be expected to do meditation techniques that require a lot of stillness. As with all activities, start each child at the appropriate level. If the idea of meditation or Listening Within is new to your children, or if they are very young, start them slowly with "silent sitting." You might have them do just a minute or two of sitting quietly with their eyes closed. This gets the child used to turning within and becoming more inner-directed. Silent sitting is appropriate before moving on to a new activity. In school, it can be used at transition times. A child can reflect on the activity just completed and mentally prepare herself for the experience to follow. I find my own days much more productive and joyful when I take just a few minutes to sit quietly between activities.

GUIDED IMAGERY MEDITATION

The literature abounds with examples of this type of meditation, and it's usually an easy type for beginners. Two excellent books by Deborah Rozman, *Meditating with Children* and *Meditation for Children*,[5] are full of beautifully scripted-out meditations with specific suggestions for the various age groups. You will also find useful meditations in Gay Hedricks' books—*The Second Centering Book* and *The Family Centering Book*.[6] I encourage you to create your own exercises to meet the particular needs of your children.

An example of guided imagery is the following "Cloud Meditation":

> Imagine you are seated on a soft white cloud and it comes up to your waist. The cloud lifts you gently as it rises up, up, up into the blue sky. You feel so free, so warm, so joyous. In the distance you see a great waterfall of warm golden light. Your cloud carries you to the base of the fall. You look up and feel the warm drops of light pouring down over your head. The warm golden light trickles down over your face past your neck to

your shoulders and chest. It bathes your stomach, legs, and feet. Still sitting on your cloud, you're aware of your white cloud being immersed in the warm golden light. It's now a golden cloud. You now feel the light from the waterfall pierce your head. The warm golden light is entering your head and flowing down into the rest of your body. It is healing and energizing each cell it touches. You are cleansed with light inside and out. Any darkness is gone. Your golden cloud now carries you back to your home and you joyfully roll off it onto your soft bed.

In reciting this or any guided imagery be sure to go very slowly so as to give the participants plenty of time to visualize.

OBJECT MEDITATION

A candle flame is a popular focus of object meditation. Light a candle and place it before you. Sitting in a meditation posture, gaze at the flame until you feel that the image of the flame is clearly impressed on your mind. Slowly close your eyes and bring the image of the flame into your head between the eyebrows. Send this flame down into your heart. Let the light of the flame fill your heart. Next, take the light of the flame to all other parts of your body, and watch it push back the darkness. Let the light spread out from you and shine all around you. See circles of light envelop your family, your friends, humankind, all living things, and the entire world.

A variation of the candle flame meditation is to feel as though you are sitting safely inside the flame, becoming one with it. Bring your family and friends inside it with you, and include anyone or anything else that comes to mind.

As mentioned earlier, you can use a variety of objects to provide a calming focus of awareness—a rock, flower, crystal, watch, etc. Do not think about the object, but just let the mind rest on it until mental activity stills.

SYMBOL MEDITATION

For ages people have meditated on symbols such as mandalas and yantras. A simple balancing meditation is based on one used by initiates in the Mystery School of Pythagoras, who invented geometry and developed some basic principles of mathematics, astronomy, and the musical scale. It consists of five minutes of concentration on each of three geometric symbols in sequence, making a total of fifteen consecutive minutes.

The symbols are: (1) a circle with a dot enclosed, (2) a plus sign, and (3) an equilateral triangle. They must be focused on in 1–2–3 order, with only one symbol in view at a time. Each should be carefully drawn on typing paper or on a plain 4 × 6 card. A child can sit with the symbol on lap or desk, or a class can view it on a chalk board.

Instruct the child to "draw" the symbol with the eyes or mind and to keep drawing it so as to avoid extraneous thoughts. The circle should be drawn in a clockwise direction; the plus from top down and then left to right; and the triangle clockwise, starting at the lower left-hand corner. Encourage the children to be as aware of the symbol as they possibly can be and, when the mind wanders, to bring it back and "feel" the symbol.

Research shows that, done daily as instructed, this meditation will bring people's mental and emotional levels into balance. Walter and Marta Burleigh give instruction and monitoring, through the mail, in the use of this balancing technique.[7]

As with all techniques, ask for guidance to see if it is appropriate for your child, and honor any resistance. *Never insist.* We don't know what is right for that soul's growth.

COLOR CENTERING

Color is a vital force. It can exert a powerful influence on mind and emotions. I recently heard researcher Barbara Vitale tell how she walked into a classroom and asked the teacher which student was having trouble getting work finished on time. The teacher pointed to Sally, who was struggling with her math assignment. Barbara went over to her desk and asked what her favorite color was. She then placed a piece of felt that color on her desk. For the first time, Sally finished her math assignment. Was it just the extra attention or the adult expectation? Research says no—color has a lot more effect on children than we may realize. In many classrooms, thanks to researchers like Barbara, there is a stack of felt colors on a chair in the back of the room. A child may go back and choose a favorite color and sit with it or place it on his desk until centered.

Color may also be used for healing or energizing. Focus the recommended color on a specific body area and breathe through the nose rhythmically: five cycles of inhaling slowly to the count of five, holding to the count of ten while visualizing the color, and exhaling to the count of five. Authors differ quite a bit as to which color to use for which purpose, but we can't go too far wrong if we trust ourselves or our children to choose the appropriate color for the need at hand. The child can look at an actual color, or simply visualize it. The results will be the same, since whatever affects our mind affects our body.

Because of the personal effect of color on us, it is important to let children of all ages choose the color of their clothing. They will instinctively know what colors they need to be wearing.

Two of the many books that explain the attributes and powers of the various colors are *Color Meditations* by Ouseley[8] and *Colour Healing* by Anderson.[9] I can offer here only a few generalities: the three universal healing colors are golden orange, turquoise, and green; sky blue is the color for peace, harmony, and serenity; rose pink is the color for love and affection; purple represents transformation, purification, and forgiveness; yellow stimulates wisdom, thought and visualization; silver can trigger intuitive and creative channeling, as well as artistic endeavors. The use of color is a science and an art well worth investigating.

You may wish to use color to create guided imagery meditations for your children. Here's an example, from nature. After a relaxation or breathing exercise say, "Picture a sheltered bay surrounded by towering evergreen trees. The calm blue sea rolls tranquilly in toward the barnacle-encrusted rocks. The waves break upon the shore and splash the rich brown seaweed with white foam. Silvery gray driftwood dots the beach. On the horizon is a radiant sunset of flame and purple colors. Every cloud is bathed in rose." Be sure to allow plenty of time for visualizing. Such color meditations can awaken in the child the spiritual faculty of color consciousness, help develop the power of concentration, and assist in self-healing.

MANTRA MEDITATION

A mantra is simply a word, phrase, or sound used to still the mind in meditation. Popular words are peace, love, harmony, God, light, and *Om*. *Om* is known as the great mantra because it is considered to be the universal vibration—the matrix of the universe. The *m* in *Om* should vibrate as a humming sound. Many feel that the mantra should be a word or sound without meaning so that concentration might be more one-pointed and not distracted by any associations. You listen to the sound of the mantra as you exhale.

A THOUGHT FOCUS

Closely related to using a word as a mantra is using a word or thought as the focus of meditation. We might choose attributes that we wish to align with or better understand, such as joy, love, wisdom, imagination, strength, faith, and gratitude. By listening within, we can sense how to bring more of that attribute into our being. We might also use passages from Scripture or meaningful quotations as our focus.

LISTENING FOR GUIDANCE

A Course in Miracles says: "It is quite possible to listen to God's Voice all through the day without interrupting your regular activities in any way. The part of your mind in which truth abides is in constant communication with God, whether you are aware of it or not."[10]

I can think of no more valuable habit to model for children than that of listening within for answers to specific questions or concerns. As children learn to be more inner-directed than outer-directed, they will grow more in touch with their inherent joy.

Two resources I've found useful and can highly recommend are Lee Coit's *Listening*[11] and the chapter "How To Use Meditation for Guidance" from *The Inner Power of Silence* by Mark Thurston.[12]

In seeking inner guidance, it is helpful to formulate a specific wording for our question, and to write it out. The wording should make clear what we are looking for: a direct answer, more information, or confirmation of something we are already inclined to do. It is sometimes a good idea to use common sense, intuition, and our highest ideal to form a tentative decision and then seek guidance regarding it.

A true listening attitude requires that we desire no special answer to our question and that we truly wish to know what is best for us. Being open is the only condition necessary for listening.

It may help children to have some idea of what they can expect to receive in the way of inner guidance:

> ☆ A strong feeling or intuition regarding the wisdom of the action they are considering.
>
> ☆ A feeling, intuition, or image of what is likely to happen if the tentative decision is followed.
>
> ☆ A previously unconsidered solution or piece of the puzzle.
>
> ☆ A new perspective on the question being considered.
>
> ☆ Recognition of another question that must be dealt with before the present question can be resolved.

Or the answer may come from an *outside* source. Spirit can use anything and anybody to give us guidance. Once we have asked for an answer it may come in the form of a song, something read or heard on TV, an overheard conversation, or even advice from a friend. Such things may not mean much alone, but in the light of asked-for guidance they take on special meaning.

JOURNALING

Used as both a form of prayer and meditation, journaling is a popular way for young people to listen within. The journal notebook can be a child's vehicle for exploring inner space.

Journaling easily lends itself to use with the two forms of meditation just described. For instance, children can focus on a question or word, once the body, emotions, and mind are stilled. They then write down the thoughts that flow through them. Or they may rely on inner guidance and start writing after a meditation without deciding what they are going to write about. Spirit may give us ideas and information we would never have thought to ask for.

A journal should be kept absolutely private—with no thought of ever sharing any of it. Only by keeping our journal strictly to ourselves can we feel free to say what is in our hearts. A journal is a gift to help us see ourselves better. If we worry that others may see it, we may start judging and block the flow.

We can also write more freely if we forget about spelling, grammar, and punctuation. The only rule is to write clearly enough so that we can easily read what we have written. Reviewing the journal is important because it will help us see patterns in our lives—what keeps happening, what doesn't, how we've changed or not changed in handling situations, which things we find important or unimportant, and so forth.

The journal is a tool to help us listen to ourselves and to the Spirit within. There are books with suggestions to get the process started. These range from writing conversations with real or imaginary people to asking oneself questions on such topics as happiness, creativity, stubbornness, purpose, interests, family, honesty, authority, sharing, shyness, humor, self-control, money, death, playing, liking oneself, and many more. I feel a child old enough to journal is old enough to listen within for the subject to write about.

When we are feeling less than well, an appropriate journal subject is "What is my body trying to tell me?" Our body is a finely tuned instrument that tells us, through physical signals, when we are out of alignment with the Universe.

TAPED MEDITATIONS

Music meditations have become very popular and there are a great number of lovely tapes available. Music can give us a focus and help calm our mind and emotions, but by definition it cannot take us into silence.

There are also beautiful guided meditation tapes for both adults and children, which may serve as a first step to listening within. Tapes for young children are often used in place of the bedtime story. When this is done it is important for the parent to share the experience and to watch reactions. The child may need to be taught how to relax. It's preferable for the child to lie flat on the back with legs and arms uncrossed, and eyes closed, for the entire tape. Encourage the use of the imagination to become part of the story.

Always let the tape play until the particular story or meditation is finished, even if you're sure the child has fallen asleep. Research shows that a person's mind registers and reacts to the things it hears even while asleep. That is why we must never say anything in front of a sleeping child that we wouldn't also say if that child were awake.

Don't let children have tapes every night, or they may feel they have to have a tape to go to sleep. Help them realize that they can imagine beautiful experiences even without a tape. They can use their imaginations to make up their own story.

You might want to create your own meditation tapes for children—with, for example, an introduction of relaxing music and a guided imagery trip that will take the child to a place where answers are available. Be careful not to include anything that hints of manipulation.

You might also create similar tapes for yourself. One meditation teacher suggests a simple format: a music introduction for relaxation and then silence, with a reminder every minute or so to bring the mind back to the point of concentration. The reminder can be a bell, a sound, or your own voice gently saying, "Where is your mind now?"

TIMES OF SILENCE

In quietness are all things answered,
and is every problem quietly resolved.
A COURSE IN MIRACLES

To underscore the value of listening within rather than always talking, plan some family silent times. Try a silent weekend, or a monthly day of silence, or a weekly evening of silence. Silence, of course, means no TV, music, or telephoning. Observe the ego, which will try to take over and keep control.

Author Barbara Scarantino says, "If silence is golden, it is also necessary. . . . Your brain and body need a rest now and then from the constant intrusion of voices, environmental noises, and, yes, even musical sounds."[13]

The meditation techniques described are only a few of those available. You'll find some techniques are more appropriate at certain times than others. Whichever ones you choose, try not to get caught up in the techniques themselves. Make sure you give yourself and your children the time and encouragement to meditate.

AFTER MEDITATION

Bring your children out of meditation gently by making them aware of where they are, and by having them wiggle their toes and fingers and stretch. This helps them return to their bodies, which they may have been away from during the meditation. Tell the children to remain seated in the silence for a while and then to get up slowly.

Most children need some grounding after meditation. Grounding implies contact with the earth—being centered in our earthly self. When grounded we focus on the present, the here and now. Because food is of the earth, eating is automatically grounding. So is getting up and walking around and, where appropriate, going outdoors and hugging a tree or sitting on the ground. Running and sports that involve continuous, nonviolent activity also have a grounding effect. In classrooms, probably the most popular form of grounding is some sort of creative expression—art, writing, creative movement, and dance.

In *Joy in the Classroom*, Stephanie Herzog states, "After meditation, children have a heightened, dynamic energy that is just waiting to be used. Failing to do something with it is like opening a door to the child's potential without realizing what a precious gift it really is."[14] She reports that, in her classroom experience, one of the best ways to direct that energy is to have her children play awareness games from *The Ultimate Kid*[15] and *Exploring Inner Space*.[16] She says, "I have never seen such vibrant, joyful expressions on children's faces as I invariably see during and immediately following an awareness game."

Other teachers, upon the close of meditation, let each child choose how to record the experience. The children are given about fifteen minutes to journal, tape-record, paint, draw, write poetry, cut and paste, or whatever else they choose. They do this while their impressions are fresh. Then they are brought together to share and discuss. This is a good time to ask them questions and let *them* be the authority. With the stimulation of new ideas, children can usually go back and finish what they started.

Recording what they have experienced during meditation not only offers children grounding, but helps them develop communication skills and gives them the opportunity to find out what is stirring inside themselves.

GROUP MEDITATION

This Aquarian Age is a time for group work, and many groups now include some form of meditation, listening within, or centering in their time together.

A particularly effective formula for meditating with a willing group is outlined in Carlin Diamond's delightful book, *Love It, Don't Label It*.[17] Suitable for use in family, classroom, office, and committee work, this technique can set the tone for the day and for the gathering. Here, in brief, are the steps Diamond suggests: (Vary according to the situation.)

1. Sitting in a circle with hands joined, the group enters the silence for 20 to 30 seconds, or sings, or says a verse.
2. They let go of hands; with eyes closed, each person thinks about what she would like help with for this day and says, "Ready," when she has her request in mind.
3. One person serves as a recorder; he writes down each person's request or concern and leaves space for any answer that may come from the meditation. (This step can be skipped, but it has a lot of merit.)
4. Each person closes her eyes and asks the Universe or her inner teacher for help with her particular concern.
5. One person leads the group, through guided imagery, to the something or someone that will give them each an answer. Examples suggested by Diamond:

   The phone rings . . . the person on the other end
   gives you the answer.

> You're by a stream . . . a fish comes up to the
> surface and gives you your answer.
>
> You go to a Chinese restaurant . . . the answer is in
> the fortune cookie.
>
> A beautiful plant grows before your eyes . . . it
> blooms and your answer is in the blossom.

6. Each person says, "Ready," when he has his answer, and the
   recorder writes the answer down.
7. The session is closed by joining hands and singing, or by
   saying a familiar verse, or sitting quietly and sending love.

Diamond stresses the importance of releasing what is past and of following the guidance received.

> *. . . our time in the silence is the most*
> *productive and creative time in the day.*
> *Being is more important than doing.*
> JACK AND CORNELIA ADDINGTON[18]

Joyous Self-Talk

*Every single statement you make about yourself,
to a friend or even to yourself becomes a
truth.*

ORIN

How would you like your stream of internal chatter to supply you with only uplifting, encouraging, joyous messages—messages that free you, instead of limit you? We can learn such self-talk and teach it to our children. Joyous self-talk aligns us with universal principles and, hence, with our inner joy.

Self-talk comes in various forms: silent, spoken, and written. Generally, I'm referring to the silent verbalization that goes on within us most of the time, and that tells us what we think about ourselves or about anything else. But self-talk also includes speaking to ourselves out loud, or about ourselves to someone else. This can range from a conversation with ourselves ("Nice job, Peggy.") to a gripe session with a buddy, ("Seems like I can't do anything right these days.") And, of course, there is written self-talk, which ranges from letters to friends to scripts of self-talk statements or affirmations. For a thorough definition of self-talk see Chapter 9, "The Five Levels of Self-Talk," of *What to Say When You Talk to Yourself*, by Shad Helmstetter.[1]

Self-talk is self-management—through choice of words. Our words create attitudes; our attitudes create feelings; and our feelings determine our actions. In this way, our words control our lives—they create our reality.

The Power of Words

Our words are like seeds we plant in our minds. They take root and sprout. If repeated often enough, words grow into attitudes and beliefs.

Never doubt the power of words—whether self-talk or talk we have accepted from others. Words are the primary tool of the hypnotist, and I have seen some amazing living room demonstrations. Two examples should suffice:

Alan, a first-time subject, was quickly put into an altered state, although he seemed alert and natural to me. He was told to lie down on the carpet and that he would be stuck to the floor, unable to sit up. When he was commanded to get up, we all witnessed his struggle and inability to do so. The demonstration was repeated with Alan standing but being unable to pick up his right foot. The onlookers were all invited to offer him any help we wished. "Raise your toe, raise your heel, lift your knee"; none of these suggestions worked—he was hopelessly "stuck." Consider how we might also be getting our children stuck in a feeling of unworthiness by thoughtless words. Words and thoughts can make an indelible impression on subconscious minds.

A second subject, Constance, was told to count to ten and that each time she did, she would forget to say the number three. It was fascinating to watch her struggle to count correctly but each time skip the number three. Is there not a powerful message here about how our subconscious can be programmed with limitation? These adults were simply put into the same brain-wave state that children are naturally in below the age of seven. Young children are as affected by their self-talk and by our statements as if a hypnotist had put them under.

We can also use words to *remove* limitation—to affirm. A true story that I've told for years in teacher-education classes illustrates this point beautifully. A seasoned kindergarten teacher had a new boy who screamed and cried from the moment his mother dropped him off. After days of this, the teacher decided Tommy was just not ready for school. However, she also decided to try one last thing she had only heard about—affirming for a child.

When Tommy arrived, screaming as usual, she shouted (in order to be heard), "Tommy enjoys school!" She shouted it many times that morning, and Tommy kept bawling. Many of the children chimed in and also yelled, "Tommy enjoys school!" By that afternoon he had stopped crying and even joined the other children at snack time. The teacher kept affirming this for several days, and each day Tommy participated in more and more activities. The subconscious mind will believe anything we tell it—if we tell if often enough and with emotion. Children as young as Tommy are in a naturally receptive state, so it doesn't take long.

We can teach our children to develop self-talk that will imprint their subconscious mind in a positive, joyful way. Much of what they now say to themselves is disheartening, even debilitating. This has been demonstrated by muscle testing. I have witnessed a volunteer hold an arm out stiffly while the demonstrator tested his natural strength. She then asked him to talk positively (but silently) to himself. When she pressed down on his arm it would not budge. Next she requested that he talk negatively to himself. This time his arm gave little resistance and she could easily lower it.

Muscle testing, properly done, is a fun and informative activity to do with children. Suggest first that they put themselves down or think of a time they failed. Let them test their muscles. Then suggest that they switch to positive self-talk or think about being successful. Let them test their muscles again. The difference in results can make a lasting impression.

Limiting Self-Talk

Most of us recognize the obvious harm of derogatory remarks that invalidate the self, although we may not be aware of subtler language that makes us feel powerless and limited. Learning joyful self-talk begins with an awareness of the words we're currently using. To move to a higher level of self-communication we must understand how the words we choose may limit us. There are several books on this subject, but the most comprehensive treatment I know of is in one that you could easily give your teenager—*Talk Sense to Yourself: The Language of Personal Power*, by Chick Moorman.[2] It can help you evaluate your own language so as to be a model of non-limiting self-talk.

"MAKES ME" LANGUAGE

Moorman presents a wonderful exposé of "makes me" language. It's the language of blame—"He made me do it." "That makes me angry." "She makes me happy." "He embarrasses me." "Tests make me nervous." It's a mistake to attribute any feeling to an external source, because *we* are the ones who choose our feelings. As Moorman says, "Emotions are your personal response to an outside act and are within your power to control."

Some familiar variations of "makes me" language include: "You disappoint me." "That annoys me." "He offends me." "That's depressing." "She let me down." "He changed my mind." The list could go on for pages. "Makes me" language reinforces the false idea that we're not in control. It is a form of giving our power away. Start modeling the language of self-responsibility for your children. Instead of "He made me angry," here are three choices that put you in charge: "I made myself angry." "I chose to be angry," or simply—"I was angry."

Listen intently to your children and note any limiting language. Don't interrupt or offer corrections. Just plan for the perfect time and way to explain to them the power of words. Most children relate well to the computer analogy. They can understand that the subconscious mind is a human computer that is programmed with words. Poorly chosen words rob us of joy, love, self-esteem, and a sense of personal power.

"HAVE TO" LANGUAGE

"Have to" language is another pitfall. As you get clear about "have to," you can help your children get clear.

Have you ever done something you didn't want to do, but *had* to do? Most people, especially children, will answer yes, but the answer is really no. Many of us have mistakenly equated the word *want* with the word enjoy or like. "Want to" really means "choose to." When we choose to do things we don't enjoy, we still want to do them. An example from *Feeling Good*[3] is, "Do you want to go to the dentist?" "No," is the response if the person is thinking of want as enjoy. Why are you going then? Most people respond that it is the lesser of two evils. By that token, they are *choosing* to go.

"I have to do my homework," complains the child. Having to do anything gives our computer mind the message that we're powerless. When we have to do something we don't want to do, we feel victimized and joyless, and we block out our alternatives. There's really nothing that we *have* to do if we're willing to pay the price for *not* doing it. By making the *choice* to do it, we are saying we *want* to do it. We would rather do it, than not do it. That gives us back some of our power.

I have caught myself saying, "I have to work on this book," as I turned down invitations to swim and camp or participate in other summer activities. The truth is I *wanted* to work on the book rather than pay the consequences of not meeting the publisher's deadline. When I get into a "have to" frame of mind, my energy is blocked. "Want to" frees my energy and releases joy.

A clear treatment of this subject is in *Feeling Good:* "Anytime you think you are doing something you don't want to do, but have to do, ask yourself: 'What is the price I'd have to pay for not doing this?' And if you are unwilling to pay the price, you may be sure that you want to do it (even though you don't enjoy it at the moment)."[4]

When we come to see that we have never done anything we didn't want to do, we are no longer infected with "victimitis." Our actions were our choices. "Children who realize that they are not the helpless victims of their parents' arbitrary decisions, but that they make their own choices and are responsible for the consequences, often give up their blanket resistance to authority figures."[5] Encourage them to use "I choose to," not "I have to," in their self-talk. The choice to feel good or bad is theirs, and it begins with what they tell themselves.

"Need" is another word to eliminate, because it develops a feeling of dependency. Food, water, and love are our most basic needs, and almost everything else is a want. Saying "I want" helps us feel more in charge.

LANGUAGE OF DENIAL

Little need be said about eliminating "I can't" from our self-talk. "Can't" obviously implies no choice on our part, no control. Teach children to take responsibility and to use "don't" or "won't" or "choose not to" in place of "can't." "I don't resist ice cream," "I won't resist ice cream," and "I choose not to resist ice cream" are all more accurate than "I *can't* resist ice cream."

Just imagine how much we limit ourselves and our children by "can't" thinking! When we tell ourselves over and over again that we can't, we directly affect our subconscious minds and eventually our beliefs and actions. And, as explained in Chapter 3, when we *think*, over and over again, that our *children* can't, we directly affect *their* subconscious minds and eventually *their* beliefs and actions.

"Can't" clearly belongs to the language of limitation. But have you caught yourself or your children using these other self-limiting words?—"It's *impossible*." "It's *no* use." "I'm *too* tired." "I'm *never* chosen." "I'm *always* late." "That's *just* the way I am."?

Encourage children to use the language of confidence. This means they let go of passive words like "hope" and "wish." Instead, they *expect* to do well on the test, or they *know* it will be a great trip. It also means they eliminate the language of denial—language that denies their worth or ability. This includes apologizing before beginning an activity (e.g., "I'm not as prepared as I hoped to be."), bragging, exaggerating, watering down (e.g., "This is only my opinion."), and justifying or defending themselves. Encourage them to use positive self-talk instead—to tell themselves, "I know," even when they're thinking they *don't* know the solution to a challenge or problem.

"SHOULD" LANGUAGE

Another word that should be eliminated from our self-talk if we wish to keep it joyous is the word "should," unless it is followed by an "if," as I have done in this sentence. "I should help out." "I shouldn't have lied." "I should call her." When we say, "I should," there is usually an unspoken ending to the sentence—"but I can't," or "I won't," or "I don't want to."

"Should have's" and "shouldn't have's" often imply a need to control the past—something that is out of our control. Encourage children to let go of the need to change what can't be changed. Since what we focus on expands, it only makes sense not to keep looking at our past mistakes. "Should have" and "shouldn't have" keep us feeling guilty. Guilt is anger turned inward, and it is a way of giving up our power. Ganz and Harmon suggest a better way:

Feel Good Self-Talk

"Should haves" don't count.

The past is out of my control.

> I have always done the best I could do with the awareness I
> had at the time.
>
> I deserve to feel good all the time, in spite of my mistakes,
> failures, and shortcomings.[6]

Instead of "should have," encourage your children to say, "could have." "I could have helped them." "I could have invited him." "But I didn't. So what do I do now?" Remember, they'll learn best from your modeling.

LANGUAGE OF JUDGMENT

Let's look at some more self-talk that needs eliminating: the language of judgment. This includes put-downs, blaming, self-criticism, fault-finding, complaining, labeling, gossip, evaluative praise, and the use of "only" and "just." Examples are hardly needed—"I'm just a kid." "I'm only in second place." "How silly of me." "Nice going, stupid!" "I'm not creative." The list is endless. For a deeper understanding of the "judgment trap," see Moorman.[7] Remember that judgments are generally self-fulfilling, are based on insufficient evidence, and usually reveal more about the judge than the person judged.

SPEAKING FOR OTHERS

Collective speaking is another form of self-talk that gives our power away. "We resent that." "Joe thinks this is a good idea, and I agree." "People don't like it when you do that." These are saying that I am not enough, so I need to surround myself with all these other people. Speaking for ourselves by using "I" promotes self-responsibility, hence greater joy.

Be on the lookout for the many other limiting self-talk words that program children for self-doubt instead of self-confidence—words that make them feel powerless rather than powerful, irresponsible rather than responsible.

Affirmative Self-Talk

At least as important as avoiding negative self-talk is using positive self-talk to build sound self-esteem. A good place to begin is with affirmations. I define an affirmation as a positive declaration about who we are and what we can become or experience. Affirmation is a method for changing our consciousness, for bringing it into harmony with the Divine Perfection that already exists within us. Our subconscious creates what we *feel* is true for us. It accepts negative thoughts as readily as positive. Through conscious use of affirmations, we counteract the negative messages we've told ourselves or accepted from others—and we replace our limited beliefs with higher ones.

"I AM"

In creating affirmations, I suggest a special emphasis on the words "I am." *I am* is the name of the God in us, so the words that follow "I am" have an especially powerful influence on us. It is important to avoid negative "I am" statements, such as: "I am dumb." "I am slow." "I am sick." Saying, "I am dumb," is equivalent to saying, "The God in me is dumb." Encourage children to use esteem-building "I am" statements —"I am a winner." "I am lovable and capable." "I am friendly and helpful." "I am one with the Universe." "I am full of light and love." "I am a good influence on others." "I am a unique and valuable person." To help build an "I am" awareness, see the "I am" game in Chapter 13.

CREATING AFFIRMATIONS THAT WORK

Effective affirmations speak to us directly and powerfully. Use the following guidelines to make yours work:

1. Personalize your affirmations, when possible, by using *I* and your name. "I, (name), am a stronger swimmer."

2. State your affirmations in the present tense. The subconscious mind is very literal, and if an affirmation is worded to take place in the future, it will always be in the future.

3. Your affirmation should indicate that you've achieved what you want to, not that you are "growing into it," e.g., "I express myself clearly."

4. Affirmations work best if accompanied by a mental picture. A strong picture is worth a thousand words. Our formative subconscious responds well to detailed visualization.

5. Your affirmation should describe what you wish to cultivate and not what you want to move away from. Instead of "I don't lose my temper," say, "I am even-tempered."

6. Specify exactly what you want to achieve: "I can swim three laps of the pool." Vague directions, such as "I am a good swimmer," beget vague results.

7. Inject feeling words into your affirmations: "I enjoy getting up on time." The more joyous the feeling, the more effective your affirmations will be.

8. Your affirmation needs to be simple so that it is easily recalled when needed.

9. Avoid affirmations that depend upon the action of others.

10. Make sure your affirmation is in keeping with your highest ideal, your highest purpose—the best that is within you. Don't sell yourself short. When we're focused on our highest purpose all doors are opened to us.

The most important self-talk you can get children to use is esteem-building self-talk—such as "I feel warm and good about myself," or "I love myself totally and completely," or "I always find ways to put myself and others up." If you want a script of self-esteem self-talk, I suggest Chapter 17 of *What to Say When You Talk to Yourself*.[8] An example: "I really am very special. I like who I am and feel good about myself. I am unique—from the top of my head to the bottom of my feet."

BUMPER STICKER SELF-TALK

These are affirmations which are so short and concise that they've been labeled bumper stickers. When, through many repetitions, they are programmed into our subconscious they support us with their messages when we need them most.

Here are some I like:

I'm enough	Go for it
I can do it	Act as if
I can handle it	Now is all there is
Feelings create	Do it now
I receive as I give	Divine Order
We are one	I deserve the best
Think love	Think joy

SELF-ACCEPTANCE

Joyous self-talk is talk of acceptance, acceptance of self and of others. To be accepting, we let go of judgments—the critical thoughts we have about ourselves or about anyone else. And when *others* criticize us, put us down, insult us? What we tell ourselves about what others tell us is all that matters. Positive self-talkers go into action at this time. We immediately start feeding into our mental computer statements that cancel out the effect of the insults.

Here's a technique that works with children of almost any age. When someone has called Johnny a dummy, *you* start calling him Sam. "But that's not my name," he'll object. Point out that just as he objects vehemently to being called the wrong name, he can also refuse negative labels. They belong to him no more than the name Sam. If he does not feel it is safe to object out loud, he can in his silent self-talk declare "I am John, not Sam." This can stand for rejecting all that is not positive and good. One parent started calling his little boy "car" when the child was receiving insults from playmates. By being able to reject the label "car" as not him, he was able to mentally reject the put-downs.

Before I became aware of the power of the subconscious, I would let a criticism or insult of me echo in my mind. I would not mentally agree with the put-down, but I would hear it over and over and over, like a broken record. Knowing now how the subconscious works, I realize that I was being my own worst enemy. I had not learned the tools, the positive self-talk, to cancel out those painful statements. How important it is to teach children to talk lovingly to themselves. Not only do we all need to counteract criticism from others, but some self-critical temperaments (such as the high C's) need especially to counteract their own criticisms.

Pick out areas where you suspect your children may be doing *limiting* self-talk and help them think of happy, positive statements to feed into their computer mind. You might also say affirmations for them. How quick we can be to criticize our children, and how seldom do we offer them positive statements about themselves that they can relish, cherish, and roll around in their mind.

The same goes for us. If we are used to talking lovingly to ourselves, we will not overreact to barbs and insults. So often such remarks simply mirror our attitude toward ourselves.

When we are experiencing emotional pain, it is important to embrace the emotion in love, just the way it is. This frees the energy that is repressed by our judgment. When we are judging or criticizing ourselves, others, or the situation, we are blocking energy. This adversely affects our thinking and our body.

Another way of dealing with emotional pain, the sages tell us, is to repeat inspiring words as often as we can: their very vibration will begin to calm our emotions. If your older children get overwhelmed by feelings, you might suggest they write out appropriate affirmations, ones that remind them that the Universe is purposeful and that they are beloved children of God. Examples: "Everything happens for my higher good." "I'm a joyful, loving child of God." "I see a universe of order and harmony." "I am always doing the best I can at the moment—and so are you." "I am an expression of God and God makes no junk." "I chose this experience for the lesson in it."

The same idea can work for physical pain. A true story I heard many years ago made an indelible impression on me. A boy of eight was alone in the apartment when his pajamas caught on fire from an electric heater. He ran screaming into the apartment house hallway. By the time help came, he was severely burned. He kept saying over and over the one affirmation he knew, "I am a happy, healthy child of God." In the ambulance and in the emergency room he was heard repeating it. He kept focusing on that one thought. In the ward, in the bed next to him, was a girl who had also been burned, but much less severely. She died. The boy was released in record time.

Activities for You and the Children

Here is a potpourri of suggestions that can be used in any order you wish and whenever appropriate.

1. **Listen to yourself.** It's important to listen to your current self-talk so you'll know what needs to be changed. Chick Moorman calls it monitoring your head-

stream. Ask your Higher Self to help you be conscious of every thought you think and everything you say for the next three days. Listen for both positive and negative self-talk and notice whether you are basically negative or positive in outlook. Listen internally when you wake up, get dressed, eat, study, drive, watch TV, face problems, and so forth.

2. **Checking in.** A parking meter timer or small kitchen timer that you can carry around with you is a useful tool for checking in on self-talk. You set it to go off at random intervals (e.g., 3 minutes, 10 minutes, 7 minutes, 20 minutes, 5 minutes), and when it rings you notice what you have been telling yourself in the last few minutes. Were you feeding your computer with positive or negative programming? A teacher can do this for an entire class, allowing everybody to check self-talk at the same time. Of course, no one should be put on the spot to share.

3. **Uplifting words.** If your self-talk tends to be troubling or worrisome, replace it with a stream of catchy, uplifting words—words that feel joyous to you. Phrases from some of the songs in Chapter 6 help me. For instance, "I feel wonderful, I feel wonderful, and I'm going to stay that way," or "I've got the joy, joy, joy down in my heart." A bumper sticker affirmation like "Think God" or a mantra like "The Father and I are one" might be useful to you. Some people like slogans such as "When the going gets tough, the tough get going." The idea is to crowd out negative thinking.

4. **Keep a language journal.** There are many ways to keep such a journal. You might start by having the children list the negative self-talk suggestions they catch themselves saying the most often. Include those you've heard them use—such as "I can't" or "It's just not my day" or "I have to go to the dentist." Have them find a way to rephrase each example and record these in their journals. Offer suggestions if they want help.

Older children can be encouraged to do this activity on their own, but the parent or teacher might do it for younger children. A teacher could have a large journal with a page for each member of the class. Some of the activities that follow would also be appropriate for a journal.

5. **Make a list.** Have older children make a list of what they want to accomplish in their life in the next few months. It could include overcoming a problem or fear, developing a sports skill, talent, or self-esteem, making friends or getting along with someone, and so forth. Next have them choose three items on the list and write out a self-talk script that would help them achieve results.

They might begin with an "I am" affirmation and then add sentences to facilitate the affirmation: "I am a punctual person and enjoy getting places on time. I allow plenty of time to get where I'm going and always arrive on time or early. People can depend on my punctuality."

6. **Play "How are you?"** This suggestion from Moorman is one we can all use immediately. Simply agree with yourself ahead of time how to respond to this perennial question: "just so-so," "incredible," etc. Have the children list all the ways they could answer "How are you?" or "How's it going?" or "How are you doing?" They

can decide on two or three they'll use. Help them understand that this is taking conscious charge of their programming—of how they feel about themselves.

7. **Play detective.** This could be another journal activity. Encourage the children, when they listen to TV, radio, and the conversations of others, to catch language that limits people, that makes them feel powerless, not in control. Have them sleuth out words that create self-doubt, indecision, and irresponsibility. As they become language detectives, they'll learn to choose self-talk that creates joy.

8. **Muscle testing.** Look into the art of muscle testing and expand on the exercise at the beginning of this chapter. The mind can reveal important information through muscle testing but it takes a lot of practice to become good at it.

9. **Describe yourself.** Without using any judgmental language, describe yourself to a partner or in your journal: your physical appearance, abilities, behaviors, everything—but don't evaluate.

10. **Describe others.** Again, without evaluating or judging, describe to a partner (parent, friend, fellow student): your teacher, a brother or sister, a parent, your school, the day, your bedroom, a pet.

11. **Use a tape recorder.** Tape-record your conversation at the dinner table or a group discussion at school. Play it back and note any language of limitation, denial, judgment, etc.

Make a tape of the affirmative self-talk you want programmed into your mental computer. In preparing the script and recording it on tape, talk as if you really liked yourself and were confident that you deserved only the best. Play the tape as you fall asleep or wake up: your mind is in a most receptive state at these times. Also listen to the tape as many other times during the day as you can. Repetition is vital for re-programming.

12. **Reminder cards.** What we view often also affects our programming. Place affirmation statements where you'll see them frequently. You might also make a set of language cards to remind you of the new word choices you wish to make. For starters, print on 3 × 5 cards the following:

> Change *should have* to *could have*
> Change *need* to *want*
> Change *can't* to *choose not to* or *won't*
> Change *have to* into *choose it*
> Change *but* to *and*
> Change *if* to *when*

13. **Affirmation box.** As a classroom activity for most ages, prepare an attractive box to hold simple affirmations written on slips of paper. Make sure both the words and the thoughts are appropriate to the students' level of understanding. At the end of the week, invite students to draw out a special thought to take home for the weekend. Spend a few minutes of class time to have them get a visual image for their affirmation, to get a *feeling* for it, and to say it aloud with meaning. Discuss

ways they might incorporate it into their self-talk over the weekend. When the children return to class, have them share experiences with their affirmations. They may decide they want to do this activity more than once a week.

14. **The penny jar.** Some families have a penny or nickel jar and each time a member is caught or catches himself saying a certain word, a coin goes in the jar. "Can't" is a good one for starters, and when that is almost eliminated, move on to other limiting words. This activity is similar to what is done in Toastmaster Clubs where there is an "uh" counter who fines the speakers for the number of "uh's" they used.

15. **Reward system.** Encourage a child to set up a chart of self-talk activities and plan a system of rewards for every so many that are checked off. Although joyous self-talk is ultimately its own reward, some may need an extra incentive to get this new habit started.

16. **Elimination techniques.** Certain negative words or phrases may have become so habitual, that we need something dramatic and visual to help us eliminate them. Write the offending words on sheets of toilet paper and flush them down the toilet. Or write them on slips of paper and ceremoniously set a match to them. Practice affirmative self-talk while you watch them burn. Some children enjoy writing words they wish to eliminate on slips of paper—"I now let go of 'I can't.'" "I release 'makes me.'" "Goodbye to 'you know.'"—and putting them inside a balloon. The balloon is then blown up and released into the sky with a happy "Goodbye!"

These activities can also be visualized through guided imagery meditation, since the subconscious cannot tell the difference between a real experience and one that is vividly imagined. Visualization is a major tool for manifestation on this planet, and should be encouraged. Use it to see miracles in your children's lives—and in yours as well. A miracle is simply the speeding up of universal laws.

> It is the habitual thought that frames itself into our life. It affects us even more than our intimate social relations do. Our confidential friends have not so much to do in shaping our lives as the thoughts have which we harbor.
>
> J. W. TEAL

The Power of Songs
and Quotes

Songs and quotes have a unique programming power and can be effective instruments for joy. Songs are especially powerful because they speak to the heart—they energize our feeling nature.

Have you ever had the words of a song go round and round in your head? You fall asleep or wake up mentally singing the refrain. Most of us have. Children often experience this with TV or radio commercials. Because of this common effect, songs can be a potent programming device for the good we want in life. If its words are simple, its tune catchy, and it is heard often enough, a song can plant valuable seed-thoughts in a child's subconscious mind.

Songs get a concept into the subconscious mind through the combination of repetition and intensity of vibrations. Psychologists have found that music works 80% faster than affirmations or the spoken word in programming our subconscious.

This brings to mind the mystical marriage discussed in Chapter 2, which explains that a thought and feeling must come together to create manifestation. The ideas in the song are quickly emotionalized by the music. The music creates feeling, which greatly magnifies the impression made by the words. The ideas then go into our subconscious and are reproduced in our life and daily affairs. Remember that the subconscious mind is the memory bank where habitual actions and reactions are stored, including emotional reactions and attitudes toward others and ourselves.

I urge you to collect or create jubilant songs, and songs that remind you of the universal principles. You can create these for your children by putting a message you find important to a familiar melody. Examples follow. Some were created, and others were acquired from a number of sources.

Introducing Songs

Introduce a song to young children by singing it yourself—while driving, doing chores, walking, and so forth. Most preschool children are not conscious of voices or tone, but are very observant of attitudes. The "I love singing" attitude is contagious. And children really appreciate your wanting to share songs with them. Sing a lot, but don't expect the children to sing something back to you right away. You must sing a song many times over if you want them to know it. They'll absorb it and give it back to you someday—not always in the form of the song, but certainly in an awareness of the concept.

If the children know the original words to the tune, you may wish to sing it that way first and then explain why you prefer the new version. Encourage the children to create new words to old tunes or even to make up their own tunes. Be sensitive to their feelings. Sometimes they aren't ready for us to repeat their song or sing it with them.

Please remember not to refine or polish a child's song. The important thing is not the musical value of the song, but what happens within as it is sung. Both creativity and that precious feeling of self-worth can be undermined by well-intentioned criticism. Also, keep in mind that retaining the child's song is not as important as retaining the climate that inspired creative expression.

When teaching or sharing a song with children, make sure that they understand the meaning of the words. Don't take anything for granted. Children often have a distorted understanding of words. In the songs offered below, I would make sure that they understand what is meant by such words as "radiate," "expand," "focus," "forgive," "forget," "unconditional love," "trusting," "perfect," and "negative." You might ask them what they think these words mean. They may surprise you with how much they do know and the misperceptions that were hidden until you asked. Discussions around the meanings of such words can provide a great learning opportunity for both you and the children.

Use your own discretion about which songs are appropriate for which age groups. And don't underestimate your children *or* the power of songs.

Familiar Tunes, New Words

I Am Happy
(Tune: "Frère Jacques" or "Brother John")

I am happy, I am happy
Yes, I am, Yes, I am
I am fun and cheerful
I am fun and cheerful
Joy, Joy, Joy
Joy, Joy, Joy.

You may substitute "joyful" for "happy" and end the song with "love, peace, joy."

I Am Grateful

I am grateful, I am grateful
Yes, I am, Yes, I am
I am very thankful
I am very thankful
Joy, Joy, Joy
Joy, Joy, Joy.

Use at Thanksgiving or Christmas time or on other special occasions. It could be a mealtime blessing or a bedtime song.

I Am Joyful
(Tune: "Alouette")

I am joyful, I am very joyful
I am joyful, joyful all the time
Smile with me and spread the cheer
Radiate from ear to ear
   (point to each ear)
Spread the cheer—Spread the cheer
Radiate from here and here—Oh . . .
   (point to forehead and heart)

Clapping or rhythm instruments make a nice accompaniment to these songs. Pieces of dowels make great rhythm sticks for preschoolers.

What I Focus on Expands
(Tune: "Twinkle, Twinkle, Little Star")

What I focus on expands
My life is in my own hands
My thoughts and feelings
   they create
So I can choose a joyful state
What I focus on expands
My life is in my own hands.

What I have, if I don't want
I can change it by my thought
Joy's a feeling I now choose
Negative thoughts, I will refuse
What I have, if I don't want
I can change it by my thought.

Help children realize that their focus is their attention and includes thoughts, feelings, and visualization. With young children, you may wish to change the words to "What I think about expands." This is a powerful universal principle, and the song can help children remember that they are in control of their lives.

The Now Song (#1)
(Tune: "Rain, Rain, Go Away")

Now, now, stay with me
Past 'n future I set free
(a) Now is all I'll ever see
(b) Now is all there'll ever be.

Young children are in the Now, but as we grow older we need reminders not to spend time regretting the past or worrying about the future.

The Now Song (#2)
(Tune: "Row, Row, Row Your Boat")
Now, Now, Now is All

All we have to live
When we concentrate on Now
We have much more to give.

Forgive and Forget
   (Tune: "Mary Had a Little Lamb")

It is joyful to forgive
            to forgive
            to forgive
It is joyful to forgive
That's the way to go
It is wisdom to forget
            to forget
            to forget
It is wisdom to forget
Simply let it go.

Forgiving and forgetting are an important key to inner joy and they help us stay in the Now. This is a good song for older children.

Unconditional Love
   (Tune: "The Farmer in the Dell")

Unconditional Love
Unconditional Love
Loving unconditionally
Unconditional Love.

It brings me Inner Peace
It brings me Inner Peace
Loving unconditionally
It brings me Inner Peace.

(b) It keeps me in good health
(c) It brings me many friends
(d) It keeps me full of joy
(e) It fills me full of light
(f) *(Make up more verses)*

A wise teacher has said that un-conditional love does not mean loving in spite of conditions. Unconditional love means rec-ognizing that loving is the only condition. No right or wrong; no good or bad—just pure love.

Three Good Thoughts
   (Tune: "Three Blind Mice")

Three good thoughts
Three good thoughts
Joy, Love, Peace
Joy, Love, Peace
I use them with all I meet
In each the Light I'm sure to greet
With these three thoughts I am complete
Joy, Love, Peace.

Let the children know that "Peace" refers to Inner Peace— the Peace of God—the Peace that must precede the peace between people and nations.

All Is Perfect
(Tune: "Frère Jacques")

All is perfect, all is perfect
When I see, when I see
With the eyes of God
With the eyes of God
Peace, Love, Joy
Peace, Love, Joy.

If it were possible to see this world from the perspective of God, we would see that all is perfect because all is operating according to the Law of Cause and Effect. Each person is creating his lifetime to learn the lessons he wants or needs to learn.

I Am Trusting
(Tune: "Frère Jacques")

I am trusting, I am trusting
The Universe, the Universe
It brings me only good
It brings me only good
Peace, Love, Joy
Peace, Love, Joy.

The more we grasp the inherent perfection of the Universe and how all is truly in Divine Order, the more trusting we can be.

Changes Don't Bother Me
(Tune: "Shoo Fly, Don't Bother Me")

Changes don't bother me
Changes don't bother me
Changes don't bother me
Good is all I'll ever see
I know, I know, I know
I know there's nothing to fear
I know, I know, I know
I know there's nothing to fear
Changes don't bother me
Changes don't bother me
Changes don't bother me
Good is all I'll ever see.

The more we trust the Universe and its Divine Order, the less we'll be disturbed by the changes that are inevitable. We can help children embrace change as a positive, not a negative experience.

Our Feelings They Create
(Tune: "The Farmer in the Dell")

Our feelings they create
Our feelings they create
By attracting their own kind
Our feelings they create.

I attract what I feel
I attract what I feel
I let go of fear and doubt
I attract what I feel.

We can't remind ourselves too often about the potency of feelings as a creative force in our life. The self-esteem section in Chapter 2 speaks of this. Feelings attract their kind more than simple thoughts do. This is why what we fear sometimes happens to us.

I choose a joyful feeling
I choose a joyful feeling
'Cause joy is the real me
I choose a joyful feeling.

*You might use "love" or "peace"
in place of "joy" in this stanza.*

I Am Full of Joy and Sunshine
(Tune: "I've Been Working on the Railroad")

I am full of joy and sunshine, happy all day long
I am healthy and courageous; I feel so well and
  strong
God's joy and love and wisdom are in my life all
  day
Health and peace and many blessings go with me
  on my way.

The Joy of Life is Mine
(Tune: "Farmer In The Dell")

The joy of Life is mine
the joy of Life is mine
Radiating all the time
the joy of Life is mine.

*In place of "Life," alternate with
words such as "Love," "Peace,"
"God," or "Health."*

Joy Is Here
(Tune: "Row, Row, Row Your Boat")

Joy, joy, joy is here
  filling every heart
Merrily, merrily, merrily, merrily
  laugh and play your part.

*With older children, you can
teach them the deeper meaning of
the original words to "Row, Row,
Row Your Boat."*

I Radiate
(Tune: "My Bonnie")

I radiate joy when it's gloomy
I radiate health and good cheer
I radiate love to all people
I radiate good far and near.
  Shining, shining,
  I grow with the light in my heart today,
  Loving, loving,
  I give love and joy to the world.

A Good Day
(Tune: "Auld Lang Syne")

This day is full of joy for me
I'll choose for love and peace
I'll bring good cheer to everyone
And let my worries cease.

I'll think good thoughts and speak good words
Of Truth that sets us free
It's joy for me to be my best
Each day in harmony.

This Little Smile of Mine
(Tune: "This Little Light of Mine")

This little smile of mine
I'm going to let it shine!
This little smile of mine
I'm going to let it shine!
Let it shine, let it shine, let it shine!
Hide it under a frown—No!
I'm going to let it shine!
Hide it under a frown—No!
I'm going to let it shine!
Let it shine, let it shine, let it shine!
(b) All over our classroom
(c) All over my house
(d) All over (child's city)
(e) All over the planet
(f) All over the universe

A Smile Is Quite a Funny Thing
(Tune: "Auld Lang Syne")

A smile is quite a funny thing
It wrinkles up your face
And when it's gone you never find
Its secret hiding place
But far more wonderful it is
To see what smiles can do
You smile at one, he smiles at you
And so one smile makes two
He smiles at someone, since you smiled
And then that one smiles back
And that one smiles until, in truth
You fail in keeping track!
And since a smile can do great good
By cheering hearts of care
Let's smile and smile and not forget
That smiles go ev'rywhere.

Joyous Health
(Tune: "Hark! The Herald Angels Sing")

Joyous health and healing
   power

Vibrate through me every
 hour
Joyous health and healing
 power
Vibrate through me every
 hour.
(Repeat to end of song)

Judgment

(Tune: "Rain, Rain, Go Away")

Judgment, Judgment, go away
Good is all I'll see today
Love is all I'll be today.

Energy Follows Thought

(Tune: "Farmer In The Dell")

Energy follows thought
Energy follows thought
I watch what I'm thinking
'Cause energy follows thought.

Form follows energy
Form follows energy
My thoughts will take form in life
'Cause form follows energy.

My thoughts bring me joy
My thoughts bring me joy
Because I choose them carefully
My thoughts bring me joy.

*Here is a basic metaphysical
principle that you may wish to
explain to older children at their
level of understanding. A couple
of analogies along this line are in
A Child of God.[1]*

A Chant

I am one with Joy
I am one with Joy
I am one, I am one
I am one with Joy.
*(Repeat, replacing "Joy" with
"Love," "Peace," "Light,"
"God," "Good," "Health," "Fun,"
"Earth," or "You")*

You are one with me
You are one with me
We are one, we are one
You are one with me.

*You and your children may wish
to create simple chants to familiar tunes or make up your own.
Chants are fun to share when
hiking, driving, or doing chores.
Be creative—let your love, gratitude, and joy flow.*

I Am Joy
(Tune: Chorus of "Jingle Bells")

I am joy, I am joy
I am joy today
I am joy, I am joy
I am joy all day.
(Repeat to end of song.)

Here's a chant to be creative with. Change words. Use "I am love . . . ," "We are joy . . . ," etc.

The More We Get Together
(Tune: "Did You Ever See a Lassie")

The more we get together, together, together
The more we get together, the happier we'll be!
For your friends are my friends, and my friends are your friends
The more we get together, the happier we'll be!

The more we work together, together, together
The more we work together, the happier we'll be!
For my love and your love are all really God's love
The more we work together, the happier we'll be!

Oh, I love to be a blessing, a blessing, a blessing
Oh, I love to be a blessing from morning 'til night
For God's light is my light, His presence is my might
Oh, I love to be a blessing from morning 'til night.

Talk To God
(Tune: "This Old Man")

When I play, when I sing
When I do most anything
I can talk to God in my own way
And feel Love's light throughout the day.

I say thanks, sometimes please
On my bed or on my knees
I breathe in feelings of peace and love
And pray for guidance from above.

Deep in the Heart of Spirit
(Tune: "Deep in the Heart of Texas")

My mind and heart are full of Joy (*clap 3 times*)
Deep in the heart of Spirit
My mind and heart are full of Joy (*clap 3 times*)
Deep in the heart of Spirit.

Sharing
(Tune: "Bicycle Built for Two")

Sharing, sharing, sharing our very best
Sharing, sharing, sharing brings happiness

We're happiest when we're sharing
Because it shows we're caring
We give our best. Love does the rest
And we're blest with true happiness.

God Has a Plan
(Tune: "Farmer in the Dell")

God has a plan; God has a plan
God has a perfect plan; God has a plan.
(b) I listen for God's plan
(c) God shows me the plan
(d) I now accept God's plan
(e) I am happy in God's plan

You may know this as "Spirit Has a Plan." I think younger children relate better to the word "God." Adapt the words to your group. I like to emphasize listening for God's plan.

Songs That Uplift

Carmen Moshier has written a joyous and uplifting songbook. This passage explains:

> A good time to sing fun songs is when you are feeling un-happy. Sing them even if tears are falling down your face. Sing them when the world looks blue . . . and watch the corners of your mouth start to turn up—even if you have to sing them over and over.
>
> And that isn't all that will turn up. Watch the good begin to turn up in your life! So let's be bathtub singers and walking-down-the-street singers. Let's be car singers and get-together singers. Let's sing on Saturday night with the gang, and on Monday morning as we get our minds ready for the week. We don't have to worry about "carrying a tune." The tune will carry us through the day, through the week and through life. The happy tunes will carry us over the rough places, from sadness to joy.[2]

It's a rewarding habit to start the day, as soon as you wake up, with a song on your lips, even if you only sing it under your breath. Some favorites my friends use: "Oh, What a Beautiful Morning," "Love Is the Only Power," "Zippity Doo Dah," "This Little Light of Mine," "He's Got the Whole World in His Hands," "When the Saints Go Marching In," and "High Hopes." One of my favorites is "I Feel Wonderful." Even when I don't, it helps me start feeling that way. If you don't know the tune, there is an arrangement by Charles King on the next page, followed by two others from his songbook.[3]

Other songs that can get me going in the morning are "I Let Me Be Happy Today," "Say 'Yes' to Life!," "It Can Be Done," "Just Imagine It," and other songs by Carmen Moshier. These catchy tunes are on a cassette designed for trampoline exercising—

a great way to start the day![4] Two of them follow the popular gospel song, "Joy, Joy, Joy." Some people prefer to use "I have the joy" or "I feel God's Joy." You may wish to consider substituting other words for "joy" such as "peace," "love," or "truth." This section closes with a couple of songs from *Sing—Be Happy*, an inexpensive book full of easy tunes to remind children of God's love and the good in our world.[5]

I Feel Wonderful

Verse 2: You'll feel wonderful! You'll feel wonderful!
For this is a glorious day.
You'll feel wonderful! You'll feel wonderful!
And you're going to stay that way.

Verse 3: We are wonderful.

Come Over on the Sunny Side

arranged by Charles King and Daisy Robinson

Verse 1:　We're happy, we're happy, over on the sunny side.
　　　　　There's joy and gladness ev'rywhere.
　　　　　We're happy on the sunny side.

Chorus:　Come over, come over, over on the sunny side.
　　　　　There's joy and gladness ev'rywhere.
　　　　　Come over on the sunny side.

Verse 2:　We're moving, we're moving, over on the sunny side.
　　　　　There's joy and gladness ev'rywhere.
　　　　　We're moving on the sunny side

(Chorus)

Verse 3:　Come join us, come join us, over on the sunny side.
　　　　　There's joy and gladness ev'rywhere.
　　　　　Come join us on the sunny side.

(Chorus)

I Am a Child of God

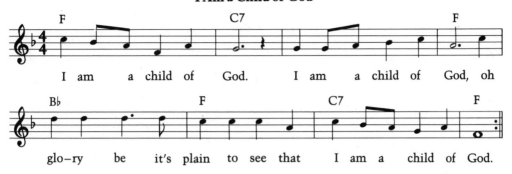

I am a child of God. I am a child of God, oh
glo—ry be it's plain to see that I am a child of God.

By Dorothy Kanuer

Verse 2: You are a child of God,
You are a child of God.
Oh, glory be, it's plain to see that
You are a child of God.

Joy, Joy, Joy

Chorus: I've got the joy, joy, joy, joy down in my heart, down in my heart,
down in my heart! I've got the joy, joy, joy, joy down in my heart,
down in my heart to stay! And it's the grand—est, great—est
feel—ing, and it's a feel—ing here to stay! And it's a
joy that needs re— veal—ing, so I just want to say: *return to chorus*

I Let Me Be Happy Today

© 1980   *Carmen Moshier*

Say "Yes" to Life!

© 1984   Carmen Moshier

Good, Better, Best

Good bet–ter, best! I'll ne–ver let it rest, 'Till my

good is bet–ter And my bet–ter best.

Good bet–ter, best! I'll ne–ver let it rest, 'Till my

good is bet–ter And my bet–ter best.

from Sing–Be Happy

Sing and Be Happy

Sing! Sing! Sing!—— Sing and be

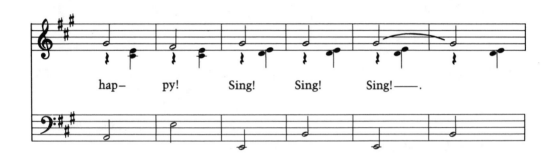

hap– py! Sing! Sing! Sing!——.

Sing and be hap– py! Sing! Sing! Sing!

from Sing — Be Happy

Note other words: Smile, laugh, work, pray, play etc.

ADDITIONAL SONG SOURCES

A carefully selected and annotated list of children's songbooks suitable for use in the home appears in *Whole Child–Whole Parent*, pages 270–272.[6] Scarantino's *Music Power*[7] has a great list of recorded music and songs appropriate for children, pages 165–69. Rosie Lovejoy has two wonderful children's cassettes, *Wings To My Heart* and *I Claim A Miracle*.[8] Two other lovely cassettes are *For A Child's Heart*[9] and *The Joy of Music*.[10] Written for upper elementary age, Vitamin L has award winning music that promotes values. Their two tapes are *Walk a Mile* and *Everyone's Invited*.[11]

The list is endless because so much uplifting music is coming out now. There are even two Joyful Child cassettes: *The Joyful Child Sing-A-Long* contains many of the songs from the beginning of this chapter including "I Feel Wonderful;" and *Joyful Child: Songs for the Child in Each of Us* contains the Joyful Child theme song and my favorites from several artists including Carol Johnson's "Music with a Message." I share other thoughts on music in Chapters 10 and 13.

NOTES:

Consider starting your own list right here of your favorite joy songs—ones that uplift you personally.

The Daily Thought

Another inspiring way to start one's day, at home or at school, is with a "Thought for the Day." This might be a quotation or a short poem or just a word.

Like songs, catchy quotations that are memorized can help the child in time of need. Bible verses have been used that way for years. Studying uplifting quotations helps children relate to the highest in themselves. It also encourages truly human ideals, promotes analytical thinking, and develops the memory. It's a fun way to bring forth Truth Teachings and takes very little time.

You can present the thought for the day in a number of ways. The more you involve the children or make a game out of it the better.

1. Put quotes on 3 × 5 cards in a file box. Draw one out each day as the message for the whole family or class—or let everyone draw out his own. Such a box is fun to have on the dinner table, where each member of the family has a chance to draw

a message for himself. It makes for nice sharing to tell why you think you got that card or what it means to you.

2. Make up a three-ring notebook with a list of numbered quotations. When choosing a daily thought, try to tie it in with a value that is being studied or something that is going on in the child's world. Or you may simply ask for guidance as to which number to select that day. Children can be involved by getting to call out the number they want.

3. Punch two holes at the top of a stack of 3 × 5 cards and put large metal notebook rings through them. Write appropriate quotations. The cards will stand up nicely for display if you have a sufficient number. The quotations can be used in sequence or chosen randomly.

4. Select the quote for the family or class and display it on the breakfast table or write it on the chalkboard. Or put it in a different place each day and have the children look around for it. You might want to keep an uplifting thought permanently displayed. One I keep on my refrigerator is

I GIVE THANKS FOR THIS JOYOUS DAY:

MIRACLE SHALL FOLLOW MIRACLE

AND JOY NEVER CEASE

5. Simply open up a favorite book—after asking that it open to what you need to know right now. Some books used in this way are the Bible, *A Course In Miracles*, and Bartlett's *Familiar Quotations*.

Encourage the children to offer their views about the "Thought for the Day" and to keep a special notebook of poems and quotations that have special meaning for them. If they are old enough, have them memorize some of the quotations. Not only does this develop their memory but it programs their subconscious mind. In times of need, these ideas will come back to mind.

WORD OF THE DAY

Using a 3 × 5 card for each word, write in large letters words that evoke a quality that you admire or want to see developed. One group I belong to gives out cards with such words as:

Joy	Responsibility
Trust	Openness
Gratitude	Support
Courage	Acceptance
Integrity	Willingness

Make up your own list, according to the age level of your children. Place the word you're currently working on where it can be constantly seen.

The idea is to reflect on this "daily word," and to visualize how that quality can manifest in our lives. The word can affect us subliminally—below the threshold of awareness. Subtly, the quality can take form in our life, or our children's lives. Children can be asked to contemplate the word during Silent Sitting time or to write their thoughts about it in their journals.

COSMIC ANGELS

A variation on "The Daily Word" can be done with a commercial set of fifty-two little cards (about the size of your thumb) called Angel® cards.[12] These cards each have an angel picture and a key word to help us focus on a particular aspect of the inner life (e.g., freedom, peace, forgiveness, patience, love).

The cards are thoroughly mixed and laid face down. Participants then center themselves and ask within to receive the message needed for that particular day, week, or special occasion. With eyes open or closed, choose a card you feel drawn to. The idea is to affirm that you are a clear, open expression of the quality or energy named on the card, to visualize being at one with its essence, and to see it streaming into your life in wonderful ways. When it's time to choose a new card, you're asked to recognize the contribution the current one has made to your life and to release it with your appreciation. Parents and teachers can easily adapt the cards to their particular situations.

Back to Quotations

Start now to collect quotations that you feel will enhance your child's inner joy. Make sure you are attuned to them and that they are not beyond your child's level of understanding.

It has been said that the teachings of all the great philosophies can be reduced to a single idea: that we live in a world of consciousness, not a world of form. The following quotations will help your child's consciousness evolve. Explore and discuss them together. They are to get you started. If they don't appeal to you, you can readily find others in the Bible, quotation books, and elsewhere. While many of these quotations will be familiar to you, remember that they will be new to your children, and that they have stood the test of time.

SELECTED QUOTATIONS

(When no author is indicated, it means the author is unknown.)

> 1. Success comes in cans. Failure comes in can'ts.
>
> FRED SEELY

> 2. The trouble with opportunity is that it often comes
>   disguised as hard work.

3. Look fear in the face and it will cease to trouble you.

   SRI YUKTESWAR

4. The best way to have a friend is to be one.

5. The world is like a mirror
   Reflecting what you do,
   And if your face is smiling
   It smiles right back at you.

6. Politeness is to do and say
   The kindest things in the kindest way.

7. There is no pillow so soft as a clear conscience.

   FRENCH PROVERB

8. Man is just about as happy as he makes up his mind to be.

   ABRAHAM LINCOLN

9. If you fear that people will know, don't do it.

   CHINESE PROVERB

10. Of all the things you wear, your expression is the most
    important.   JANET LANE

11. Most smiles are started by another smile.

12. People who fly into a rage usually make a bad landing.

    WILL ROGERS

13. Seek not greatness, but seek truth and you will find both.

    HORACE MANN

14. Luck is what happens when preparation meets
    opportunity.   ELMER LETTERMAN

15. It is in loving, not being loved,
    The heart finds its quest;
    It is in giving, not getting,
    Our lives are blest.

16. The most completely lost of all days is that on which one
    has not laughed.   CHAMFORT

17. Happy is the person who can laugh at himself. He will
    never cease to be amused.

18. A winner never quits, and a quitter never wins.

19. A man would do nothing, if he waited until he could
    do it so well that no one would find fault with what he
    has done.   CARDINAL NEWMAN

20. There is no limit to what can be done—if it doesn't matter
    who gets the credit.

21. I'll see it when I believe it!

22. Don't find fault—find a remedy. Anybody can complain.

    HENRY FORD

23. If fifty million people say a foolish thing, it is still a foolish thing. ANATOLE FRANCE

24. To be a friend remember that we are human magnets: that like attracts like and that as we give we get. WILFRED PETERSON

25. Don't talk unless you can improve the silence. LAURENCE COUGHLIN

26. Life is like a big red apple . . . only by taking a bite of it can I enjoy it's crisp, juicy sweetness. An apple can't be enjoyed to its fullest by sitting and watching it.

27. With God's help I can do *anything*. ABRAHAM LINCOLN

28. If you don't go out on a limb, you're never going to get the fruit.

29. The feelings that we have predetermine the experience that will come. JACK BOLAND & JULIA CARNEY

30. All that we need to make us really happy is something to be enthusiastic about. CHARLES KINGSLEY

31. A man's true wealth is the good he does in this world. MOHAMMED

32. Only one person in the whole world can defeat you. That is yourself.

33. Use what talents you possess; the woods would be very silent if no birds sang there except those that sang best. HENRY VAN DYKE

34. When there is something wrong with everyone there is something wrong with you.

35. Everything comes to the one who waits, if he works while he waits.

36. We can all live on less when we have more to live for. VIC KITCHEN

37. A loose tongue often gets a person in a tight place.

38. When an optimist gets the worst of it he makes the best of it.

39. You will never FIND time for anything. If you want time, you must MAKE it.

40. Experience is a hard teacher, because she gives you the test first, the lesson afterwards. VERNON LAW

41. The chains of habit are generally too small to be felt until they are too strong to be broken.

42. If you wouldn't write it and sign it, don't say it.

43. If you think you are too small to do a big thing, try doing small things in a big way.

44. It is possible to disagree and still be agreeable.

45. Politeness costs nothing and gains everything.

46. No one can sincerely try to help another without helping himself.

47. Inner correction guarantees outer correction, just as fixing a clock makes its hands go right.

48. What the heart understands today, the head understands tomorrow.

49. The journey of a thousand miles begins with a single step.

50. It may be that those who do most, dream most.

51. A ship in harbor is safe—but that is not what ships are for.
   JOHN A. SHEDD

52. Do not let what you cannot do interfere with what you can do.

53. Procrastination is lack of conviction.   VIC KITCHEN

54. The more one gives, the more one has.   CHINESE PROVERB

55. Our greatest glory is not in never falling, but in rising every time we fall.   CONFUCIUS

56. A certain amount of opposition is a great help to man. Kites rise against, not with the wind.   JOHN NEAL

57. Nothing is too wonderful to happen
Nothing is too good to be true
Nothing is too good to last
   FLORENCE SCOVEL SHINN

58. Giving is an art of instant receiving.

59. If you think you can, or if you think you can't, you're right.

60. Cooperation is doing with a smile what you have to do anyway.

61. One of the most important trips a man can make is in meeting the other fellow halfway.

62. Some people grin and bear it. Others smile and change it.

63. If you always do what you've always done, you'll always get what you've always gotten!

64. It's a funny thing about life: if you refuse to accept anything but the very best you will very often get it.
   W. SOMERSET MAUGHAM

65. Heart has a mind that the brain doesn't understand.

66. 'Tis the set of the sail, and not the gale, that determines the way it goes.

67. Maturity is the ability to live in peace with that which we cannot change. ANN LANDERS

68. The really happy man is one who can enjoy the scenery when on a detour.

69. Great minds have purpose—weak ones, wishes.

70. Well-timed silence has more eloquence than speech.

71. Life lived just to satisfy yourself never satisfies anybody. VIC KITCHEN

72. Consider the postage stamp, my son. It secures success through its ability to stick to one thing 'til it gets there. JOSH BILLINGS

73. When you are down in the mouth, remember Jonah. He came out all right.

74. Let discouragement harden your determination, never your heart.

75. Anything you vividly imagine, ardently desire, sincerely believe in, enthusiastically act upon, must eventually come to pass.

76. If we don't stand for something, we will fall for anything. VIC KITCHEN

77. We can change our whole life and the attitude of people around us simply by changing ourselves. RUDOLF DREIKURS

78. Life is like an orchestra—if a man wants to lead, he must turn his back to the crowd. LAWRENCE WELK

79. Don't discourage the other man's plans unless you have better ones to offer.

80. Who lives content with little, possesses everything.

81. One of these days is none of these days.

82. All that is necessary for the forces of evil to win in the world is for enough good men to do nothing. EDMUND BURKE

83. One person with a belief is equal to ninety-nine who have only interests. JOHN STUART MILL

84. You can only see around you what exists within you. Viewpoint is a state of consciousness. RAYMOND CHARLES BARKER

85. A man's life is dyed the color of his imagination. MARCUS AURELIUS

86. Fear and faith cannot keep house together. When one enters, the other departs.

87. Love seeks no reward, Love is its own reward.

SAI BABA

88. If there is righteousness in the heart,
There will be beauty in character.
If there is beauty in character,
There will be harmony in the home.

When there is harmony in the home,
There will be order in the nation.
When there is order in the nation,
There will be peace in the world.

SAI BABA

89. Do not look back in anger, or forward in fear, but around in awareness.   JAMES THURBER

90. Settle one difficulty and you keep a hundred away.

CONFUCIUS

91. Hate is a weapon you wield by the blade.

92. Failure and success are not accidents, but the strictest justice.   ALEXANDER SMITH

93. Sow a thought and you reap an act;
Sow an act and you reap a habit;
Sow a habit and you reap a character;
Sow a character and you reap a destiny.

94. Man's only limitation lies in the negative use of his imagination.

95. What you can do, or dream you can, begin it.
Boldness has genius, power, and magic in it.

GOETHE

96. When love and skill work together, expect a masterpiece.

JOHN RUSKIN

97. Love may make the world go around but laughter keeps it from getting dizzy.   DON ZOCHERT

98. Men do not attract that which they want, but that which they are.

99. Surround yourself with winners: winners AFFECT you; losers INFECT you.   J. D. ROCKEFELLER

100. Being born is a lifelong process.

101. A man can fail many times, but he isn't a failure until he begins to blame somebody else.

102. The only time you can't afford to fail is the last time you try.   CHARLES KETTERING

103. Obstacles are those frightening things you see when you take your eyes off the goal.   HANNAH MORE

104. One who fears failure limits his worth. Failure is the opportunity to begin again more intelligently.

HENRY FORD

105. Gratitude is a duty which ought to be paid, but which none have the right to expect. ROUSSEAU

106. Minds are like parachutes—they function best when open.

107. We see things not as they are but as we are.

108. Knowledge is awareness of the fact that fire will burn; wisdom is a remembrance of the blister.

ROBERT QUILLEN

109. The size of a man can be measured by the size of the thing that makes him angry. J. K. MORLEY

The following quotes are from Torkom Saraydarian's *Joy and Healing*.[13]

110. You increase your joy by increasing the pure joy of others.

111. The measure of our life is the measure of our love.

112. A life lived for one's own sake does not count. It is only the life lived for the service of others that counts.

113. Every time you criticize you impose yourself on others.

114. Wherever joy is, there can also be seen the presence of beauty, goodness, righteousness, and freedom

115. There is no real true joy if that joy is not imbued with love.

The following quotes are from *A Course in Miracles*.[14]

116. Peace comes not from the absence of conflict in life, but from the ability to cope with it.

117. All anger is nothing more than an attempt to make someone else feel guilty.

118. There are many answers you have received but have not yet heard.

119. All forgiveness is a gift to yourself.

120. *Having* rests on giving, and not on getting.

121. It takes great learning to understand that all things, events, encounters, and circumstances are helpful.

122. To heal is to make joyful.

123. Do you prefer that you be right or happy?

124. Every loving thought is true. Everything else is an appeal for healing and help, regardless of the form it takes.

125. What you see reflects your thinking. And your thinking but reflects your choice of what you want to see.

The following are quotes by Orin from Sanaya Roman's *Living With Joy* (LWJ) and *Personal Power Through Awareness* (PP).[15]

126. When you put out a definite and clear message to the Universe, you rarely have to fight for what you want. (LWJ)

127. Loving yourself means accepting yourself as you are right now. (LWJ)

128. Whatever you appreciate and give thanks for, will increase in your life. (LWJ)

129. You can choose to see the world the way you want. (LWJ)

130. Inner peace is a connection to your deeper self, and it will assist you in letting go of fear. (LWJ)

131. Joy is an inner note that you sound as you move through the day.

132. See everyone as expanding and growing and you will see yourself that way too. (PP)

133. You learn to love by putting yourself into situations that challenge you to be loving. (PP)

134. Whatever you give to others is also a gift to yourself. (PP)

135. Rather than resisting or getting rid of lower thoughts, simply place thoughts of a higher nature by their side. (PP)

136. If you have trouble forgiving people pretend the next time you walk with them it's their last day on earth. (PP)

137. The mind has 40,000 to 50,000 thoughts a day. When 1,000 to 2,000 of those daily thoughts are directed to a goal, it will come rapidly. (PP)

138. If you are in a difficult situation, broadcast love. Love heals and protects you. (PP)

139. Talk of the abilities you aspire to as if you already have them. (PP)

The following are quotes from Arnold Patent's *You Can Have It All*.[16]

140. As you express joy, you draw it out of those you meet, creating joyful people and joyful events. The greater the joy you express, the more joy you experience.

141. Our consciousness is like a sponge. We can fill it with our own ideas and decisions . . . or, if we leave the sponge partly dry, the world around us gladly fills it for us.

142. Your expectation about how someone will act encourages him to act that way.

143. What we believe at any given time creates our experience at that moment.

144. When we see another person as less than perfect, we really see our own imperfection.

145. Life is just a series of events which we have attracted in order to see where we stand in our personal growth.

146. When we see only perfection in someone, what we are told about him does not influence us one way or the other.

147. The essence of each of us is not only perfect, but the same. We only believe in our own perfection when we believe that everyone else is perfect.

148. To achieve unconditional love, you think unconditional love and act unconditionally loving, moment by moment.

149. The Universe misses nothing and always gives us the perfect response to our action or thought.

150. Each of us emits energy signals all of the time, everything that happens to us is just a return to us of something we have asked for—something we have signaled others to give us.

151. We only give to ourselves.

152. What you focus on expands.

153. Using our intuition is listening only to Infinite Intelligence.

154. Following our intuition, our connection with Infinite Intelligence provides us with the perfect signals or guidance without any effort on our part.

155. Judging, evaluating or analyzing anybody inhibits our ability to respond to the real self of that person.

156. Our lives continue to expand in the direction of our existing beliefs.

157. Every attempt we make to resolve a problem by changing something outside of ourselves will be unsuccessful.

158. We are only our essence, which is always perfect.

159. The only reality is that we all love each other; everything else is illusion.

160. There is total safety in the Universe at all times.

161. Our essence cannot experience anything but joyfulness.

NOTES:

Consider adding some of your own favorite quotations below.

8

The Joy of Stories
and Storytelling

You may have tangible wealth untold,
Caskets of jewels and coffers of gold.
Richer than I you could never be;
I know someone who told stories to me.
CYNTHIA PEARL MAUS

Our joy is often sitting there under the surface just waiting to be released. Next to happy songs, inspiring stories get me most in touch with joy. They open my heart, expand my vision, renew my faith in the goodness of life, and help me establish higher ideals for myself. The story can be as short as a one-paragraph anecdote. It's recognizing a truth I know in my soul that triggers my joy.

The Value of Stories

Good stories entertain, inform, provide vicarious insights, help solve problems, stir to action, change attitudes, present high ideals of leadership, and develop a positive expectancy of life. What's more, they do all these things in language children can understand and enjoy.

☆ Stories can motivate children to do and be their very best. We are all more influenced by heroes and role models than by general principles. We can give our children solid values by sharing stories of people who embody these values. Biographies and stories of saints show how the human spirit can overcome obstacles. In the heroic myth the hero faces something that is truly a risk—if not to his life, then to his self-worth or emotional vulnerability. He has temptation to face and an impossible situation to confront. Will he give up? Or will he keep on the path and continue to listen to his inner voice?

When my son was in fifth grade and until his senior year in high school, I read such stories to him over breakfast and while he got ready for school. Sometimes he would read to me while I made his lunch. When our schedules permitted, we did the same thing at dinnertime. He'd read a few pages to me while I prepared the salad, and I'd read to him while he did the dishes. It was a time of sharing and bonding that we'll always cherish.

☆ Stories can tell a particular message indirectly, letting children discover it for themselves. For instance, when I want children to appreciate the value of cooperation or to understand that "as we give, we receive" and that we don't get something for nothing, I have three favorites:

> Stone Soup, by Marcia Brown. Remember how the soldiers tricked the peasants into helping them prepare stone soup, and because each contributed, a lovely feast was had by all?
>
> The Loudest Noise in The World, by Benjamin Elkin. For his birthday, the young prince wanted to hear the loudest noise in the world. He figured it would be everybody shouting, "Happy Birthday!" at the same time. But, as the people gathered in their public squares to participate, the idea spread that "if I'm shouting I won't be able to hear." So no one did.
>
> A West African folktale. I heard this from a talented folklorist, Harlynne Geisler.[1] The king of the village announced he was having a feast, and asked the villagers each to bring some palm wine for the communal vat. Although this was freely available by tapping the surrounding palm trees, everybody happened to be low on palm wine at the time. Since the wine looked just like water, each thought that no one would know if he only brought water instead.

✮ A story can relieve tension and calm emotions—in the classroom, on the playground, in the car, in the home. It can also nip rebellion in the bud. American Indian parents avoid giving commands to their children, and hence causing resentment, by showing them the reason for desired behavior in the form of a story. According to Jeanette Brown, "the suggested action is portrayed, with good or evil consequences to the doer or the shirker."[2]

✮ Stories can ignite and feed children's imagination. They can stir their listeners to look beyond things as they are, to how they might be.

Fairy tales, besides appealing to the imagination, have a special value for children. They can touch their souls. In the words of Almut Bockemuhl, "Up to about ten years of age, the child can understand the fairy tale pictures immediately, if not intellectually. They rest within the soul and let him sense the secret of life. Later on these pictures transform themselves into powers of understanding." And she adds, "Each character belongs to us and is part of our own soul."[3] Nothing is gained by explaining. When children begin to ask, "Is that really true?" she suggests we answer, "Here in our world it is not like that, but in the land of fairy tales it is true." Let's remember that young children see into realms beyond the third dimension.

✮ A story can be a short and effective way to drive home a point. Here's a simple example by an unknown author:

The Builder

There was once an expert builder who had worked for years in a large company and had reached the age of retirement. His employer asked him to build one more house; it was to be his last commission.

The builder took the job, but his heart was not in it. He used inferior materials, the timber was poor, and he failed to see the many things that would have been clear to him had he shown even his normal interest in his work.

When at last the house was built, his employer came to him and said, "Here, take the key, the house is yours, it is a present from me!" The builder immediately regretted that he had not used the best materials and engaged the most capable workers. If only he had known that the house was for him . . .

✮ A story can prepare a child for an experience or interpret that experience: a trip to the dentist, the arrival of a newborn sibling, the death of a friend.

☆ Stories unite all of us in a common understanding. They help us to be sensitive, compassionate, and in touch with our deeper feelings.

What Stories and When?

First, let's hear what former Secretary of Education William J. Bennett had to say in a recent speech on values in education:

> There is a wealth of material to draw on—material that virtually all schools once taught to students for the sake of shaping character. . . .
>
> Do we want them to know what honesty means? Then we might teach them about Abraham Lincoln walking three miles to return six cents and, conversely, about Aesop's shepherd boy who cried wolf.
>
> Do we want them to know what courage means? Then we might teach them about Joan of Arc, Horatius at the bridge, Harriet Tubman and the Underground Railroad.
>
> Do we want them to know about kindness and compassion and the opposite of these? Then we should have them read *A Christmas Carol* and the *Diary of Anne Frank*, and later, *King Lear*.
>
> Do we want them to know about loyalty to country? Then we should want them to know of Nathan Hale and about the Battle of Britain and the pass at Thermopylae. They should know about a man like Lt. Elmo Zumwalt, who served his country willingly and nobly. Also, they should understand the contrary examples of men like Benedict Arnold and John A. Walker.
>
> Do we want them to know what faithfulness to family and friends means? Then we tell them about how Penelope and Telemachus and even an old dog waited twenty years for Odysseus to come home.
>
> Do we want them to know about respect for the law? Then we should be sure they understand why Socrates told Crito, "No, I must submit to the decree of Athens."
>
> Do we want them to know about persistence in the face of adversity? Then we should tell them about the Donner Party, Columbus, George Washington during the Revolution, and Lincoln during the Civil War. Our youngest should be told about the Little Engine That Could.
>
> Do we want them to recognize vanity? Then we should tell them of King Midas.
>
> Do we want them to know about overreaching ambition?

Then we should have them read about Macbeth and Lady Macbeth.

Do we want them to know that hard work pays off? Then we should teach them about the Wright brothers at Kitty Hawk and about Booker T. Washington learning to read. Do we want them to see the danger of an unreasoning conformity? Then we would tell them about "The Emperor's New Clothes" and about Galileo.

Do we want them to see that one individual's action can make all the difference? Then we should tell them about Rosa Parks and about one man's discovery of a vaccine against polio.

Do we want them to respect the rights of others? Then we should have them read the Declaration of Independence, the Gettysburg Address, and "Letter from Birmingham Jail."

There are some other stories we can include—stories from the Bible: Ruth's loyalty to Naomi, Joseph's forgiveness of his brothers, Jonathan's friendship with David, the Good Samaritan's kindness toward a stranger, Cain's treatment of Abel, David's cleverness and courage in facing Goliath. These are great stories, and we should be able to use them in teaching character to our children. Why? Because they teach moral values we all share. And they shouldn't be thrown out just because they are in the Bible.[4]

FABLES. Aesop's fables are a wonderful source of stories. In them are found deep truths, wit, wisdom, and morality. They make us smile because we recognize our own inherent traits. Their characters are simply drawn and do not change: the fox is always sly; the cat always pursues the mouse; and the lion is always king, strong and majestic. Martin Luther said that, next to the stories of the Bible, students should study the fables of Aesop. They speak to our hearts and teach us by their clear examples.

You might also want to explore fables from other countries—Japan, India, China, Greece—or from the Renaissance period. Some modern fables have been written by Lewis Carroll, Charles Kingsley, Rudyard Kipling, Kenneth Graham, Beatrix Potter, Hans Christian Andersen, and J. R. R. Tolkien.

MYTHS. Mythology captivates children because its larger-than-life beings perform miracles that defy the normal order of things, and because the great mysteries of life are often explained in magical terms. Stories like Homer's *Iliad* and *Odyssey*, the Epic of Gilgamesh, the Norse myths, and countless others ignite the imagination.

FAIRY TALES. One of the most potent means of educating young children, fairy tales offer their wisdom in the form of pictures. They develop a moral sense by their examples. The good must win and the bad be defeated. The prince striving for his princess is anyone striving towards an ideal. Being lost in the forest is an allegory for our own troubles in this material world. The people the hero encounters, those who help and those who hinder, are the conflicting forces with which we have to contend in life. Bruno Bettelheim says, "The fairy tale expresses in words and action the things which go on in children's minds."[5] It is fascinating to read his detailed interpretation of a story such as "Little Red Riding Hood." There is so much more to fairy tales than most of us are aware of. I bet you never guessed that "Goldilocks and the Three Bears" really is about sibling rivalry and the search for identity.

SPECIFIC STORY SOURCES

1. In *The Radiant Child*, there is a wonderful annotated bibliography of transpersonal children's literature.[6]

2. The Sathya Sai Book Center of America has three little booklets titled *Stories for Children* that are appropriate for teaching values to children, ages 6–12. Also, they have a wonderful book, *Lesson Plans for Education in Human Values: International Edition*, in which stories are categorized according to the value being taught.[7]

3. The Ananda School has a list of uplifting books for children and young adults, free for the asking.[8]

4. The Vedanta Society has children's books available by mail order—Indian myths, fables, folktales.[9]

5. *Teaching Children Joy* is a guide for parents of preschool-age children. At the end of each of the thirteen chapters there is a lovely original story, with a reading list of children's stories appropriate to the chapter subject.[10]

6. *Whole Child–Whole Parent* has several fine bibliographies. One lengthy one is entitled "Good Books for Children," which divides stories into stages one, two, three, and four.[11]

7. *Unfinished Stories: Facilitating Decision Making in the Elementary Classroom* could be used as a different approach to storytelling, one where you build up to a climax and the children finish the story, either orally or in writing. These stories, intended for grades four through seven, focus on ethical problems in three general categories: responsibility for and commitment to others, personal shortcomings, shortcomings of others.[12]

8. Books on Indian saints and Indian legends, along with the educational principles of Sri Aurobindo, are available through Auromere.[13]

9. Aquarian Age Stories for Children are available from the Rosicrucian Fellowship.[14]

10. *The Stress-Proof Child* has a bibliography for children seven to ten and another for children ten to fourteen.[15]

11. Harlynne Geisler of San Diego is a talented professional storyteller who does workshops and lectures widely. She's developed some useful bibliographies you can send for.[16] These include "Stories To Tell," "Subject Indices and Age Lists for Stories," "Short Short Tales," "Urban Legends," "Participation Stories," "Stories with Songs in Them," and "Books and Organizations about Storytelling"—this last one lists a fine book for parents: *Creative Storytelling* by Jack Maguire.

12. NAPPS is the National Association for the Preservation and Perpetuation of Storytelling, a nationwide organization devoted to encouraging the practice, use, and application of storytelling in contemporary America. It offers a year-round program of activities and a catalog of over a hundred storytelling albums, cassettes and books.[17]

13. Most states have a storytellers' organization. In Arizona it's called "Teller of Tales," but the names vary from state to state. Such groups give you the opportunity to practice storytelling, to learn from both amateurs and professionals, and to meet with storytellers who can then come to your classroom or club. There are many storytellers who make their living this way. In Arizona, Dennis Freeman and Cat Burdulis are just two examples.[18] Dennis and Cat tell stories for assemblies, workshops, and concerts, and also hire on as resident storytellers in schools. To get in touch with the organization in your state, contact NAPPS or your library system.

STORY INTERESTS FOR DIFFERENT AGES

EARLY CHILDHOOD (ages 3–5): This realistic age-group is interested in familiar things. The child's attention is centered on the things and the people she knows—mother, father, dogs, birds, children. Consequently, she enjoys stories and jingles about these.

MIDDLE CHILDHOOD (ages 6–8): Fairy stories, folk tales, fables, legends, Grimms' fairy tales, and Old Testament stories. Middle childhood is the time of imagination and make-believe. The child delights in pretending to be someone other than herself.

LATER CHILDHOOD (ages 9–11): Nordic, Celtic, and German sagas; myths of India, Persia, Egypt, and Greece; folklore; Bible stories; Greek and Roman history. This is the heroic, dramatic, exploratory, adventurous period: these children crave action, daring, and even danger. Monitoring movies and books is important for this age group.

EARLY ADOLESCENCE (ages 12–17): Tales of chivalry; King Arthur; Renaissance and Medieval times; Reformation; U.S. history; modern Europe. This is the age of high idealism, sometimes called the "epic" period. During this time the dominant story interest may be characterized by the term "attainment." This group likes to look behind physical bravery for its motive or ideal.

The Value of Storytelling

> *A story is a mind picture painted by the human voice and the voice is far more wonderful than the hand.*
>
> EGGLESTON

We may all derive more value and joy from a story told than from a story read. As Cathryn Wellner relates:

> A man visited an African tribe which had recently acquired electricity and a communal television set. For two weeks activity stopped while the villagers sat glued to the screen. Then they lost interest. Wondering why TV had so little appeal, he asked a tribesman. They did not need television, the man replied, because they had the storyteller. The answer puzzled the outsider. After all, the television surely knew more stories than one man could. The villager thought for a minute and then grinned. "Oh, yes," he said, "the television knows many stories, but the storyteller knows me."[19]

The storyteller can meet individual needs in a way that neither TV nor books can. Here are some of the benefits of *telling* stories to children:

> ☆ An intimacy is created between the child and storyteller by being able to look at one another. A special rapport results. This focused love benefits child and storyteller alike in unseen ways.

> ☆ Making up a story can provide the answer to a difficult question or situation better than any book or written story.

> ☆ Storytelling can reach children of all ages, whereas a picture book story is awkward with a mixed age group. By focusing the story toward the youngest child but keeping eye contact with all the children, everyone can be made to feel included.

> ☆ Storytelling allows you to change or rearrange your story as you observe the children. You may build up certain parts and let go of others according to what you sense from them.

> ☆ A storyteller can make a character come alive. He can bring to life for the listeners things that might not seem real to them in any other way.

> ☆ Telling good stories can inspire and encourage in children an appreciation for literature. The child can be exposed to stories from literary masterpieces beyond his reading level. His background is enriched and his experience enlarged.

> ☆ With storytelling, children's attention span is usually longer, and their retention better—especially if puppets tell the story.

> ☆ Hearing stories told gives children practice in visualization. As they listen, they can imagine the characters, the actions, and the scenes—something TV doesn't give them the opportunity to do.

☆ There is pure joy in hearing a good story. Storytelling is the language of the heart.

Creating Stories

One of the joys of storytelling is creating your own special stories for those very special children. (By the way, let your children know frequently just how special they are—but also that *everybody* is special.)

☆ Consider creating a storybook for your preschooler of her most important experiences. Simply write a few sentences in a loose-leaf notebook. (Be sure to date your entries for your benefit.) Start about age two, when the child is getting around on his own and has developed some vocabulary. Use words the child understands.

Stories of a child's own experience give her a chance to reflect on what has happened to her. Recalling incidents will help her emotionally and intellectually make peace with past events (past is yesterday or last week). Often they have occurred too rapidly to be fully digested at the time. This seems particularly true with moments of joy, and the more these are recalled, the more she'll be able to recreate those feelings.

So take a few minutes to tell a story about your child's trip to the park, the beach, or the doctor's office, or about a visit from Aunt Jean or meeting a new playmate. The child will want to hear these simple stories over and over, because they highlight her joys, fears, questions, and adventures. They'll help her understand and grow from her experience.

☆ Write an original story. An idea might pop into your head while meditating, journaling, or driving in the car. Capture it and develop it. You might be assisted by unseen helpers if you call on them. I have included an example of such a story in Chapter 12. Written by Cindy Thomas, a young lady from Mesa, Arizona, the story appears in the second lesson plan of that chapter.

☆ Use the Forced Association Principle to create a story.[20] You can have the fun of creating such a story by yourself, or you can involve older children and make it a group effort.

1. First list six to eight characters that you might meet in any kind of situation: teacher, parent, pilot, fireman, child, coach.
2. Then list six to eight objectives that any person

might hope to attain. Include two types of goals: (a) possession of something, such as a job, skills, friends, a bike; (b) relief from something, such as illness, fear, habits.

3. Next list six to eight obstacles which might confront a person as he tries to reach his goals. Examples might be having no money, lacking education, being ill, having an enemy.

4. List six to eight possible ways one might surmount an obstacle in one's life. Examples might be force, staying awake, moving, a partnership, winning a contest.

5. Then choose randomly from each list one character, one objective, one obstacle, and one way of overcoming. A good way is to close your eyes and let your pencil fall on one idea from each column. Then let your imagination go and weave the four elements into a story plot. Keep in mind the age group of your audience. For the next story, you may wish to randomly select another four elements and weave yourself or your child into the plot as an additional character.

   This forced association approach was also used by Fran Striker, author of "The Lone Ranger" radio and television series.

Of the many good ideas for creating stories, the following six work especially well with groups of children:

A Picture-Based Story. Find a picture large enough for your whole group to see together, and create a story around it. It is best to have a "stop action" picture—one where a moment of action is captured. You might want to use more than one and force a relationship between them. I have used a lot of pictures with preschool groups. I would arrange them in a story sequence and tape a bit of sandpaper on the back so that they could cling to a felt board. With older children you can ask what the characters in the picture are doing and why, and what happened before and after.

A Group Story. I have seen an adept "storymaker," Mike Gilbert, develop a group story most effectively.[21] You might want to try it out. The "storymaker" asks for characters and lists several on the board. New kinds of characters are encouraged, unusual objects, animals, or people. Then, through group consensus, he chooses one from the list and asks the group to describe it, using their five senses. After asking questions about the character's personality, the "storymaker" then paints a word picture of the character.

Next, he elicits from his audience the setting, the time period, and the goal or problem this character has. He may ask for ways this problem can be solved. Then the "storymaker" begins the story, stopping every so often to ask questions, such as "Who did he see?" "What did the stranger say?" "What did she want to eat?" or anything else he may want help with. In this way the audience plays a vital role in evolving the story.

"I Was There." This is another fun way to let children take part in the joy of storytelling. It requires a lot of flexibility on your part. You begin a story and, at any time, a child can interrupt and say "I was there." At this point she is allowed to give her first person account of the incident. When the contributor is done, everyone says "Thank you, (child's name)," and the storyteller continues from where the contributor left off.

Tall Tales. Before using stories of exaggerated fancy (such as Paul Bunyan, Pecos Bill, and John Henry), you may wish to play the Tall Tale Game. Start out by telling a simple incident. Going around the circle, the person on your left says roughly the same thing but exaggerates it a bit. The next person exaggerates a bit more, and so on, until the tale has changed completely.

A Problem-Solving Story. Choose a problem or challenge pertinent to your group of children or a particular child. Create a story, outlining the problem in disguised form. Stop where the main character must decide what to do, and ask the children what happens next. As they discuss how the problem might be solved in this hypothetical situation, they'll gain insight into how to work out different solutions to real problems. You can end the story as you see fit, or let a child tell the ending if good ideas have come forth.

Puppet Skits. Create your own puppet skits for situations where you can't find an appropriate story or where you especially want the lesson to be remembered. An old proverb says: "I hear, but I forget; I see, and I remember; I do, and I understand."

Puppets are especially effective for problem-solving stories. They can act out misbehavior, such as not following safety rules, and give children insight into the consequences of such actions. Puppets help children see themselves. Through observing the unhappiness of the timid or the overly aggressive puppet, children may change the ways they act or react.

The more serious the subject, the more useful puppets seem to be at conveying the needed message. There are puppet scripts available now on such topics as child abuse, substance abuse, racial prejudice, sibling rivalry, low self-esteem, lying, jealousy, and understanding handicaps.[22] Kids On The Block is a special puppet troupe whose purpose is to heighten awareness of handicapped persons. Skits on such subjects as mental retardation, learning disabilities, blindness, deafness, asthma, cerebral palsy, and child abuse are put on by volunteers all over the country.[23]

Storytelling Hints

First and foremost, make sure you love the story. Remember, children sense your feelings and it will confuse them if you are saying one thing and feeling another.

Choose a story that you can tell in fifteen minutes or less. The attention span of children is roughly the same in minutes as their age in years.

Plan appropriate discussion questions while planning the story.

Don't put on a precious voice, even to tell a story to preschoolers. Children loathe a monotonous tone, so cultivate variety, but avoiding the "honeyed accent."

Set the scene in your children's minds before you start.

Tell stories with action, animation, enthusiasm, and sincerity. Live each character in your mind.

Add sound effects to the story—use your imagination or ask older children for suggestions.

Let the story speak for itself. Don't tack a moral onto the end or say, "This is what the story means." Leave it open to interpretation. Trust children to come up with more than you can tell them about what's in your story. You may wish to have them think about the story for two or three minutes first, to see what meaning they find in it. Then have them write out its moral or larger meaning. If you have the children share, they'll hear many valid interpretations of the same story.

Let younger children participate. They can say some lines or do some actions along with the storyteller. Let them repeat sound effects, make hand gestures, repeat certain words, or sing the song, if there is one. Even older children love Echo Pantomime—where they repeat stanzas and copy the storyteller's pantomime.

For younger children, repeat the same stories many times. They love it, and it implants the lesson. For older children this is unnecessary. Also, sound effects and dramatic character voices are not recommended for older children, unless you're very talented.

Use puppets to tell your story. Puppets are fun and help your story make an indelible impression. You can have a puppet tell your story instead of you, or you can adapt your story to be acted out by two or three hand puppets. Or you might use a puppet to introduce your story and describe the setting. The puppet could ask questions or make comments during the story, if that's appropriate, or lead the group discussion following the story.

Review your stories to make lasting impressions. A week after telling one you might have a child tell the story back. Or you might tell it again, making a number of mistakes to test how well the children listened. They might act out the story or have the puppets do it. This enables them to experience the value illustrated in the story. They might enjoy creating a group mural of the story or making individual cartoon strips from it, or even writing up the story as a TV program or news report.

Learning A Story

Storytelling takes careful preparation, but the advantages far outweigh the disadvantages. Be sure you have chosen a story that has a message you truly want to impart.

Familiarize yourself with the parts of your story: the introduction, the action or plot, the climax, the conclusion.

Make a brief outline of these four parts:

1. Introduction—arouses curiosity and presents the characters, setting, and situation.
2. Plot—the sequence of events that shows progress toward the climax. Somebody said that every plot can be summed up in these four words: somebody wanted . . . but . . . so . . . (e.g., Three billy goats wanted to cross the bridge but . . . so . . .)
3. Climax—the highest point of interest, where the truth is revealed.
4. Conclusion—winds everything up quickly and satisfyingly.

Visualize your characters. Know what they look like, even if you're not going to describe them. See them in various scenes.

Don't try to memorize the story. Just impress a picture or a sequence in your mind.

Decide which way you might best learn the story. Are you an aural, a visual, or a kinesthetic learner?

If you're a visual learner, decide which is better for you—words or pictures. If words, photocopy the story and carry it around, reading it many times during your spare moments. If pictures, find a picture book version of the story or use adding machine paper and draw a stick figure cartoon strip. Or sit back and watch a movie in your mind, complete with details.

If you're an aural learner, make a tape of the story. NAPPS[24] has a catalog listing story tapes, and many libraries have tapes and phonograph records of stories. When you're reading the story, read it aloud. Like the visual learner, watch a movie in the mind, but put most of your attention on the soundtrack, the dialogue.

If you're a kinesthetic learner, type or write out the story in your own words. Or you may prefer to act out the various roles in the story, props included. Props need to be used so they'll make a clear mental impression and not be forgotten during the storytelling. Where would "Little Red Riding Hood" be without her basket?

Tell the story to yourself as often as possible. Tell it to anyone who will listen. Tell it to your tape recorder. Consider what details you might add to make the story more meaningful for your particular audience.

Put joy into preparing your story, as well as into telling it, and the children will feel your joy.

> *All the world's a stage,*
> *and all the men and women merely players;*
> *They have their exits and their entrances;*
> *And one man in his time plays many parts.*
>
> SHAKESPEARE, *As You Like It*

NOTES:

As you've read this chapter, undoubtedly other stories have come to mind that teach values you deem important. Consider recording here those stories you might share with your children, and starring those you love enough to learn to tell.

"What's That For?"

SOLIDIFYING PRINCIPLES WITH VISUAL ANALOGIES

All truly wise thoughts have been
thought thousands of times;
but to make them really ours we must
think them over again honestly till
they take root in our personal expression.

GOETHE

Most of you are acquainted with visual analogies—using familiar objects to explain unfamiliar ideas, usually abstract principles. Many hard-to-understand truths can be symbolized by easy-to-understand objects.

I offer here an assortment of such analogies to illustrate the universal principles and key concepts in this book. They are meant to start you thinking. I hope you will embellish them, and others of your own making, into appropriate and complete lessons. Some of the analogies will be too abstract for the young child. You must decide which ones are suitable for your particular children.

As much as possible, I have made use of common household objects. Spare moments or mealtimes can easily become occasions to teach children to look at the world in new ways. Having the objects around will remind them—and you—of the principles.

1. If you wish to remind children that fear is at the root of all negative feelings, put the word FEAR on a card at the bottom of a small box. Invite the children, and

yourself, to write down things that elicit anger or irritation on separate slips of paper. Crumple these up and toss them into the box. Throughout the week, as more crumpled paper with irritations and angers are tossed into the box—both figuratively and actually, the box becomes a clear reminder that hidden underneath them all is FEAR.

2. Love has been called the universal solvent. Love can dissolve all that troubles us. A quick object lesson would be a glass or white bowl with pink water (use a drop of red food coloring). Love dissolves fear—and disturbance, annoyance, worry, concern for the future, etc. These can be represented by salt or something that would easily dissolve in the water of love.

3. Love has also been correctly called the glue that holds the universe together. If you think about it, this does not contradict the above. One could get a glue stick or bottle for each child and label each one LOVE (with a gummed back sticker). Explain that where there is love, there is cohesion—a coming together. When we're not feeling love, we're feeling a separateness from others or from God. Think of a gluing exercise appropriate for the children's age. One idea is to let a large sheet of paper represent the child, and have her glue to it scraps of colored paper with names of people, activities, things, foods, animals, and places that she loves.
Another idea is to use those little note pads of gummed-back paper to symbolize love. The glue on the back can show that "love sticks." The child can be given a plain piece of paper and a sticky-back piece and told to stick both to the wall. The plain paper, which doesn't stick to anything, represents resistance. The love paper sticks to the wall, because love takes away resistance. When we're filled with love, we do what is best for us.

4. Our brain will absorb the thoughts and ideas it is fed. Take an absorbent sponge and cut it into an irregular oval to represent the brain. Place it on a sheet of construction paper and have the child draw the rest of her head and shoulders. Have available a glass of clean water and a glass of dirty-looking water. Explain that these represent loving, pure thoughts and negative fearful thoughts. Offer examples of such thoughts from the child's life—school, TV, friends, family members. Encourage the child to give his own examples and let him dribble the corresponding water onto the sponge. Help him see that he has the power of choice and can choose which kind of thoughts to let enter his brain.

5. "If thou canst believe, all things are possible to him that believeth." Mark 9:23. After locating a mail order catalog, make sure the children know how the mail order system works. You may even let them place an order. Explain that when you place an order through the catalog, you have mentally accepted the item—you believe you now have it. This belief is necessary for manifestation. This is how the creative law works in our lives: "I'll see it because I believe it."

6. There are a number of ways to visualize the basic Law of Cause and Effect, often called the Boomerang Law. It is important for children to know that they live in a world of perfect justice—that they never have to worry about getting back at someone. Lacking a boomerang, I usually use a Chinese yo-yo because they're inexpensive enough to have a number of them for the children to experiment with. For older children consider regular yo-yo's, or a rubber band around an object or their wrist.

7. To remind children to lean on the God within, not on people, choose two small items that will lean against each other in a standing position. Some possibilities are soda or graham crackers, gelatin or pudding boxes. Crackers are especially effective because each child can have two, and can then eat them afterwards. Lean the two objects against each other in a standing position and show how unstable their position is by tapping one just slightly so that they both fall. Explain that the crackers or boxes are just like people. When people lean on each other they are likely to fall. When we lean on the God Spirit within, we'll always be supported. Prop a box of crackers against a solid wall-like surface, which represents God. Point out how that support won't give way with a slight tap. God is all-powerful, all-knowing, and everywhere present. God is love. What better support is there? How much wiser we would be to lean on God instead of our friends.

8. One of the things that keep us from remembering our natural state of joy is forgetting that we are all connected. We all use, as Emerson said, "the one mind common to all individual men." Show the child a hairbrush with a lot of bristles, or a whisk broom. Suggest that the base of the brush represents the One Mind. Just as the bristles are all unified at the base, so we humans are all unified in the One Mind. Mind is expressing itself through a multitude of separate human forms. Older children can come to know that there is no such thing as your mind and my mind. Mind is one—and we all use it. Be sure to differentiate between Mind and brain. Another way of showing this is with a large circle full of random dots. The circle represents the One Mind, the one consciousness, and the dots represent all of us who are expressions of it.

9. The hand is certainly the most readily accessible tool for visual analogies. It's been used to illustrate many points. Here are two of my favorites:
The fingers can represent individuals or races. Our fingers are peninsulas, not islands. The further we go back into reality—into the palm of the hand, the more "one" we become.
The hand can also be used to show right action between individuals and God. In this analogy, the thumb, which is separate from the fingers, represents God. Without the thumb, the four fingers don't work effectively. Without acknowledging God, neither do we function effectively. As each finger bows down to the thumb, or a person submits to God's will, he feels a sense of joy because right movement starts

taking place in his life. He's not going it alone. If the child is old enough, he can understand that he has four lower bodies—physical, emotional, mental, and etheric —which the four fingers can represent.

10. Older children, and all of us, can use a reminder that we're creating our future now. It is built by the thoughts, feelings, actions, and beliefs of the present. Consider purchasing a large quantity of popsicle sticks or tongue depressors. Put the initial T (THOUGHTS) on some, F (FEELINGS) on some, A (ACTIONS), and B (BELIEFS) on the rest. Suggest that your child build a structure entitled FUTURE. It may be a log cabin, a tower, a spaceship, or whatever. Offer help if it is needed. When it is finished, point out what the letters stand for on the building materials. Remind him that he is building his future with them right now.

11. A strong positive attitude can overcome most of life's obstacles. Use a raw potato to represent the challenge or obstacle and a straw to represent an "I can do it" attitude. Desire-power is the quick thrust of the hand that drives the straw through the potato. It may take two or three attempts, but it is certainly possible and a lot of fun.

12. It is always helpful to have reminders of the power of prayer and meditation. In this object lesson you'll need a tube of toothpaste (wrapped in masking tape if you wish to avoid advertising) and a flashlight. The flashlight represents Divine Light— the illumination and power of God. We draw it to us through prayer and meditation. The tube represents our consciousness, our thoughts and feelings. The more we spend time thinking about God, the one power, the closer the light comes. Shine the flashlight down on the tube. Press the opened tube gently with the flashlight so that it presses out Divine ideas (the toothpaste). The more we ask for light in our mind, the more it presses out good ideas, God ideas. This Higher Wisdom creates the harmony, peace, order, and abundance in our experience.

13. Light analogies are always useful for understanding our true identity. We are all lights (our inner selves) covered with lampshades (our ego personalities). In dealing with others, we always have the choice of focusing on either their light or their lampshade. Since what we focus on expands, we want to look for the light, or God qualities, in others and ignore the human frailties. And we want to do the same for ourselves. This can lead to forgiveness.

14. The above analogy can be amplified by using the same lamp with bulbs of varying sizes. Explain that the current flowing through the lamp is unlimited. We can either tap into it with a small bulb and experience dim light, or we can put in a powerful bulb and experience brilliant light. This current is, of course, the one power, the Source. The bulbs represent the yearning of our heart. The more intensely we want the light and are willing to let go of the negativity and judgmentalness that

blocks it, the brighter our light will shine. The intensity of our desire to be in the Light will determine the size of our bulb.

15. A universal principle is "Where my attention goes, energy flows." The light bulbs above illustrate this, and so does a lasso. Our attention can be compared to a lasso which pulls the object of our attention into our world. It connects us with the essence of what we're putting our attention on. You might make a miniature lasso for demonstration or show pictures of cowboys lassoing cattle. Also see the activity "What Gets My Attention Gets Me" in Lesson Plan 2 of Chapter 12.

16. A balance scale is useful to build an awareness of self-talk and to teach about affirmations. If you don't have one, improvise a mini-tabletop teeter-totter. I use beans to represent seed-thoughts and place the positive seed-thoughts in one pan of the scale and the negative in the other. Let your child come up with a limiting thought or feeling she has had about herself in the last day or two. Place a bean on one side of the scale. Explain that it usually takes about ten positive thoughts to cancel out one strong negative one. Help her to come up with ten self-talk statements or affirmations that would cancel out the negative thought on the other side of the scale. As she does so, she can place beans, one by one, in the scale pan and observe the shift in balance. If there is a group of children, they can take turns and help each other think of supportive affirmations. Remind them that it is not the words but our feelings that create.

17. Look at a hammer with your child and discuss how it can be used to either build or destroy. Show how the same is true with our thoughts and feelings. You might want to use a match and discuss how fire can destroy or serve us. And the same is true of our energy. Misguided energy can be destructive to the body, to relationships, to new ideas and projects.

18. Our true self is clear and perfect, like a diamond, but it is covered over with layers of illusion—with a false self—just like a child wearing a Halloween mask. The outside layers of an onion can also represent the "little self." The children can peel off layers that represent such things as unworthiness, lack of self-love, fears, guilt, limiting ideas. When they get to the core of the onion, it will represent their essence. The core is our higher self, that is totally free, unlimited, and unhampered by our dense physical body. This is the self that feels unconditional love and joy at all times, the self that knows its immortality. Another way of depicting our essence is through the use of a pearl and an oyster shell. The pearl is the real self, in all its purity and beauty. The shell that hides our true self is the body and personality. It's a dense covering hiding the light inside us, but we can go within and find it. Meditation and a willingness to look for it in ourself and others will help. Our joy will help. It is both means and end.

19. When we're faced with irritation, the above oyster and pearl can also help. Grains of sand work themselves inside the oyster's shell and begin irritating him. He tries to get rid of them, but when he can't, he turns the irritation into a highly prized gem—a beautiful pearl. We can choose to take the energy we're putting into irritation and put it into something beautiful—like a creative endeavor or helping those in need.

20. The strength of habits is fun to demonstrate. Here are a couple of analogies you can make with thread, string, or yarn. Which you use may depend on the size and strength of the children. They can break one thread, then two threads, then three threads that are twisted together. As a habit becomes more entrenched (more threads added), it becomes more difficult to break. This can be applied to habits the youngsters want to break—or to those they want to establish. Discuss what habits they may now be forming.

21. Someone has said, "To be angry is to punish oneself for another's mistake." I often remind myself that anger is a weapon I wield by the blade. A sharp knife can demonstrate this in the mind of older children. Ask them: "If you were to hit someone with the handle of the knife while holding the blade, who do you think would be hurt the most?" A less graphic, but also apt, analogy is to compare one's blood to the white of an egg. The heat of the skillet can be anger. It takes very little heat before the egg white starts to coagulate and very little anger to heat up the blood. The saying, "He's reached his boiling point," very nearly describes what is going on inside with the blood. The heating of the blood destroys blood cells, reduces memory power, and aggravates one's physical weaknesses. A scientist has pointed out that the electrical energy released by one burst of anger is sufficient to light a two-cell flashlight bulb for three months.

22. One of my friends tapes the two halves of a geode together to show to her high school students, explaining that the geode is symbolic of them. After comments about how ugly it is and how they don't want to be compared to a dull gray rock, she separates the two halves and reveals the beautiful crystalline interior. This symbolizes their inner perfection, their true nature, the real self that has been covered over. She asks them not to identify with their failings and shortcomings, but with the radiant, pure spark within.

23. Visual analogies are useful for explaining our relationship with the Source. The ocean as the Source and individuals as waves may be a hard concept to depict. I favor showing the body full of, and totally immersed in, Spirit. This can be illustrated by placing a tiny jar, like a pill bottle with the lid off, in a bowl of water. The water represents pure Spirit and it is both inside and outside the body, which is represented by the little bottle. Children learn that they are not their body and that their body is contained within their being.

Another way to show that we are visible forms of Spirit is by using a bowl of cold water with ice cubes in it. The ice cubes represent people and the water represents Spirit, the invisible power of the Universe. As water can change form and become steam or ice, Spirit, which is invisible, can also take form. We are a visible form of Spirit, just as the ice cubes are a form of water. This analogy can also be used to explain the death of a body. As ice melts and becomes water again, we simply lay aside our bodies and our spirits return to Spirit, or the so-called invisible.

A tasty lesson is showing a loaf of bread to explain our relationship to the Source. Children are each given a chunk of bread of a different shape and size. They are led to understand that even though all the pieces look different, each has identical ingredients because it is from the one loaf. The pieces of bread are like them, and the loaf is like Spirit or God. Since Spirit is everywhere present, it is in them. They have the same innate attributes.

24. There are a number of analogies to help children understand that they are not their body, and that death is only a door on the road of life—not a wall or a dead-end. We are energy, and energy never dies. At the dinner table you can pour some salt or sugar in a glass of water. It still exists—you can taste it; it's just in a different form.

You might also have children observe the blade of a small fan. When not in motion, the blades are easily visible, but when you speed up their vibration (turn it on), they seem invisible. There is a lot of life that is invisible to us just because it's vibrating so fast.

A balloon is often a useful analogy for explaining the dropping of the body and the continuation of life. The life, air, on the inside of the balloon, is what gives it its shape and size—it's the important part. When the balloon pops and shrivels, the air rejoins the larger body of air outside it. It is the same with the release of life when the body dies.

The dropping of the body could also be compared to the dropping of the outer skin of an onion, or the husk on an ear of corn. The inside of the onion, or the ear of corn, can be compared to our spiritual body. A glove, like our bodies, is merely a covering for the hand, or our spirit. Older children can learn that our real hands are etheric hands—clothed with gloves of physical matter.

25. Here is one of my favorites—an outstanding analogy for showing children that they are not their awareness. What joy is released when children can see that they no longer need to feel guilty about anything because they were doing all their awareness permitted at the time. Guilt robs us all of so much joy. It is from the Facilitator's Manual for Taking Active Charge of Your Life, a five-session self-esteem course for teens and preteens.[1] I can't do justice to the analogy in this limited space, but I'll give you the main idea. Use a toy car (about 3" × 6" in size) with a windshield. If it has no windshield, improvise one with plastic wrap.

The components of the analogy:

Car = body
Driver = you, the being
Windshield = seeing and understanding
Clearness of the windshield = clearness of your seeing and
  understanding
Streaks of marker (or dry erase) on windshield = mud

Authors Harmon and Jarmin explain:

> Is the driver a part of the car? No. Her job is to operate the car
> and make it go. Is the driver what the car does? No. She controls
> the car but she is not what it does. The driver is obviously not
> the windshield, but its clearness affects how well she drives.
> So it is with you. You are the being who controls the brain,
> and your brain controls your body. Just as the driver is not
> the car nor what it does, neither are you your body, or what it
> does. Just as the clearness of the windshield determines how
> well the driver drives, so does the clearness of your seeing and
> understanding determine how well you run your body and your
> life.
>
> Since you act on the basis of your awareness, which is how
> clearly you see and understand, then any fault lies in your
> awareness and not in you. To help you understand that better,
> let's go back and compare yourself to a car once again.
>
> Now, pretend for a minute that while you are driving along,
> this big blob of mud splashes up on the windshield so you can't
> see where you are going, and you run into a tree. Now, where
> is the actual problem? Where is the mud? The problem is that
> the mud has covered the windshield and you can't see clearly
> where to drive the car. Is there anything wrong with you? The
> only problem is your car has a muddy windshield.

The analogy is then carefully applied to things that the students feel they
shouldn't have done. They learn that the fault is never in them but in their awareness.
And they can *change* their awareness.

For more visual analogies see *A Child of God*.[2] There are 44 object lessons in it.

The above analogies are meant to trigger your thinking so that you will develop
analogies of your own that fit your needs and the needs of your children. They are
truly a memorable tool for expanding children's awareness. Here are two approaches
that I use in gathering analogies:

1. As I read, I note analogies that appeal to me and that can be
   adapted to common household objects.
2. I find a principle in my reading that I deem important and
   think about how to demonstrate it with objects.

Since I use the shoe box approach to writing, all my notes on visual analogies are tossed into a shoe box and sorted out later. Speaking of shoe boxes, put a small rubber band around one, a rubber band you really have to stretch. Observe how rapidly it deteriorates when it is kept under tension. If we allow it to return to its natural state, it will last a long time. Let this remind us to relax, to go within at least once a day to our center of peace and joy.

Before presenting your object lesson or visual analogy to the children, *try it out*. It's amazing how simple and great things sound on paper and how often they don't work out quite that way. I loved the idea that one can become a clear channel or conduit for Spirit if the pebbles of self-concern were out of the way. I pondered a piece of garden hose, but that seemed cumbersome, so I decided to use straws. A bean would represent the "little me," or ego that wants to run things and gets in the way. I used a big bowl of water for Spirit and practiced picking up the water in the straw by putting my finger over the top of the straw while it was in the water. This worked fine, but when I put the bean (blockage) into the straw (channel) it didn't want to block the flow of water (Spirit). I found that bits of cotton would block the flow, although they lacked the visual impact of the bean. The message is—try out your visual analogies *before* using them with children.

NOTES:

There are a number of visual analogies throughout this book. You may wish to make note of those you find especially useful and list them below.

Page: *Analogy:*   *Objects Used:*

The Joy of Creating

There comes
that mysterious meeting in life,
when someone acknowledges
who we are and what we can be,
igniting the circuits of our highest
potential.

    RUSTY BERKUS, *Life Is a Gift*

To help children reach their highest potential, hence their greatest joy, we fan the spark of creativity. Although children are born creative, too often the spark is extinguished early in life. Society is downright savage in its treatment of creative young people, says Dr. Torrance.[1] It stamps out abilities that could help them become more self-sufficient, productive, and joyful adults.

What Is Creativity?

Creativity is the ability and willingness to produce something that is new to the individual. It is not really a single quality, but stands for a group of related abilities. Because these abilities are often expressed together, they are referred to as an entity: creativity.

Creativity is also a way of thinking and a set of attitudes. If we are to develop our creative thinking, we need to develop those attitudes. Indeed, we can say that creativity is not so much aptitude as attitude.

The most important attitude we can develop, in my opinion, is to acknowledge God, Universal Mind, or whatever term you prefer, as the source of all creativity. Each of us taps into, or aligns with, this source in varying degrees. Much of the study of creativity is about how to do this. Prayer and meditation help, aligning with universal principles helps, and getting the ego out of the way helps. Creative thinking exercises and imagination-stretching activities are tools for accessing creativity: they expand the consciousness, opening it to new possibilities.

Young children are naturally creative because they are more in tune with the Infinite. Usually it is not until they reach fourth grade that we pressure them to conform, to grow up and face reality. At the fourth grade their creative imagination starts to decline. For a list of ways we interfere with a child's creative inclinations, see Dr. Dyer's excellent chapter on creativity in *What Do You Really Want For Your Children?* One can also find an eye-opening list of payoffs for keeping children from developing their creativity.[2]

We can counteract this decline in the creative imagination, by surrounding our children with a nurturing climate—one that encourages the expansion of their imagination and creativity. Just as there is an ideal climate for all growing things in nature, so there is an ideal climate for the growth of creativity.

The Creative Climate

What kind of climate will nurture a child's creativity?

☆ A climate of psychological safety. This means, first of all, unconditional acceptance of the child's worth, just as he is. Secondly, it means the absence of external evaluation. Neither the child, nor what he does, is measured by external standards. Patent says, "If we judge the result, no matter how excellent the product or the expression, we limit rather than encourage free expression."[3] Even praise can be threatening. (See "The Question of Praise" in Chapter 3.)

☆ A climate that fosters psychological freedom. The child is free to think, to feel, and to be whatever is most within herself. Behavior may need to be limited, but not symbolic expression.

☆ A climate where there is adult reinforcement of creative efforts. Any effort that is sensitive, honest, and unique is encouraged, accepted, and respected. In a creative climate both adults and children value uniqueness, not conformity; differences, not alikenesses. Comments such as the following are heard:

> I enjoy different ideas.
>
> It's fun to try it different ways.

If I do it, it won't be yours.

You can do it if you keep trying.

Everyone makes mistakes.

How nice you could figure it out for yourself.

☆ A climate devoid of demeaning comments. Statements like the following undermine self-confidence and courage, two necessary ingredients for creativity:

It's just not done that way.

Where did you get that silly idea?

Whoever heard of doing it like that?

Can't you ever do anything right?

Don't ask such stupid questions!

Whoever heard of a purple cat?

☆ A climate where adults have positive expectations about the greatness within the child and let him know it. Wayne Dyer says that we interfere with creativity by "letting children believe that they are average or normal, and that they do not have greatness or genius within them."[4]

☆ A climate that provides a balance between input and output time. Taking in and giving out must be given equal turns: both active and receptive states are necessary for producing creativity. If a child's school day is primarily a time of taking in, then time must be planned at home for self-expression. Be certain that her after school hours are not so filled with passive TV viewing, homework, or organized sports that there is no time left for true output—output that comes from the heart and allows the child to make a pure statement about herself. This can take the form of arts and crafts, puppetry, playtime, drama, or writing, to name only a few possibilities.

☆ A climate that provides "time out" periods. These are "do nothing" times, when the day's normal activities are suspended and the child is free to be quiet with his own thoughts and feelings—to just be. Quiet times can be informal, such as periods of daydreaming, reverie, and reflection, or they can be more formal, such as centering and meditation. The idea is to allow your child some time to focus inward, to get beyond his conscious mind to the wealth of ideas that exist on other levels of consciousness. This is a direct way for him to tap into the source of creativity.

☆ A climate that encourages risk-taking over being safe or doing what everybody else is doing. Risk-taking involves going against tradition, challenging authority when it's appropriate to do so, trying something new, experimenting. Dyer says it so aptly: ". . . if you want your child to be creative, do not try to get her to be one more sheep in the herd, bleating away to a tune being orchestrated by someone else."[5]

☆ A climate that builds self-esteem. A child who does not feel innately worthy and valuable finds it hard to take risks. "It takes courage to be creative. Just as soon as you have a new idea, you are a minority of one."[6] The needed confidence is instilled by esteem building. With high self-esteem, the child has the confidence to stand up for his own ideas and opinions. With low self-esteem he will set aside his ideas to gain the approval of others.

☆ A climate that develops sensory awareness—awareness of *what* one is seeing, hearing, touching, tasting, and smelling. It is using the eyes, not only for seeing, but also for observing; the ears, not only for hearing, but also for listening; and the hands, not only for touching, but also for feeling. Sensory awareness is the basis of creativity—it puts the pieces in the kaleidoscope drum that our creative thinking turns.

☆ A climate where the adults understand what creativity means and how the creative process works. As said earlier, creativity stands for a group of related abilities —such as fluency, flexibility, originality, elaboration—and the more we understand these, the more they can be encouraged. Knowledge of the creative process can also help in guiding a child's creativity. Read widely on the subject so that it will permeate your consciousness and allow you to be less restrictive at important moments. My book, *Art For the Fun of It*, which is about developing creativity, not artists, has chapters on the creative process, the creative child, and the creative climate.[7] Akin to the creative process are the steps of creative problem solving. These are listed and discussed in the last chapter of this book.

☆ A climate that encourages inquisitiveness and a sense of wonder—where children are allowed to indulge in fantasy. It's been found that adults with low levels of creativity usually had parents or teachers who deprived them of fantasy at an early age. Keeping the imagination alive and well is particularly important, for any activity that is truly creative originates in the imagination. "Reason can answer questions, but imagination has to ask them."

Imagination Stimulation

> It is the imaginative
> use of knowledge that is
> essential for actual
> creative productivity.
> SIDNEY J. PARNES

Imagination—what is it and why is it such an important attribute of creativity? Imagination is the ability to form images not present to the senses. It's a function of the intuition. Our imagination has four different parts or aspects: The *creative* imagination, which thinks up ideas, like the different ways to use something; the *visual* imagination, which forms pictures in the mind; the *anticipative* imagination, which lets us look ahead and plan; and the *vicarious* imagination, which lets us put ourselves in the place of others—and "feel" for them.

It is imagination that fosters our capacity to love. We can fall in love easily, but to continue to love takes an act of imagination. It is what sees the perfection in the loved one, along with their potential and possibilities for growth.

The following are imagination-stretching suggestions to introduce your children to the joy of "imagineering":

1. Put an article in a paper sack and suggest ways a child might identify it.

> Have the child imagine herself very tiny. She climbs a rope and enters the paper bag at the top.
>
> Have her imagine that she has X-ray vision (like Superman) and she can see into the sack.
>
> Have her place her hands gently on the sack and name some attributes of the object (size, weight, color, shape). Naming the article is not important.

2. Display a can of cherries or green peas and a jar of peanut butter. Invite the child to make himself very tiny and go inside one of the containers. He imagines himself playing around in there and then shares what it feels like.

3. Set a plant before the children and have them imagine themselves tiny enough to go inside it. Have them figure out how and where they'll enter the plant. Ask them to observe what they see as they travel through the plant. Invite them to share their feelings and observations.

4. Choose a past setting and have the child imagine herself in it. For instance, suggest she see herself as an Indian child playing by a river or walking through the woods. Encourage her to become that person, not just an observer. Have her pay close attention to what the child is wearing, doing, and feeling. In such an exercise, the human mind selects from past data, so don't be surprised if she claims she was an Indian child "really." It may be that the experience triggered a past life.

5. Play mental "Simon Says" games. Since there is nothing you can't be in your imagination, let the child practice being all sorts of different things, "Be an eagle, be a duck, be a dolphin, be a giraffe, be a mosquito, be a whale, be a cricket, be an ant, be a rabbit, be a goldfish in a bowl, be something scary, be something really nice, be something soft and furry . . . be yourself, be your father, be your mother, be a neighbor, be your teacher, be someone else, be yourself . . . be something no one has ever been before. What is it?" This exercise is adapted from *Put Your Mother on the Ceiling*, a book full of imagination-stretching games for children.[8]

6. Strange Comparisons. Comparisons help children use their imagination to see the world in a new way. I'm especially fond of the mind-stretching analogies and metaphors in *Making It Strange*.[9]

Here are some examples. (Remember, there are no right or wrong answers. We are simply rearranging what we know to get a fresh look at it.)

Which takes up more space—a pickle or a pain?
Which is thinner—day or night?
Which weighs more—zero or one?
Which is quicker—yellow or black?
Which is heavier—a mountain or an ocean?
Which is funnier—3 or 4?
What color is surprise?
Which is crisper—winter or celery?
Which weighs more—a cough or a sneeze?

There are many other kinds of comparisons in *Making It Strange*. For instance:

A calendar is like a mirror because _____ .
A sandwich is like _____ .
A dentist's drill is like _____ .
A soap bubble is like _____ .
A printing press is like what animal? _____ .

I use some of these comparisons in the puppet skit at the end of this section. Another comparison exercise is to assemble some objects and ask the children whom they represent.

7. Cartoon captions and vice versa. This is a lot of fun for older children. I cut the captions off cartoons and photocopy two or three on a page. It always amazes me and them that their captions are often funnier than the original. The reverse is also stimulating. Photocopy two or three captions from cartoons on a sheet and let them sketch or describe in words a picture for the caption.

8. Forced-relationship product improvement. Older children have fun with this one. Place in a basket or box small slips of paper with a name of a different object on each one. Just look around the room and put down what you see—telephone, pen, cup, candle, chain, table fan, basket, painting, flowers, TV, shoes, watch, etc. The basket is passed and each child draws out two slips. The challenge is to use an attribute of one object to make an improvement in the other object. Attributes can include size, shape, color, weight, function, fragrance, sound, and so on.

9. Picture completion. Draw a random shape, squiggle, or geometric form on a piece of paper and have the child use her imagination to work it into a picture or design of some sort. Another aspect of this is to see how many things she can make from a triangle, or circle, two parallel lines, etc. Or put a torn piece of construction paper in the middle of the child's working paper and have her use it as the basis for an imaginary character.

10. People watching. A different use of the imagination is to observe people from a distance and discuss with your child what they might be thinking and feeling. The clues will be in facial expressions, gestures, and posture. This can also be done by looking at photographs or by looking at an unfamiliar show on TV—with the sound off.

11. "What if" games. What if this improbable situation happened? Let the child

use his imagination to think out all the things that could happen because of it. What would be the consequences? (The following are adaptations of *Turner's Story Starters*.)[10]

> What if people were born full-grown from eggs—and they grew down instead of up until, as adults, they were the size of babies?
>
> What if you had been away on a long trip in the woods—and when you returned home all your family and friends acted as if they didn't know you, but thought you were a stranger?
>
> What if you were given the power to have all your wishes come true, but every time you made a wish your fingernails would grow an inch and if you cut your nails even a little all your power would disappear?
>
> What if you woke up one morning and all the world had turned pink?

12. A Puppet Script. Use puppets for imagination stretching. Here is a script for an adult and two hand puppets. The only preparation you need is reading the script over and gathering your props.

IMAGINATION STRETCHING

The imagination, like a muscle, needs to be frequently exercised. This is an accordion-type puppet skit that can be shortened, or lengthened, depending upon the age level and attention span of the youngsters.

CHARACTERS: Elmer (Any type of authority figure puppet will do, but one with a moving mouth would be best because he talks so much) and Sasha (puppet with moving hands).

PROPERTIES: A wishing rock (rock with white stripe around it.) A sponge of average size. A piece of driftwood with interesting shape. (If unavailable, make paint blots in the middle of a piece of paper, and then fold the paper in half to make a double image.)

At rise Elmer is peering around the room and at the audience.

ELMER: Hi, boys and girls! I'm Elmer and I'm here to do some imagination-stretching exercises with you. What do you know about imagination? Do any of you know what it can do for you? (*Such questions can help Elmer size up the children's level of understanding.*)

Now, let's pretend we can hold our imagination in our hands like we'd hold a grapefruit. Everybody holding it? Okay, now let's pretend that it's made of clay or silly putty. Stretch it as far as your arms can reach. Good! That's what I want you to do with your imagination today—stretch it so that it's bigger than it is right now. That's what imagination exercises are for.

SASHA: (*Enters, carrying a rock*) Hi, Elmer. Look what I found at the beach.

ELMER: Let's see. Why, it's a wishing rock. A wishing rock always has a white line around it.

SASHA: Yes, I know; and I thought I'd let you wish on it, too. You can share a wishing rock with others, you know.

ELMER: Thanks, Sasha. The last time I wished on a wishing rock I got my wish.

SASHA: You didn't tell anybody what it was, did you? That's against the rules.

ELMER: No, I always keep my wishes secret. Sasha, I'm just about to do some imagination exercises with these children. Can we share the wishing rock with them and let each of them make a special wish, too?

SASHA: Sure! The rock doesn't care how many wishes are made on it.

ELMER: Okay, boys and girls, I want you to imagine now something good that you would like to have happen to you, or to someone you know. See it happening in your mind. Maybe you know someone who is sick and you want to see them well. Or maybe there's something you'd like to learn to do better, or a place you really want to go. (*Pause.*)

SASHA: And after you decide on your wish, keep it to yourself. That's *your* secret.

ELMER: Can you stay and help me while I give the boys and girls some imagination-stretching exercises, Sasha?

SASHA: Sure, I'd love to, Elmer. What can I do?

ELMER: To begin with, hold up that interesting piece of driftwood so they can all see it. Show them both sides of it.

(*Sasha holds it up, turning it from side to side.*)

ELMER: Girls and boys, I'd like you to use your imagination now and try to see something in this piece of driftwood. You might see people or animals or things. Everybody's mind is different, so each of you will see things a little differently. There is no right or wrong to these exercises. (*Pauses for observation time.*) Now let's hear about some of the things you saw in the driftwood. (*Waits for responses.*)

SASHA: (*After the boys and girls are finished.*) Can I say what I saw, Elmer?

ELMER: Of course, Sasha.

SASHA: (*Offers a response different from the others.*)

ELMER: Sasha, would you put the driftwood down now and hold up that sponge?

SASHA: (*Does so.*) This is like the one my mother uses to wash things in the kitchen.

ELMER: Boys and girls, now I want you to use your imagination in a different way. I want you to think of all the different uses you can for a sponge.

SASHA: Does it matter what size the sponge is?

ELMER: No, it can be the size of a football field if you want.

SASHA: Oh, that would be funny seeing a football team playing on a sponge.

ELMER: Here's something else you can do. Make yourself really tiny and crawl inside the sponge. (*Pauses.*)

SASHA: Oh, what fun! Boys and girls, imagine what you would do with the sponges if someone gave you a truck full of them? (*Pauses.*) Now, can you think of any art projects where you could use a sponge? It's okay to cut it up. (*Pauses.*)

ELMER: Now here's another way to use our imagination. Let me tell you about the little girl in the department store yesterday. (*Names a large store they're familiar with so they can get a visual idea of it.*) She had tears running down her cheeks and she was whimpering, "Mommy, Mommy, Mommy," as she wandered up and down the aisles. There was no one around that looked like Mommy and no one seemed to notice her. How do you think she felt? (*Pauses and waits for responses.*)

SASHA: I'd like to ask you, boys and girls, what would you do if you were at a parade or a fair and got separated from your parents. What if you couldn't see them anywhere? What would be your plan of action? (*Pauses for responses.*)

ELMER: These are all good examples of using your imagination.

SASHA: It's fun to play imagination games. What's next?

ELMER: I've got some questions I'm going to ask the boys and girls. There is no right or wrong answer to any of them. Whatever answer comes to your mind is okay.

SASHA: Oh, I like questions like that. May I answer, too?

ELMER: Sure. First one is "Which is rougher, purple or green, and why?" (*Pauses for answers.*) Now this question is about you. "What animal are you like and why are you like this animal?" (*Pauses for answers.*)

SASHA: I'll be first to answer that one. I see myself as a bunny rabbit because I'm always hopping around from one thing to another, and I've been told I have big ears because I always hear what's going on.

ELMER: Thanks, Sasha. You seem more like a squirrel to me, but whatever you say is right. Who else here will tell me what animal they are like? (*Pauses for answers.*)

SASHA: Boy! Those were great answers. What's your next question, Elmer?

ELMER: The question is, "What fruit are you most like and why?"

SASHA: That's a fun question. Let me think. There are berries, cherries, apples, oranges, peaches, pears, bananas, apricots, lemons, grapes, and lots more.

ELMER: What do you think, boys and girls? (*Pauses for answers.*) Okay, are you ready for the last question for the day? (*Pauses.*) "Which is faster, a table or a chair, and why?" (*Pauses for answers.*)

SASHA: I pictured my dining room chairs and table and I figured because the table is made of heavy marble, it wouldn't be very fast. The chair would be faster.

ELMER: How many of you pictured in your mind a specific table and chair like Sasha did? (*Pause.*) To learn to visualize, to picture things in your mind, is a very valuable ability to develop. I want you all to take a minute right now and picture your bedroom the way it was last night when you went to bed. See the furniture, the closet, your clothing, your toys . . .

SASHA: (*Interrupting*) Oh, no! Do I have to? It's so messy!

ELMER: Look around your room and see every detail you can remember—just the way it was last night. (*Pauses.*) That's enough for today, boys and girls, but another day we'll practice visualizing some more. You can bring a lot of good into your life by learning to picture yourself and others having a good and happy experience.

SASHA: Remember to stretch your imagination! If you just sat all day, your legs would grow very weak, and if you don't use your imagination, it becomes weak too, and then you can't think up new ideas.

ELMER: That gives me an idea, Sasha. The boys and girls have sat still so long I think I'll have them stand up now and do some stretching exercises.

(*Use exercises and ending appropriate for the circumstances.*)

Someone has said, "Man's only limitation lies in the negative use of his imagination," so let's keep in mind that it's not enough to help our children develop their imaginations. We must also nurture in them human values and universal principles.

Magic of Puppetry

Puppets fulfill a need because they allow children to enter the world of fantasy so easily. They are magic because they can be anything the child wants them to be. They free children to create whatever is needed right now in their lives. Because puppets often reveal the inner world of the child, a great deal can be accomplished through puppetry. Here, I'll just highlight their role in promoting creative thinking.

WHAT IS A PUPPET?

A puppet is any sculptural or pictorial representation that is made to move by the efforts of an operator. It can represent anything—animals, people, inanimate objects, or abstract ideas. This means almost any inanimate object can become a puppet if it's brought to life by a performer. The performer's imagination is the catalyst. A spatula, hammer, twig, or detergent bottle, when used in a creative way, can become more of a true puppet than an elaborate commercial puppet that hasn't been given personality by the puppeteer. There are seven types of puppets in common use: string, rod, stick, shadow, hand, finger, and people puppets. In general, I favor hand and stick puppets for most purposes.

I urge you to think of puppetry as a performing art, not as a craft. The primary value of puppetry for children is in the *use* of puppets, not in the making of them. When puppets are made, I recommend quick-to-make "instant" puppets, so as to leave as much time as possible for their use. Keep in mind that the puppet is a means to an end, rather than an end in itself.

Here are four puppet-making activities to challenge the imagination of older children. Following them are suggestions for creatively using puppets.

> **A 10-Minute Puppet.** The child goes to any one room in the house (kitchen, bathroom, garage) and, using only

the materials found there, makes a 10-minute puppet. Beforehand, a box is placed on the table with items that can be used, such as scissors, glue, tape, pins, needle, and thread.

Nature Puppets. These puppets are made entirely from materials found in the backyard, woods, or beach. A real test of ingenuity!

Grab-Bag Puppets. The teacher puts a variety of "puppet stuff"—enough to make a puppet or two into paper sacks or grocery bags. The bags are stapled shut and distributed to the students. The challenge is to create a puppet out of the items in the bag. Of course, tape and scissors, etc. are available.

Common Object Variations. A common object is assigned, and each child comes up with his version of a puppet based on this object. Then to stretch the imagination, the same object is given again and the child is asked to create another puppet using the object in an entirely different way. For example: paper bags can make moving-mouth puppets or be stuffed for stick puppets; paper plates and envelopes can have moving mouths or be stick puppets; styrofoam cups can be used upside down with a finger poking through for a nose, or they can be used right side up with hair coming out of the cup. Other objects with varied possibilities: clothespin, detergent bottle, wooden spoon, balloon, egg carton, milk carton, toilet paper tube, a fly swatter, some fruits and vegetables.

Dramatic Play. For younger children, just providing puppets, a few props, and a simple cardboard box stage is all that is needed.

Puppet Activity. Older children can use their imagination in getting puppets to perform such activities as a tug-of-war, washing windows, sweeping floors, doing a song-and-dance act, searching for something, carrying something that requires two puppets, putting props on stage for an imaginary play.

Personal Encounters. Working alone or with another puppeteer, older children can enact:

a telephone conversation	a salesman and a customer
a nurse and a difficult patient	a farmer and a crow
a policeman questioning a witness	a boy and his dog
a mother teaching son to cook	a giant and a fairy
animal conversations about their owners	two ghosts

Fables and Folktales. As a step toward creating their own puppet plays, children often like to do original twists on old nursery rhymes, fairy tales, and fables. They might combine characters of one story with those of another, substitute animals for people, put them in a modern setting, or make up a surprise ending.

Using Uniqueness. Puppets have a unique ability to do things people can't do. Encourage children to create a skit where the puppets fly, disappear, and do other things impossible for people.

Creating Puppet Personalities. Give each child a puppet and have them create a funny voice and some interesting mannerisms for it. Maybe the puppet giggles constantly, is always eating, bounces instead of walks, or likes to walk backwards to see where it has been. After the personalities are developed, two puppets can go on a nature hike or grocery shopping together.

Creating Skits Around Puppets. Give the children three or four specific puppets and the challenge to create a story around those characters. For instance, they may be given a king, a bear, a girl, and a witch.

Creating Skits Around a Background. The child first selects a background and then chooses three or four characters suitable to the background. Actions are planned that connect the characters to their background. Some possible backgrounds:

castle	farm	seashore
cave	zoo	museum
circus	kitchen	woods
picnic	library	ocean floor
army camp	elevator	on the moon
schoolroom	space rocket	on a train

Let the children add to the list.

For more puppet activities, for ideas on teacher and parent use of puppets, and for many kinds of "instant" puppets, see if your library has *The Magic of Puppetry*.[11]

Art Adventures

> *The source of art is not visual reality,*
> *but the dreams, hopes and aspirations*
> *which lie deep in every human.*
> ARTHUR ZAIDENBERG

Art generates joy. There are certain sets of conditions that release our inherent joy and allow it to bubble forth. Art experiences, when not directed, usually meet these conditions. There is joy in expressing our uniqueness or individuality which valid art experiences allow. Art offers the deep satisfaction of discovery—both of ourselves and of what various materials can do.

Much joy comes from our being aware of and alive to beauty, in everyday objects as well as in art forms. Also, joy comes from releasing pent-up emotions in a constructive manner.

And what joy and delight can accompany creating something that never existed before! This can give real meaning to existence.

Art includes other values, as well: it develops our creative thinking, strengthens our sense of self, provides a means of communication and self-expression, challenges us to make decisions, makes us appreciate the individuality of others, and helps integrate our thinking through balancing the right and left hemispheres of our brain.

None of these values of art will be realized if we impose "dictated art," on the child—art in which the result is determined by the adult. Obvious forms of dictated art are picture outlines the child is asked to color in; shapes or patterns he is asked to duplicate; likenesses of models, pictures, or designs he is asked to copy; or any directed art in which the child must follow a prescribed, step-by-step procedure established and controlled by the adult.

There are also subtle forms of "dictated art," such as placing a sample picture or model before the child, or even holding strong expectations of the end result. Remember, children can tune into our thoughts and can feel pressured by our expectations.

You may wonder how "dictated art"—coloring books being a prime example— blocks a child's joy. Here are just a few of the ways:

> It dulls the child's imagination by denying it needed stimulation.
>
> It undermines the child's self-confidence and discourages independent thinking. He feels his own ideas are unacceptable.
>
> It deprives the child of individual expression, since she cannot express her own relationship to the subject.
>
> It frustrates the child's own creative impulses because it conditions her to believe she cannot produce alone.
>
> It provides no emotional release because it gives the child no opportunity to express his experience.
>
> It offers the child only a limited feeling of achievement or pride in his work.

Art in which the end result is predetermined by the adult puts the emphasis on the product and not on the process happening within the child. I spoke earlier about balancing input and output time. Art is not truly output time for the child unless he is allowed to express himself in his own unique way.

A wonderful thing about art is that all ages can use the same media, be given the same instructions, and achieve satisfying results.

Here is a list of the more popular art categories along with a few suggestions in each category. For a more complete listing and for detailed descriptions of the activities that follow, see my *Art for the Fun of It*.[12]

1. Arranging and Decorating

> Flowers and natural forms
> Room arrangement
> Holiday and party decorating
> Shelf displays
> Bean layering—also layer colored rice, macaroni (eat later)

2. Pasting and Assembling

> Collage—frees children from clichés and allows them to be
> more inventive
> Materials—nature, tissue paper, found objects, pebbles,
> assorted paper, geometric shapes, fabrics, torn paper
> mosaics
> Adhesives—glue, paste, dough, tape, staples,
> gummed-back paper

3. Drawing and Rubbing

> Crayons—peel-and-break crayons: use on the side, tie two
> together, collect rubbings; cut and paste into a design on
> paper
> Paper—experiment with corrugated paper, sandpaper, paper
> towels, wax paper, paper doilies, paper plates, crepe paper,
> tracing paper
> Chalk—use wet and dry, on wet paper, dry paper, with hair
> spray fixative
> Fingerprint pictures—using ink pad, put several fingerprints
> on piece of paper. With felt pen, turn them into animals,
> people, etc.
> Pebble pictures—drop a handful of pebbles or beans on paper,
> put dot where pebble lands, make drawing that incorporates
> all dots.

4. Painting

> Tools—having a variety will stimulate flexibility and inven-
> tiveness:
>
>> Sponges held by clothespins
>> Brushes—tooth, bottle, paint, paste
>> Hands and feet, straw
>> Toothpicks, cotton swabs, sticks
>> Roll-on deodorant bottles, string, rope
>
> Painting liquids—add sand or coffee grounds to tempera paint;
> add soap flakes, food dyes
> Painting surfaces—paper doilies, windows, wood, rocks, gift
> boxes, cartons for hide-aways, paper plates, paper bags,
> classified pages

5. Printing

Finger and handprints
Sponge printing
Gadget printing—print with buttons, corks, hair rollers, keys,
   jar lids, potato mashers, lego blocks, forks
Vegetable and fruit printing
Styrofoam printing
Eraser and cork printing
Nature printing—use leaves, weeds, shells, feathers

6. Modeling

Clay has a magical attraction for children. Those who show little interest in drawing or painting usually find much satisfaction in clay. It has great therapeutic value.

Materials—natural potter's clay, play dough, sawdust clay,
   baker's clay, cornstarch clay, whipped soap, papier mâché,
   edible play-dough cookies

7. Constructing and Woodworking

Cardboard construction—make box sculpture; use cylinders/
   tubes
Fruit and vegetable figures
Straw structures—cut up plastic flex-straws
Pipe cleaner figures
Rock creatures
Foil figures
Toothpick sculpture
Pine cone characters
Mobiles—from branches or clothes hangers

8. Stitching and Weaving

Children can learn to use the needle as a brush, the yarn as paint, and burlap as canvas. They can start stitchery at three and weaving a year or so later. Boys especially should be encouraged to do stitchery, since it has been found they can sometimes do better and more imaginative work than girls.

Materials—meat trays, hardware cloth, burlap, mesh dish-
   cloth, styrofoam sheeting, onion sacking, rug canvas,
   plastic-coated shelf paper
Threads—household string, rug yarn, butcher twine, embroi-
   dery floss; length should be length of arm.
Weaving—branch and wheel weaving

There is so much value in art for children that author J. C. Pearce says it should be the foundation of all education—not just something tacked on. Because of the way our midbrain operates, he urges us to saturate the children with art, storytelling, and "let's pretend's." Only by incorporating all five senses in the activities of early childhood can functional intelligence be fully formed. And that is why, he states, TV is killing intelligence.[13]

Creative Writing

Many older children find writing a powerful form of self-expression. The activities that follow are often used in schools, but can be easily adapted for home use.

1. **Journaling.** This is probably the most comfortable writing activity to be used in the home. In Chapter 5, I described it briefly, emphasizing the importance of keeping the journal absolutely private so the child can explore her feelings freely, without worry that prying eyes might later see what she has written.

There is another type of journal, however, one that is used to communicate. In some classrooms the children write in journals on general themes and include anything they especially want to say to the teacher. Once a week the teacher reads each journal and writes in her response. Children value this personal form of communication: it forms "bonding" between them and the teacher that offsets the lack of personal time together. In fact, it meant so much to one sixth-grade boy that when he moved out of state, he asked if he could continue to send his journal once a week to his teacher. They are still communicating in this way.

Here are some excerpts from the school journal of a fifth-grade girl:

> 12/17
> I have a problem with my friends. Just because I don't swear and do the things they do they call me a goody-two-shoes. What should I do and who should I play with?

> 1/12
> Today was fun. I especially liked the group discussion. When we were relaxing, everyone laughed. I didn't because I really was relaxed. Now I can concentrate on things more clearly. Today my decision was to pay more attention. I've also made a decision to not watch more than two hours of TV tonight. I am going to be friendlier. I think _____ was kind. She didn't tell any jokes or funny stories. She was quiet, listened, and worked hard.

> 2/25
> The friends that I play with at school don't like any of my ideas. They want to do their own things. Whenever I go to do something else on my own for a change, they start to hate me. What can I do? I finished one of my questions. I got 1/4 finished of a second question. I trust _____ because she is a friend to me and she is always kind. She goes out of her way to do things for me.

As you can see, the communication journal helps knowing "where the child is coming from." It provides insight into the relationships between her students. The students also appreciate the teacher's private advice.

2. **Clustering or Patterning.** For children who want to get out ideas but don't have the patience or perhaps the skill to keep a journal, clustering or patterning is a viable alternative. It is a visual form of outlining, sometimes called mind mapping. The child starts by putting a word in the middle of a page. Maybe it's a happy word like JOY because he wants to get more in touch with it—or it could be FEAR because he is aware of some fear he wants to better understand. Or maybe it's BROTHER because he has energy around his brother that he needs to release. It could be an evocative word on a card drawn for that day.

After putting the word in the middle of the page, the child proceeds to draw lines from it, and branch lines out from those. On these lines go the words, thoughts, or memories evoked by the central word.

Children can quickly gain many helpful insights and creative associations in this way. Sometimes a pattern will show up that the child may want to look at more closely. Sometimes he may get an idea for a poem or story from his pattern.

3. **SWISH.** The acronym stands for "Sustained Writing Is Sustained Habit." This is a classroom technique for encouraging free-flow writing. The children are given about 45 seconds to choose a topic from the three or four listed on the board. The teacher then sets a timer for 3 minutes and everyone begins to write. They are told that their pencils must continue to move. If they are stuck and cannot think of the next word, they can keep on writing the last word over and over. They are not to be concerned with capital letters, punctuation, or spelling. When the timer rings, they complete the sentence they are on.

Those who wish to share their writing then do so. So many may wish to share that they'll have to break up into small sharing groups. The next time they SWISH, give them an extra minute. Gradually increase the time as you think they can handle it. One third-grade class got up to 45 minutes.

It is helpful to offer the students a choice of four topics, three of which are ridiculous:

> "I am a cactus overlooking a city in the desert, I wonder . . ."
>
> "I am a dustball under a bed. Two feet are approaching . . ."
>
> "Look at that other spaceship heading our way! What do you suppose . . . ?"
>
> The fourth might be on an upcoming holiday or a current event.

This could be an intriguing family activity where adults and children of writing age all participate together.

4. **Picture-based stories.** Using pictures to stimulate writing is always fun for groups or individuals. If the group is small, a picture could be handed to each child. For a large group one or two pictures can be tacked on the wall. The writing can

go in several directions: What's happening in the picture—and what happens next? What happened prior to the scene in the picture? Describe the mood of the picture or write poetry about it.

5. **Add-on stories.** These are continuation stories that can stimulate creative thinking in a classroom. The teacher puts a list of words on the board and asks the students to write a story using as many words from the list as possible. After a couple of minutes the students are told to pass their paper to the next student, who is to "add-on" to the story. The papers are passed five or six times and then are read aloud.

6. **Unfinished stories.** Chapter 8 refers to this technique for telling stories, and it is especially appropriate as a writing activity. An ethical problem is presented in story form and the children use their moral reasoning to complete it (See Chapter 8 for a source book).

7. **Forced relationship story plotting.** This was explained in detail in Chapter 8 as an approach to creating a story. A simplified version is to have students fold their paper vertically into four columns and write the lists mentioned in that chapter. For each of the characters they list, have them fill in the character's goals, obstacles, and so on.

8. **Group story writing.** Have the students put slips of paper with "off-the-wall" characters into a basket. Put one in yourself, if you like. Each student draws a character, and then they work in groups of four to come up with a setting, a problem, and a solution that would involve all four characters. After they decide, the students work by themselves to write up a story.

9. **Recipe Writing.** Suggest writing a recipe for joy or some other abstract quality, such as freedom, justice, happiness, friendship, etc. Here is a recipe for "Peace Stew" from Thomas Turner and another for "misery" from an unknown author.

> Peace Stew:
> Begin with a sense of awe and love for the Creator. Blend two parts understanding with two parts of love for fellow human beings. Mix well with generous portions of sensitivity. Add a willingness to share. Put in a dash of humor, pour into an empty world and allow to slowly simmer until everyone feels it in their hearts.[14]

> Recipe for Misery:
> 1 cup guilt
> 1 cup dwelling on the past
> ½ cup saying "poor me"
> 1 tsp. criticism
> ¼ cup blame on others
> Blend and let it set until it rises to twice its size. Divide into equal portions and bake in hot oven of judgment and self-righteousness.

10. **Fame At Last.** This activity could release great joy for children. It makes them aware of the purpose, contribution, or service that their life could stand for. They are to pretend that their picture has just appeared on the cover of a popular magazine. They can design a mock-up and then write a story explaining how they became famous and why they are famous. Or they could write it in the form of an interview by a well-known reporter. (Adapted from *Creative Activities Resource Book for Elementary School Teachers*,[15] a tremendous source for creative writing ideas and creative thinking in general.)

Some of the activities in Chapter 11, under "Joy Exercises" and "Doing Kits," can also be used for creative writing.

Music and Movement

> *Your children deserve to be bathed in beautiful, melodic music—the best that you can find for them.*
>
> HAL LINGERMAN,
> *The Healing Energies of Music*

Here is a potpourri of ideas for using music and movement to release the great joy within children. Music gives children wonderful ways to express themselves and, through the environment it creates, to get in touch with what is best within them.

☆ Music can enhance learning. Research is showing that instrumental music affects the way the brain receives and stores information. In *Music Power*, Scarantino explains: "The largo movements of works by Baroque-era composers have been tested and recommended, because the slow tempo (60 beats per minute or less) calms the body and relieves the tension associated with learning. The music occupies the right side of the brain, while keeping the left side of the brain alert to receive the data to be learned more easily."[16]

Besides some baroque classics, she mentions Steven Halpern's *Comfort Zone* and *Learning Suite* as appropriate for study sessions. Actually, whatever keeps the mind alert and the body relaxed will aid learning as long as it is something the child is willing to listen to. Never force a child to listen to something she doesn't want to hear.

For further information on music and learning, see *Super-Learning* by Ostrander and Schroeder.[17]

☆ Music can release your child's energy. Lingerman offers a wonderful list of music to stimulate children three years and older "without attacking them or causing them to feel fragmented and confused." He says such music can help them concentrate on their homework, while the chaotic sounds of rock music will make them feel jumpy, even when they do not have work to do.[18]

☆ Music can stir the imagination and release inspiration. Certain music can "paint pictures inwardly," as Lingerman puts it; both he and Scarantino present an extensive list of such music.

☆ Music can stimulate mental clarity. When a child suffers from "information overload" and needs to refresh his mind, music can be the answer. Barbara Scarantino offers a lengthy list and suggests using it for light mental tasks, such as balancing the checkbook.

☆ Music can nourish and sustain a happy, constructive emotional nature. We can use it to release our children's emotions creatively and to clear out their emotional blockages. Lingerman discusses this area thoroughly and offers musical selections for: airing out and calming anger; relieving boredom, depression, and fear; increasing strength, courage, love, and devotion.

☆ Music can heal. It will be one of the major healing arts of the Aquarian Age. Music can reduce the trauma of hospitalization, alleviate pain, heal memories, and encourage growth in social skills. Healthy sounds invigorate, energize, and balance us, according to musician and author Steve Halpern. Simply by playing harmonious music daily we can raise the vibration of much of the discordant energy in us and around us.

Both Scarantino and Lingerman offer specific suggestions of music to play throughout the day—music for waking up, music for meals and good digestion, music for your plants and animals, and even music for driving, such as Halpern's *Driving Suite* with subliminal messages to keep you alert.

There is an abundance of inspired music available now—everything from joy songs to meditation music. I suggest you ask your Inner Teacher to lead you to the ones that will most benefit your family. A few resources are mentioned in Chapter 13, where I speak about music to counteract stress and mention the dangers of rock music.

THE TEMPERAMENTS AND MUSIC

The elements of earth, air, fire, and water have been recognized throughout the ages as the four modes for life expression. All four are present in us to varying degrees, with one or two usually predominating. The unique blending of these energies helps to create our temperament or behavior style. Some researchers feel that the earth, air, fire, and water energies correlate with the **DISC** styles discussed in Chapter 4 —fire (**D**), air (**I**), water (**S**), earth (**C**). We can choose the music that fits our temperament, and we can also be caring enough to choose music that is appropriate for our children and friends. Lingerman lists music for each element and even lists composers according to air, fire, earth, and water.[19]

You also might be interested in knowing that there are studies relating the four temperaments or behavior styles to musical elements (melody, rhythm, harmony) and instruments. According to Dr. Rudolf Steiner's research, we can help children align with their higher selves by offering instruments that suit their behavior style. We can accept the Dominant style child's inclination to choose percussion instruments and the likelihood of the Conscientious style child's preferring melody and singing, especially solos. The "C" style child also responds to instruments such as the violin or flute, that create pure melody. The Supportive style child's needs are often met with an instrument such as the piano or xylophone. The Influential style child expresses his needs with a wind instrument."

Pythagoras taught that music is a sacred science and should be an essential part of each person's training. Whatever instruments you get your children, it's important that they be of good quality—not toys. Even the rhythm instruments that toddlers so enjoy should have a pleasant sound to the ear. Have a real tambourine, drum, or bell, for instance. But most of all, encourage your child's attempts at music making. You may wish to read in *Music Power* or elsewhere about some of the methods of instruction for children, such as the Orff-Shulwek method and the Suzuki method.

HEART SONGS

There is a type of singing I want to encourage here, one that has a different purpose from the singing suggested in Chapter 7. It is spontaneous singing from the heart, using nonsense syllables. This "beyond-the-mind" singing can express more joy than actual words can. And it gives the child an opportunity for impulsive creativity without preparation or materials. It is one of the purest forms of creativity possible.

As with most behavior, this form of expression needs to be modeled for children. Modeling gives them permission to do the same. A heart song begins with a desire to express oneself in song, but instead of pausing to think "what do I know? what song is appropriate now?" you just start singing nonsense words and syllables without thinking what will follow. The results can be very soul-satisfying because you reach a level beyond words. Heart songs let us express what we need to express but probably can't in any other way at that moment. They let us express our joy, unhampered by words or form.

MUSIC AND OTHER ART FORMS

Music is a wonderful medium to enhance other art forms such as drawing, painting, writing, and movement.

A music drawing activity. Have children sit in a relaxed position with eyes closed and see, on the "movie screen" inside their heads, a picture of themselves enjoying a favorite activity. Then put on some music and ask them what pictures they now see. Stop the music after a few minutes and ask them to draw one of the things they saw.

Painting to music. As a child paints, notice a particular rhythm and make up a song or chant to go with it. Or play dance music to encourage rhythm in painting. After the children have listened to a selection of classical music with their eyes closed, have them paint the mood or picture it evoked.

Sounds and images (creative writing). Give the children a sheet of typing paper and ask them to fold it horizontally into thirds, labeling the columns A, B, and C. Have them listen, with eyes closed, to some colorful classical music—music that paints a story with sound. *Grand Canyon Suite* is an example. Others are:

> *Chariots of Fire* – Vangelis
> *Piano Concerto No. 21* – Mozart
> *Hungarian Rhapsodies* – Liszt
> *Slavonic Dances* – Dvorak
> *Star Trek* – motion picture soundtrack
> *An American in Paris* – George Gershwin
> *Scheherazade* – Rimsky-Korsakov

Stop the music at some point and ask the children to write a word picture evoked by the music in column A. The column is then folded back. The same selection is played again. This time they are to use their imaginations to get different images from the music. Again they write and fold back column B. The same process is repeated for column C. This is an excellent imagination-stretcher and underscores the creative-thinking principle of not stopping with one's first idea. It has been shown that quantity yields quality. Or you might simply play a different piece for each of the three columns and have the children write the scene it evokes.

Movement to music. Sometimes it's appropriate to just turn on some music and encourage your children to move to it in whatever way they feel. Often it's more effective if scarves are used. Scarf dancing is done with pieces of colorful light-weight fabric that the children can swirl around them, toss out and draw back like a wave, or whatever the music suggests. Where cost is a factor, you can make crepe paper streamers: cut across the package about every two inches; staple several strips to a small piece of cardboard about 3 × 4 inches; mix colors for attractive color combinations.

Scarf juggling. This is a fun activity for children and may also be done to music. Three small chiffon scarves of three bright colors are a good way to begin. After the child has some dexterity in juggling, he can adapt the activity to music. Scarf juggling is a no-risk way to learn juggling, especially in a group. There is more willingness to try because it is not so noticeable to others when one drops a scarf. (Check your toy store for a booklet called *Scarf Juggling*.)[21] Juggling balloons is also fun.

CREATIVE MOVEMENT

Creative movement is creation
for the sheer exuberance and
ecstasy of creation.
THOMAS TURNER

Such movement is a rewarding experience for children, because it escapes the "product trap," as Turner so well expresses it. This is one of the few avenues of expression for children that are not product- or performance-oriented. How freeing it is for children to do something no one can look at and judge.

Besides providing a spontaneous means of creative expression, creative movement develops body awareness, a sense of rhythm, and physical and communication skills.

Many of my favorite movement activities are found in the beautiful book *Leap to the Sun*.[22] Here are some condensed adaptations:

Scribbling. Each child pretends to be a colorful felt pen or crayon. Using the entire floor as a sheet of paper the children are instructed to scribble designs.

Paint cans. This calls for even more body movement. The child jumps into an imaginary can of paint—maybe polka dot paint or striped paint—and splashes it all over himself, even dunking his head. He then paints in space, using arm, leg, and head movements to create brush strokes.

Sounds. Sitting in a circle on the floor, each child or adult suggests a sound, and then the participants improvise corresponding rhythmic sounds with an instrument or with their hands. All those who wish stand up and interpret the idea, while the others continue the sounds. Interesting sounds might be:

> a ball in a pinball machine
> a train going into or out of a station
> boiling water or soup
> popping corn
> a rabbit hopping on crisp leaves
> bubble gum or crackers being chewed

Catching butterflies. With imaginary butterfly nets, the children try to catch imaginary butterflies, creating interesting movements as they do so.

Gusts of wind. Children pretend to be propelled forward by a strong gust of wind. With head high, chest out, and arms out to the sides, they wait for an imaginary feeling of wind behind them and run across the floor, chest leading.

Surprises. In this game the children show surprise by a dynamic pose or sudden movement. Walking down the street, they suddenly hear an explosion above them or see a spaceship. Or walking down the street, they suddenly whirl around because they heard a scream from behind them.

Things to be: A snowflake, aluminum foil being crumpled, oil floating on water, a thundershower, a blizzard, a melting snowman, thread on a sewing machine, witches or goblins, flying reindeer. Such a list could go on for pages.

For those who wish to explore the field of creative movement, the publications and records listed in *Leap to the Sun* are a good place to start. The Turner book mentioned earlier is also full of suggestions.

☆

The following section, a most beautiful statement on creative drama, was written especially for this book by a guest contributor.

The Dramatic Arts: Joy Creatively Expressed

by Marjorie Timms, Ph.D.[23]

Dramatic play is joy in its most immediate, accessible, spontaneous state; it is a direct link to the Creative Source as well as a magical gift, existing in and for all children. Creative drama is a developmental process designed to serve as a key to understanding the world and adjusting to it; an expression of the child's universal need to "act as if"; a method for releasing fear and for opening pathways of expression and communion; most of all, it is fun.

Joyful educators have long recognized that drama and all related drama-forms (dance, music, theater, visual arts) are critically important to the development of the child; ironically, the arts are generally assigned lowest priority in traditional educational programs. This is a great tragedy for the spiritual growth of children, particularly when children evidence such hunger for this work. It is vital to provide adult support and guidance at all stages of creative growth; otherwise the gift may remain unexpressed or disappear entirely.

Drama was created by the Universe as a daring innovation, paradoxically supplying children with a way to exist in a world of illusion by applying the illusions of the dramatic form. By making up stories and scenarios, children can sense their unique place in the Universe, and with guidance, can act from a sense of self-worth. Drama is a way of rehearsing for life's tough lessons, and yet it has a life of its own, exuberantly expressed. Each child has a secret drama-world where scripts are written and rewritten, tapes are made and stored. The wonderful news is that through educational drama, unhealthy tapes can be erased and truthful ones inserted in their place.

Two classic elements of drama are vital: catharsis and insight. Catharsis is the gestalt experience of moving all thoughts, words, feelings, and the utterances of spirit to expression. It occurs when the child "lets it all hang out." Insight occurs only after long experience with the cathartic process and is a way of learning about joy or relearning after negative experiences have occurred. Catharsis results from trusting adults. Children must feel they are playing in a safe environment: supportive, nonjudgmental, and unconditionally loving. Our greatest contribution in child drama is to provide such an environment; the child's own creative spirit will direct and support the work.

One such child found it necessary, in a group creative drama class, to play the role of Policeman for a year and a half! He was expressing a need to deal with feelings of fear, ego, and authority-confusion. In other learning environments his behavior was classified as emotionally disturbed; in drama, he was an individual with a greater than average need to express. After eighteen months, the little boy finally chose to become a second character: a woman who danced about in a gorgeous lime green ballgown! Many children display a natural, developmental need to portray opposite-sex roles, just as they need to portray any confusing role. In this case, the Lime Green Lady was more than just a breakthrough. In short order, the boy was portraying a rich variety of characters—all of whom displayed surprising qualities: generosity, sensitivity, love. In one enactment, he became a Magical Mailman who delivered handwritten love letters to all the other children in the group. He was seven. And deaf. What a beautiful transformation for this child—and what powerful evidence that each child has an internal clock. If we wait for the child's right time and offer unconditional joy and love, joyful things will emerge.

Child drama is allegory. Underneath the story are important truths that must be expressed. In this sense, child drama is a way to let off spiritual and emotional steam. It is important to express negative emotions, negative characters, to clear the way for positive, creative thought. Child drama has rules; the adult can best learn the rules through observation. The rules change with the form of the enactment: vocal play, with its sounds and rhythms, verbal play, with explorations in language, and nonverbal play, through gesture, movement, facial expression, and body language.

Creative drama is not "acting"; it is *real* in the sense that one completely trusts a thought or feeling and lets it flow freely. Children can express all sorts of bizarre or awe-inspiring truths through this simple belief in the here and now. Adults must get in touch with spontaneity: living in the moment, becoming at one with the scene, mood, character, emotion. Any non-involved, inhibited, or judgmental response will be joy-depleting. This does not mean that adults must necessarily join in the enactment; often nonverbal responses are sufficient. Sensitivity is the key issue—knowing when to interact with the child and when to be there and allow the child to pursue the problem or role. It is, however, not Theater; drama is Truth.

The child owns the dramatic experience and has a sense of joy and oneness with that experience. I became aware of the depth of this truth years ago, when I was serving as a creative drama teacher in an inner city project. Classes there were large and enthusiastic, despite the fact that children had to literally fight their way to class past street gangs, thugs, and bullies. On one occasion, a little fellow arrived at the door with torn clothing, a black eye, and a bloody nose. He looked around, sized up the situation, marched to center stage and claimed his right to be there: "Okay, guys, . . . Quiet on the scenery!"

For some children, this urge may be deeply hidden under layers of misinformation and fear, but without pushing or insisting, the creative adult can lovingly and intuitively know the right moment to allow this need to blossom forth. How can we best awaken the creative flame in children?

1. *Give permission.* Your words, as well as your body language, facial expression, and actions will let the child know that you will unconditionally support this activity. Remain positive, but neutral. Let the child feel comfortable in entering into dramatic play in the child's own right time. Permit child observers. You may be the only one playing at first. After all children become actively engaged, you can retreat—entering the play when approached or when you want to intensify the experience for the child by questioning (The Neutral Interviewer) or interacting (Adult as Character). If you boldly move forth into this adventure, the children will usually follow soon after. If you exhibit fear, the children will follow suit. If you are embarrassed, the child will feel discomfort. Allow your child to emerge and the play will flow spontaneously; the children await your unconditional "Yes! This is a wonderful thing to do!" You may not hear applause from the Universe, but I'll wager you'll get a few chill bumps as you watch the joy bubble forth from the children.

2. *Select the stimulus.* Dozens of excellent books are now available to help in the design of exercises in drama, depending always on the age and developmental levels of the children. A few of the classics can be found in the reference list for this section. Remember, however, your creative genius can design the very best drama experiences for your particular children. It is no accident that you are together, to share in the learning experience. Anything and everything—from the crudest set of wooden spoons and pots and pans, to elaborate hats, dolls, puppets, wigs, costumes, makeup, movies, videotapes, storybooks, an "event" from out in the world that day, bits of cloth or long streams of fabric, magic wands, angel wings, clown noses, suitcases, boxes, masks, and so on, ad infinitum—all can be used to let the drama unfold. The Play's the thing!

3. *Supportive attitude.* Try to be open to all actions within the drama "space," unless they result in harm to self or others. It is most important for children to feel that they may express everything they need to express and that the limits—although present—are different from those of traditional learning experiences. Certainly children are very tolerant of "antisocial" behaviors; they clear away anxieties, anger, fear, and doubts. Let the Monsters, Soldiers, Fighters, Witches, and Goblins appear! Eventually they will transform into joyous, accepting, courageous, peaceful, loving children. The process takes time—and it is very much a process. When positive behaviors emerge, these can be gently reinforced. In time, the child's own catharsis and insight will lead the way to intuitive knowing. Let there be as much clamor

and chaos as seems necessary to express *all* the emotions. Let the children "make a joyful noise." What is expressed without, will grow within.

4. *Safe environment.* This is related to the last principle, but refers also to the protection of the rights of all children. Sometimes one or more children need to express negative emotions. Recognize this need and support it. Give support also to the children who are observing the scene: "It's okay to act this out in drama. We know you are acting out a feeling." Or: "Sometimes we need to show our strong feelings and sometimes we don't need to. It's okay to do that in drama if we don't hurt ourselves or other children." Then move quickly to those who are working constructively and reinforce their work. "This work is wonderful. I like this story. Interesting idea. Who are you right now?" Let them return to their work and again focus attention on the acting-out child. You may want to mirror the child, take another counter-role, or express empathy so that the child feels safe and supported. After the feeling has been expressed, safely and without going out of control, then reinforce the child with body language or touching and introduce a neutral, but related scenario: "Now let's rest here under this (imaginary) tree"; "Let's look for some butterflies"; "Let's move this river (fabric) to the (quiet) music."

5. *Accept the results without judgment.* On any given day, no new moral truths may emerge, no great insights, no unique creative contributions may occur. However, trust the process, and know that the child's truth has been expressed or felt within, and know, too, that wonderful things are happening in the creative consciousness—moving the child to the full expression of self. Along with this, let the child's story emerge. Do not try to engineer the creative work to cause it to fit your conception. It is the child's inner guide who becomes the teacher. Watch, observe, laugh, and learn as the child's world view expands. Be careful not to over-praise; a lot of praise is extraneous and insincere. Take care not to focus on the child whose gift is more readily apparent. Praise the ideas as your own style dictates, but don't forget that some children may be doing all their work vicariously within.

Drama is joy in action—a kinetic/kinesthetic process through which learning occurs rapidly and involves the whole child—a form of learning that can literally save years of working through less immediate, direct, totally involving forms of education. It is also a most exciting interchange, and offers, for children and for the adults in their environment, a sharing that touches our hearts and heals our emotions. I wish you great joy in this adventure!

SAMPLE ACTIVITY: "THE BEAUTIFUL DUCKLING"

(In response to Hans Christian Andersen's fairy tale. A story theater exercise for children in kindergarten or early elementary stages, easily adapted for older groups.)

MATERIALS: Notes and resources on Andersen and the story
COSTUME PIECES: Bits of paper or fabric for water and setting, the Duckling or

Swan transformational costume, feather or paper wings and feet for players, small amount of symbolic makeup

WARM-UP: "The Ugly Duckling" may be described, read, retold by volunteer story-tellers, or used as a meditation. To enhance the imagination, refrain from showing illustrations until later. Photographs or illustrations can be used to add to individual interpretations. Use the Duckling or Swan symbol or costume as a warm-up to increase identification with the activity.

ENACTMENT: Allow the children to develop the story completely as *they* experience it. Change roles and repeat, reinforcing truth principles as they occur. Focus also on the time period *after* the "Ugly Duckling" transforms into the "Beautiful Swan," noting elements of acceptance or forgiveness if they occur. Replay the story with a different focus: acceptance of the Duckling "as is" from the outset of the story. Creative but minimal side-coaching from the adult can be helpful during this process. For good discussions of this technique, see Spolin[24] and Heathcote.[25]

SHARING: This is the most important time in any drama session, the time of quiet reflection and leaning into each other's insights and perceptions. Note the children's responses to roles, themes, and talking about feelings. Note children moving to their own personal responses and insights relative to their own life experience.

VARIATIONS: (1) Use the "Unfinished Story" technique for older groups (See Shaftel)[26] by encouraging various children to develop alternate endings to the story. Act out one or more of the alternatives as part of the enactment portion of the session. (2) Use Johnathan Fox's[27] Playback Theater Technique by letting children *tell* their own similar stories on this theme and then selecting *other* children to act them out as the storyteller watches the enactment. A "Musician" can accompany the enactment and support the emotional energy of the work.

WARM-UPS FOR OTHER EXERCISES

1. Children take archetypal opposites and develop a "living statue" of that quality: Love/Apathy, Energy/Depression, Acceptance/Rejection. In scenes between two actors portraying the qualities, using sounds, movements, or nonsense syllables for communication, we see if the positive quality is more powerful than the negative quality. Each player assumes a certain quality and then communicates that in a "nonverbal" dialogue with an actor who is portraying the opposite quality.

2. Introduce an animal, live or imaginary, into the circle. Notice how the children interact with it (comfort, play, tease). Then substitute a child into the animal's role. Do things appear to be different?

3. Children pick out musical instruments and costume pieces, placing their "goods" in front of them in the circle. They develop "conversations" with each other, first using musical instruments and then those same feelings as they are acted out in costume. Notice what is happening and how it feels/sounds/looks. Move around

the circle, letting the "essence" of each assumed personality (role) be communicated through the costume. Move to an experience of each child expressing joy in their character, expressing caring for others/resolution of conflict with self or nature or others.

Fun and Games

Calling all children
hiding out in their grown-up bodies
who long to be
joyful, funful
freeful
come out, come out, wherever you are
and play in the now-sun
of your
Life
RUSTY BERKUS, *Life Is a Gift*

Play is one of the easiest ways to express our joy. The human need to play is powerful—and instinctive. We miss out on a lot of joy when we don't allow time for play in our lives.

The Importance of Play

There are educational, physical, and psychological benefits to play. To name just a few:

    ☆ Play promotes empathy, rapport, and compassion.
    ☆ Play is one of the most powerful ways we learn, and retain what we learn.

☆ Play allows children to discover and define themselves.

☆ Play is a socially acceptable way of releasing negative feelings and frustrations.

☆ Play provides an avenue of expression, where words would be inadequate.

☆ Play offers us a chance to work through unresolved problems of the past and to deal with current pressures.

☆ Play encourages spontaneity, which can later lead to creativity.

☆ Play is the source of inventions and aesthetic creations.

☆ Play allows the child to try various forms of social interaction.

☆ Play is a way of giving joy to oneself and others.

If parents have a true respect for the value of their child's play, they won't interrupt it unless there's a real emergency. They will give children the same respect they want for themselves when they are absorbed in a task.

It's great to play with our children, but if we have an ulterior motive in mind it will mar the experience for the child. Children know if we're entering the pure joy of playing or just seeking to teach, entertain, or diagnose them.

Mencius said, "The great man is he who does not lose his child's-heart." This is the man who can still play. I love the words of author Leo Buscaglia, "I play with the leaves. I skip down the street and run against the wind. I never water my garden without soaking myself. It has been after such times of joy that I have achieved my greatest creativity and produced my best work."[1]

A middle-aged husband and wife I know initiate their playfulness through a small stuffed bear and bunny who play together as their alter egos. Buddy and Flopsy even accompany them on trips and add a humorous dimension to their experiences. On a recent trip, Buddy struck up a conversation with a young boy at the next table in the restaurant. The result was four tables of strangers communicating with each other —something you rarely see nowadays.

Last week the husband, Charlie, left to climb Everest and took his bear with him. I'm sure Buddy will add life to the expedition. He went with Charlie to get the necessary inoculations for the trip, and the nurse gave him a shot and put a Band-Aid on him also. Charlie has been doing practice climbs with his backpack, and Buddy's head peeks over the top. A climber behind him noted, "I see you have your pack down to the 'bear' minimum." "No, the 'bear' essentials," retorted my friend.

This little bear, who stutters when he speaks, *is* an essential in the sixth-grade class Charlie teaches. The children clamor for him to give the spelling test, because he sometimes goofs and starts to spell the word. They willingly accept advice when it comes from Buddy. He's the most popular one to play with at recess time.

Don't we all need a Buddy in our life? Maybe you have your own unique way of sharing your inner child.

Games versus Play

Most games are not play activities—at least not the familiar games in our culture. The young child's *play* is characterized by freedom from all but personally imposed and flexible rules, by the absence of goals beyond the activity, by imagination and pure enjoyment. Most *games*, however, have strict rules and involve tension because there are sides with winners and losers, criticism and competition. Equipment must be used in just the way it's intended, and not with imagination. Bruno Bettelheim tells us that, for a child, a game is not "just a game," but a real-life experience: on its outcome rest his feelings of self-esteem and competence. Losing is not just part of "playing the game," as it is for adults, but something that undermines the child's self-confidence.

Cooperation versus Competition

Players can be molded by their games. The competitive approach to games encourages physical and verbal aggression. The put-down statements children hurl at each other erode self-confidence. Just as damaging is the self-deprecating talk that such games encourage: "I'm not coordinated," "I'm always chosen last," "I'll never be any good." Weinstein and Goodman explain that if the pressure to win is removed, the urge to verbally humiliate other players soon disappears.[2]

Notice the games your children play. Is there more importance placed on rules than on people? Is winning emphasized? Does only one person win and everyone else lose?

There is a beautiful movement toward cooperative rather than competitive games. "Despite our cherished belief in the virtues of competition, study after study shows that nothing succeeds like cooperation," says Alfie Kohn, author of the book *No Contest: The Case Against Competition.*[3] In cooperative games there are no losers: everybody wins. All players strive toward a common goal. They play *with* one another, rather than *against* one another, and there is no fear of failure. No one is left out—all are fully involved, and all leave happier than when they began. A far cry from the competitive game.

This obsession with competition is not found in all cultures. Terry Orlick, in his superb *The Cooperative Sports and Games Book*, tells how some native cultures run their races as ties. The challenge is to reach the finish line at the same time. He includes many examples of games played by native children that are based on cooperation, not competition. He says, "Children nurtured on cooperation, acceptance, and success have a much greater chance of developing strong self-concepts, just as children nurtured on balanced diets have a greater chance of developing strong healthy bodies."[4]

A Look At Cooperative Games

One of my purposes in this book is to direct you to valuable source material, since one book can't say all that needs to be said. One of my favorites is Terry Orlick's book mentioned above. He has many descriptions of cooperative games conveniently categorized by age groups. I include here a few abbreviated examples.

For the very young children, there's **Cooperative Musical Hoops**. The hula hoop, Orlick says, is "a very effective means of promoting initial cooperation among three- and four-year-olds." In this activity two children stand in a hula hoop and hold it up. They skip around to the music, and when it stops they must join with another pair. The hoops are stacked, and the four children are inside holding them up, while skipping to the music. This continues until about eight are in a hoop.

Big Turtle is a game where a group of several children get on their hands and knees under something that represents a turtle shell, such as a large sheet of cardboard or plastic, a tarp, a blanket, or a mattress. The point is to make the turtle move in one direction, perhaps through an obstacle course or over a bench representing a mountain.

I love the name **Tug of Peace**. Contrary to tug of war, in this activity, winning comes from pulling together.

Little People's Big Sack is where about eight to twenty children get in a big sack and try to maneuver it. Orlick suggests using material that can be seen through, such as burlap or durable old white sheets.

Beach Ball Balance is one I'm eager to try. In this activity one beach ball is shared by two people, who hold the ball between them without using hands. They discover all the ways they can hold the ball between them, such as head to head, back to back, or side to side, while moving around the room doing designated activities. I want to find out if it's really possible to balance a beach ball forehead to forehead while touching your toes.

Frozen Bean Bag was designed by Orlick as a game to help your friends. The leader has children move around the room with bean bags on their heads while she gives instructions to skip, hop on one foot, go faster, go backwards, and so forth. When a bean bag falls off, the child is "frozen." The object of the game is to help friends by keeping them *unfrozen*. This is done by a child picking up the dropped bean bag and placing it back on the frozen player's head without losing his own bean bag in the process.

Orlick presents old games in new ways. For instance, **Nonelimination Musical**

Chairs and **Nonelimination Simon Says**. It is heartwarming to think of such games being played without anybody having to be left out.

In **Nonelimination Musical Chairs**, as with most cooperative games, the object is to keep everyone in the game. Even though the chairs are systematically removed when the music stops, as in the traditional version, the children aren't removed from the game. They team up together, sitting on parts of the chairs or on each other to keep everyone in the game. In the end, all the children are on one chair with no disappointed children standing on the sidelines.

In **Nonelimination Simon Says**, there are two games going on simultaneously, so instead of being eliminated from playing, a child just transfers to the other game and joins in when "Simon Says."

The traditional **Pin the Tail on the Donkey** has been revised by concerned mothers. It can be played in a couple of cooperative ways: (1) children call out directions to the blindfolded person; (2) they work together to assemble the entire animal on the wall, each taking turns adding a different body part—leg, head, tail. Directions are called out as in (1). The result is cheers, not tears, says Orlick.

Cooperative Hide and Seek was invented by another inspired mother. Two children, hand in hand, begin as the seekers, and each time they find someone he or she joins hands with them. It ends with all the children holding hands and looking for the last hider.

Take a careful look at the games your children are playing. What are they learning about themselves? Are their games releasing the joy within?

For older children—the eight- through twelve-year-olds—Orlick offers a vast variety of games including **Hug Tag**, **Frozen Tag**, water games, quiet games, relay and carrying games, and collective score games. It's fun to read about them even if you don't plan to play them, because they're beautiful examples of creative thinking. You can also sense the joy children would have in playing them. The child in you may have a vicarious experience.

I'd also like to mention a few games from another of my favorite game books, *Playfair: Everybody's Guide to Noncompetitive Play*.[5] As the title indicates, these games are for everybody: many of them are great for adults to use at retreats, conventions, church socials, and other gatherings.

The book has a couple of revised tag games—**Brussels Sprouts** uses the concept previously mentioned in **Cooperative Hide and Seek**. "It" links arms with the person caught, and together they become "it." The "it" gets larger and larger, until it encompasses everyone, and that's the end of the game. This game has some special features. It starts out in slow motion, and players call out "Lima Beans!" or "Carrots!" You'll have to read the book to find out what happens then.

The authors also give some food for thought about the negative connotation of the word "It" when used in competitive games and suggest "center person" as an alternative.

Finger Dancing is one of the less active games in the book. It is done with a partner and with eyes closed. Each partner puts an index finger (the pointer) into the space between them. The fingers find each other, fuse together, and the dance starts. The movements may be subtle or big, but they come from the fingers themselves.

One game I'd really like to see played is called **Roll Playing**. Participants sit on the floor close together in a tight circle, with legs extended. A basketball is placed on the lap of one person. The object is to move the ball around the circle as quickly as possible from lap to lap, without using hands. There are some innovative features you can add to make the game even more fun.

Imaginary Ball Toss is one of several games designed to help players get to know each other's names. Participants stand in a circle, and starting with an imaginary tennis ball, a player calls another's name and throws the ball to him. When she doesn't know his name, she just asks. Whoever catches the ball can change it into something else—a basketball, a watermelon, an egg, a live chicken, or whatever he likes. He calls out what it is, names the person to receive it, and then tosses it.

There are a number of books now that offer games to give children confidence and a feeling of worth instead of rejection. You may wish to check out *Everybody Wins* by Jeff Sobel.[6]

Choosing Partners and Teams

Choosing partners is wrought with anxiety. Weinstein and Goodman say, ". . . it is important to invent ways to get the players into pairs and groups without anyone being left out, and without putting the players into anxiety-provoking positions."[7] Here are three of the many ways they suggest for pairing people up:

1. Put from zero to five fingers in the air and find one other partner whose raised fingers added to yours make an even number.
2. Start hopping around on either your right foot or your left foot and find a partner who is hopping on the same foot.
3. Find a partner who is wearing one item of clothing the same color as you are.

Choosing teams is also a tense situation for children and often spoils the joy of the game itself. "Forced choice" is the team selection process *Playfair* recommends. For example, the leader would say to the group, "Decide if you would rather eat grapes or a banana right now," and have them divide up accordingly. Or she might say, "Would you rather go to the beach or the mountains for a vacation? Mountain people over here, beach people over there." The authors say it seldom matters if the teams are even.

Orlick relates methods used by the North American Indians to choose sides so that no one felt humiliated by being chosen last. I like the one where the leader has placed strips of two different colors of paper in a covered basket. Each player draws out one slip of paper and the color designates his team.

Constructing Your Own Games

It's fun to invent your own games. You can do this by altering existing games or by creating a game from scratch. Weinstein and Goodman offer a checklist of ten playful ingredients for noncompetitive games.[8] It's the Playfair Recipe and they suggest you use it "in concocting your own playful confections." In abbreviated form, here it is:

1. Does the game have a good sense of humor? Does it encourage the players to laugh with, not at, one another?
2. Is the game cooperative in nature? Do participants play with, not against, one another?
3. Does the game take positive action? Do people feel better about themselves during and after playing the game?
4. Is the game inclusive in nature? Are people encouraged to play, rather than to spectate?
5. Does the game provide opportunities for the players to be imaginative and spontaneous, and even change the rules?
6. Do the players have equality in the game? Is the leader also one of the players?
7. Does the game avoid putting players on-the-spot by having them "perform" in isolation and be "evaluated" in front of the group?
8. Is the game challenging? Is there a sense of adventure to it?
9. Does the game put people before rules?
10. Is the game fun?

If you wish to revamp an old game to make it more cooperative and fun, I suggest the checklist on page 194 of *Playfair*. To create a new game from scratch, the authors suggest a technique like the Fran Striker creative story writing idea I suggested in Chapter 8. Instead of the four elements of a story you use the six elements of a game:

1. Who will play the game? (e.g., preschoolers, college students, a Sunday school class)
2. What is the focus or task on which the players are to concentrate?
3. Props—this can range from none to a parachute.
4. Leader control—this can range from the facilitator having complete control to the players having most of the control.
5. Energy level and size of groupings—is the game a quiet one or an active, high-energy game? Do players play in pairs or large or small groups?
6. Ending—it's important for the players to know in advance how their game will end.

According to Weinstein and Goodman, if you list ten choices for each of the above six elements on a grid, and then mix and match them, you'll have the possible yield of one million games!

Probably the best source of new game ideas is the children themselves. Orlick says, "With a few simple guidelines they can often think in a way that has been conditioned out or made obscure by blinders in everyday adult life."[9] As evidence, he offers many games invented by children. One group of children created fourteen games in a half-hour session. What are we waiting for?

You may wish to peruse the *Animal Town Game Co. Catalog*. It features cooperative board games, as well as books, tape, and educational playthings.[10]

The Gift of Laughter

> *A person without a sense of humor is like*
> *a wagon without springs—jolted by every*
> *pebble in the road.*
>
> HENRY WARD BEECHER

Fun and games to me mean laughter. Laughter is the result of our humor, and humor comes from our joy. And, in turn, our joy is expanded by our humor. I'm referring here to uplifting humor, the capacity to laugh at ourselves and with the world. Such humor, it is said, "is born of awareness of the almost universal lack of proportion in human life."

Laughter is healing. When we laugh we are actually releasing chemicals into our bloodstream that reduce pain and, by bolstering our immune system, help prevent or cure disease. Laughter also expands the lungs and clears the respiratory system, as well as providing us with extra energy.

Besides contributing to our physical well-being, laughter relieves tension and defuses many stressful situations. Making children laugh when they are in disagreement makes them forget their differences. Even with adults, humor dissolves differences and harmonizes the atmosphere. Barriers come down and people begin to relate to each other. A favorite example of this is a true story I read in *Christopher News Notes* a few years ago: A San Francisco policewoman was sent to investigate a family disturbance. As she approached the house she saw a television crash through the window. She could hear a heated argument when she rang the bell. A gruff voice called out, "Who is it?" Instead of saying, "Police," she responded with "TV repairman." The angry shouts dissolved into laughter and a peaceful solution was reached.

Wayne Dyer says it is a parental responsibility to help children "develop an ability to laugh a lot in life, to see the fun side of everything, and to be a little crazy now and then." "Make it your commitment," he urges, "to help them have as many laughs as they possibly can."[11]

With some families the dinner hour is the time they can plan on laughter. Laughter aids digestion, fosters fellowship, and feeds the soul. How much healthier than fussing over manners and food, dwelling on problems, or watching the news. I once heard a public speaker tell about her childhood family dinners, where everybody had a hilarious time laughing. She said they would laugh so hard they would cry, fall off their chairs, or wet their pants. Their dinner hour often became a couple of hours.

Another family passes a drawstring laugh bag around at the dinner table. Each member loosens the drawstring, inhales the contagious laughter, and then refills it with laughter before passing it on. This can be fun in Sunday school, at birthday parties, or on a car trip. Joyful Child now has Laughter Bags and many suggestions for their use.

If humor is a lost art in your household, recover it by getting some joke books. Each member could bring a humorous anecdote or funny joke to the table. Teachers could have similar joke sessions in the classroom or start a joke bulletin board. Teach your children that humor can harm if it is exercised at someone else's expense, such as sick jokes, or ethnic jokes.

A great sage suggests that people laugh 15 minutes a day in order to raise their vibratory frequency, which can heal the entire body. Laugh your troubles away, he advises. Laugh at mistakes and calamities. If you laugh when an earthquake begins, he says, you can accelerate into the higher vibrations, where fear cannot exist, and you will simply pass it by. He has people start slowly by vocalizing the "ancient mantra of ha-ha-ha." Gradually they build up momentum until there are giggles and belly laughs. It's contagious.

Another way of getting laughter started is laughter tapes, cassettes of continuous laughter. Commercial ones are available, or you can make your own with a group of friends. When you are sick, depressed, bored, or your group needs a lift, put on a laughter tape.

Remind your children that it's easier to smile than frown. Smiling requires fewer muscles. Also, it is said, "A smile confuses an approaching frown."

Create laughter games. In one family, the members take turns sitting in the laugh chair while the others go through antics to get the person in the chair to laugh. Of course, those who are trying to provoke laughter have the biggest laugh of all. Since laughter is contagious, the person in the chair usually succumbs.

"I Love Ya Honey, But I Just Can't Make Ya Smile" is a similar family-type game. The object is to sit in another's lap and say, "I love ya honey, but I just can't make ya smile," in such a way as to get the other person to laugh or smile. For details, see *Playfair*.

Let's remember the words of Victor Borge: "Laughter is the closest distance between two people."

Intuition Games

Intuition is a power we all have, but we're usually unaware of using it. It is the immediate apprehension of untaught knowledge. It is knowing without knowing how we know. Our rational, logical way of knowing is not nearly as important or trustworthy as our intuition.

Helping children develop their intuition is offering them a lifelong skill, a skill that will help them make decisions, perceive the future, relate with others, and grasp higher levels of awareness. The highest function of the intuition is to tune into Infinite Intelligence. Then they'll know what's right without necessarily knowing how.

You can help children become aware of their intuition by recalling together the times it has worked for you, for them, and for others. Encourage them to practice their intuition in small matters so as to get used to experiencing this part of their mind. Who is on the phone? How hot will it get tomorrow? Which check-out line will move faster? What questions will be on the test? Which store has what they are looking for?

TELEPATHY EXERCISES

Telepathy, a form of intuition, is the ability to read what is in another's mind. It most often takes place between people who have close emotional ties, so the family is an excellent place to practice telepathic communication. Simple exercises done right after waking or before bedtime bring the best results.

Being relaxed is necessary for experiencing telepathy at the conscious level. It's already going on at the unconscious level, but to be aware of it or to play with it, you must be relaxed physically and mentally, and you must have an open mind.

In telepathy, there are senders and receivers. The sender must project clear, distinct images to the receiver by concentrating, but not straining. The sender can silently chant the name of the image while visualizing a flow of the image to the receiver. The receiver maintains a relaxed state of anticipation while silently asking the subconscious mind to send the image now.

EXERCISE ONE: Have the children prepare for this activity, and all the others, by closing their eyes and quieting their minds for a few minutes. The teacher, or the children, as appropriate, can ask questions such as the following:

1. What do I have in the surprise box today?
2. What color has Judy written on her tablet?
3. What animal has Bobby written on his tablet?
4. What are they doing in Mrs. Scott's class right now?
5. Add to the list.

EXERCISE TWO: Pair off in partners and face each other. Decide who is sender and receiver. Close eyes and hold hands. The sender's hands go on top, the receiver's on the bottom. Or the sender can hold the receiver's wrists. The sender pictures in his mind one thing that has special meaning to him. It could be a favorite object, food, pet, or person. For a minute or two he sends a mental image of this to the receiver. Then they open their eyes and the receiver shares the impressions that came. Change roles and after that switch partners if a number of people are playing.

Stephanie Herzog reports that after some practice her entire class was able to send messages with about 80% accuracy.[12] A number of the children became very close friends because of this activity.

EXERCISE THREE: For two players or a whole class. Prepare ahead of time some image charts on 3 × 5 cards as follows:

A. 5 numbers – one on each card
B. 5 letters – one on each card
C. 5 symbols – e.g., cross, triangle, square, star, heart
D. 5 basic colors – tape or staple a vivid color to each card

Show the cards to the players before beginning. Give each player a blank white card to represent a movie or TV screen. After everybody has done a relaxation technique, the sender calls out a category (e.g., letters, colors) and focuses on the image for a minute or two. The receiver looks at the blank "movie screen" card and anticipates a mental image. When there are just two players, the receiver calls aloud the image he's receiving. When more than two, each player writes down the image on a "call sheet," any lined paper, and when the categories have been run through once, the sender calls out the answers.

For a variation of the game make other five-item category lists. Examples:

Places: zoo, Disneyland, park, beach, school
Fruits: banana, kiwi, lemon, orange, peach
Cities: New York, Seattle, Phoenix, Tokyo, London
Gems: diamond, ruby, pearl, emerald, opal

EXERCISE FOUR: One person takes off an item of clothing (e.g., shoe, sock, watch) and leaves the room while the other player or players hide it. When the player comes back into the room, she stands in the middle and gets centered. She then tunes into the minds of the other players, who are concentrating on where the object is hidden. This can be done with any object, but it is a little easier when the child's own clothing is used, because it has her vibrations on it.

EXERCISE FIVE: A good small party game. Everyone stands with their backs to the leader, who chooses one person to focus on. He sends energy and a message of some sort to that person (e.g., scratch your head, clear your throat). Whoever is feeling a message responds. After a couple of minutes the leader tells who it was and what the message was. Then another leader is chosen.

The above activity and many other intuition games are in Rozman's *Meditation for Children*.[13] I especially like the one where everyone stands, one at a time, in front of a blindfolded person, who guesses who it is from the vibration he picks up.

Another good resource for intuition games is *The Ultimate Kid*.[14] For the classroom, the game "To Tell The Truth," based on a popular TV show, could be great fun.

Color sensing is popular in her classroom, says Stephanie Herzog.[15] After a meditation exercise, she'll hold up sheets of colored construction paper, and these seven-year-olds, with their eyes still closed, will sense the color. Children can practice this on their own, by laying out squares of bright colors and sensing them while blindfolded. I had heard of such experiments in Russia a great many years ago and am delighted that they have now reached our public schools.

Kinship with All Life has true stories of telepathic communication between animals and man.[16] I consider it "must" reading.

Since imagination and intuition are closely related, look up the imagination exercises in the creativity chapter for related activities.

Mind Games

The I Am Game. This is a simple game to build an awareness of "I am" affirmations and of the importance of putting the words "I am" with only what is good and true. Explain that "I am" are two of the most powerful words we can say, because that is the name of God in us. Whatever we repeatedly say and feel after the words "I am" can come true in our life.

The game can be played by a large group or just a couple of people. Starting at the beginning of the alphabet, the first player makes an "I am" statement using a word starting with *A*. Since the words must be positive, "I am angry" wouldn't count. The second player uses the letter *B* and so on. If only two are playing, each participant can give a word for every letter of the alphabet. This makes a good game for the dinner table, car, doing dishes, or at bedtime. It's fun to do with puppets. Consider speeding it up, and singing or chanting the "I am" statements. Each participant might want to pick out an appealing statement as his or her special affirmation for the day.

Following is a short list of words for when you, or your children, get stuck. Add more of your own to the list. Vocabulary building is a nice by-product of this activity when the game is played frequently.

Reminder List

A: affectionate, able, alert, awake, ambitious
B: beautiful, bold, brave
C: cheerful, careful, creative, caring, capable
D: daring, divine, decisive, dependable
E: enthusiastic, eager, energetic, efficient
F: fun, fantastic, fortunate, faithful, free, forgiving
G: generous, gregarious, gracious, good, grateful
H: healthy, happy, humorous, hopeful, helpful, honest

I: imaginative, intelligent, interesting, intuitive
J: joy, joyful, jubilant, jolly, joyous
K: kind, kingly, knowledgeable, knowing
L: loving, light, learning, life
M: magnificent, marvelous, miraculous
N: nice, neat, nifty, noble
O: optimistic, orderly, open-minded, organized
P: patient, peaceful, perfect, persistent, positive
Q: quick, quiet, questioning
R: rich, right, regal, remarkable, responsible, reliable
S: successful, sweet, strong, super, serene, secure
T: terrific, trustworthy, truthful, talented
U: uplifting, useful, unique, unusual, understanding
V: victorious, vibrant, visual, visionary
W: wonderful, wealthy, well, wise, whole
X: (excited), (extraordinary), (excellent)
Y: youthful, young
Z: zealous, zestful

An appropriate ending for this game would be to sing the "I Am Happy" or "I Am Joyful" songs in Chapter 7. Since "I can" is the child of "I am," you might make up an "I can" version of this activity. "I can be helpful," "I can swim," "I can be patient," etc.

The Freeze Game. Throughout the day or class period the leader (teacher, parent, or child) calls out, "Freeze." The participants freeze mentally and physically and check out the nature of their thoughts and feelings. Are they such that they would contribute to joy and peace? They ask themselves if they would want to have those thought impressions frozen in their mind and ultimately in their body. They also become aware of their body posture and facial expression at that moment. What does it say?

There are several ways this game could be introduced. Younger children could play freeze tag to get used to the idea of freezing. When the leader calls "freeze," each player becomes like a statue. Frozen foods or petrified wood could also be used to introduce the concept. Abraham Lincoln said that any grown man is responsible for his face. There is a whole science of personology that supports this. If you have some of this knowledge, you could display pictures of faces to show how thoughts become frozen.

The Silence Game. Choose to remain silent for an entire day. In order to get the most insights, it should be a day when you're around family and friends. As with the previous game, we listen to our thoughts about everyone and everything, especially about ourselves. We catch the criticism that separates us from others and keeps us from loving ourselves. And we become aware of many ways we communicate nonverbally. Keep in mind that the purpose of outer silence is to cultivate inner silence. We don't want to continue talking with our mind, when our tongue is silent.

"Think Your Happiest Thought." A mind-stretcher for young and old. Participants write down a happy thought in several categories that would be appropriate for the age group (school activities, trips, job, sports, health, relationships, possessions, solutions to problems).

Now ask them to take one thought at a time and make it happier. Have them keep thinking of other ways to make it an even happier thought. A variation that you may prefer is "Think Your Biggest Thought"—and now make it bigger. This is a way of stretching the imagination and stimulating creative thinking. Writing isn't necessary. Let it be a fun guided-imagery exercise. Some say it is easier to do big things than it is to do little things. A big clock uses less energy than a little one. A big idea calls forth more enthusiasm and energy, not only from ourselves, but from others also. So encourage children to believe bigger and think happier.

VISUALIZATION EXERCISES

Visualization is primarily a skill of the imagination (see Chapter 10 for related activities). It is a tool that facilitates the manifestation process. As such, it is an important skill for Light Workers who are using the colors of the various rays and other visual symbols to heal situations on the planet. Many people are working with the Violet Flame, the Threefold Flame, the White Light, and various combinations of symbols and colors which have been given us from the higher dimensions. Part of the work of The Radiance Technique is done through visualizing symbols. Even very young children are being taught visualization for healing their bodies. For instance, children with catastrophic illnesses are being taught to visualize white blood cells attacking the red ones, or to lift their brain out of their head and hose it down.

It has been predicted that this picturing process will be utilized frequently in the schools of the future. In the sports and therapy fields visualization has long been recognized as a valuable tool, since our creative subconscious doesn't know the difference between a real or vividly imagined experience. Now in the academic area imaging has been found to aid comprehension and retention. A guided imagery trip through an historical event or foreign country can have more impact and be more motivating than ordinary textbook study.

The word "visualize" is confusing, and a block to those who don't see mental pictures. It is not necessary to mentally see an image to visualize. Some just get a feeling or an impression. If the child can recall her bedroom, lying down on her bed, her dinner plate last night, or eating a favorite food she is doing visualization.

Here are some simple ways to start young children consciously visualizing:

What's Missing? Have a tray with several small objects of various kinds. Allow the children to look at the tray carefully and then cover it with a dish cloth and remove an object. They tell you what's missing. To make it more challenging, add more objects.

Seeing In A Different Way. Pick an object from the tray and have them visualize it in a different way. Start with an easy object and have them change its color (e.g., see the apple as gold or as purple). Next you could have them mentally use an object in an unusual way (e.g., see themselves taking a spoon from the tray and cutting a piece of red paper with it). Have them turn an object into something else (e.g., hold up a lemon and have them turn it into a pig).

Neighborhood Walk. For young children, start visualization practice by having them see familiar scenes in their neighborhood. Include their house, yard, and pets also.

The Drop of Water. Have the children get the feeling for a drop of water, and then guide them as they follow it on a journey. You might take the drop of water over a waterfall, into a river, into a pool, onto a rocky beach; have it evaporate into a cloud, fall as rain onto a daisy that's leaning over a pool, and so on.

Light Visualization. Start by lighting a candle and looking at the flame. Have them visualize a fire in a fireplace, then an outdoor bonfire, then change the colors of the flames to other colors. Have them make the flames cold and stand in their midst. Change the cool flame to purple, and let its coolness blaze through their body washing away negative feelings and memories.

Have them think of people that need more love and see these people wrapped in a cocoon of pink light. Have them see themselves standing in a pillar of protective white light. The possibilities are as endless as your imagination.

Alphabet Cake. This is one of many fun visualization games in the book *Scamper*.[17] You use the letters of the alphabet to trigger ideas for new kinds of cakes. Starting with *A*, you think about what an applesauce cake or an asparagus cake would look like and taste like. How would you make it? Would you put chunks of asparagus in it or just asparagus juice? Go through the alphabet as far as the children are willing to go.

Remember, we are all not equal in our ability to visualize. No child should be made to feel "less than" because she doesn't see in vivid color or detail. Encourage visualization, but allow children their differences. (See Joy Exercises for more visualization activities.)

Doing Kits

Doing Kits are in a class by themselves. They are no-cost kits made of discardable items, and they can provide many, many hours of creative activity for children of all ages. Doing Kits were conceived by Alice Rice, a teacher of elementary-age gifted children, and they are the basis of her new book, which has 99 Doing Kit activities.[18]

You'll want a Doing Kit for each child. If you're in the classroom, have the children bring containers and suitable objects from home. The container can be a nut or potato chip can with a plastic lid, or a large cottage cheese carton, or anything to hold a variety of small objects. The objects are discards that are found in average American homes, schools, and offices. Conservation and recycling are being taught indirectly. Avoid items that are flimsy like paper and fabric, that are not safe because of sharp points, or that are too fragile.

Here are some items that end up in Doing Kits:

toy parts	spools	nuts and bolts
game pieces	jacks	bobby pins
pen parts	nails	barrettes
key rings	keys	feathers
toothbrushes	buttons	Christmas ornaments
buckles	hinges	eye droppers
batteries	beads	film, film cans

When children are first introduced to Doing Kits, they enjoy some unstructured time for exploration and discovery. Left to their own devices, they will begin to see various ways of making relationships between the items. They may categorize them by color, material, function, etc. They may experiment to see what they can do with them and try to fit them together to look like a machine or object of art. You can learn a lot by observing your children when they are given materials like these and the freedom to explore them.

Following, in abbreviated form, are a few of the 99 Doing Kit activities:

Classification Activities

1. Group the items together according to how they feel to the touch: rough, smooth, sandpapery, velvety, etc.
2. Group the items together according to what they can or will do: grip, stretch, stack, cover, slide, etc.

Organizational Activities

1. Put items in alphabetical order according to their names.
2. Group together items that are alike in some way.

Art Activities

1. Create a cost-free display. Arrange the items in shoe boxes, egg cartons, etc., so that they would be attractive to a prospective buyer. Decorate the back-drop to entice the buyer.
2. Make a crayon rubbing by placing some textured items under newsprint and rubbing with the sides of crayons to create designs.

Creative Thinking Activities

1. Put several items together to create a Thingamajig and sell someone else on the idea of buying it.

2. Name something that each thing could do that it wasn't intended to do.
3. Choose an item, imagine it fifty times bigger than it is, and tell what it could do.

Creative Writing Activities

1. Write a paragraph for each of three different items, telling all the things they remind you of and why.
2. Describe the location where an item would be found; if this item could talk, what it would say. If you were selling this item, how would you describe it?

Math Activities

1. Find out the percentage of your items that are: plastic, non-plastic, metallic, non-metallic, wood, non-wood, etc.
2. Using a balance scale, find three items that weigh the same as one item does.

Social Studies Activities

1. Name ways you could get people to save one of the throw-away items in your Doing Kit. (Solutions suggested by children: advertising its uses, paying them for it, praising them for saving it, penalizing them for discarding it, criticizing them for tossing it away.)
2. If you could recycle an item, name five ways it could then be used by people.

Science Activities

1. Using a magnet, see which items are magnetic.
2. Using a pan of water, find out which items sink or float.

Rice says children experience the joy of sharing when they share their Doing Kit with relatives, neighbors, and friends. She encourages them to take it along when they're babysitting, traveling, visiting someone who is sick or bored, or when making a new friend. "Everyone's a Winner" is a game she's developed that makes use of the Doing Kits.

JOY EXERCISES

The first six are simplifications of exercises from the magnificent book *Joy and Healing*.[19] These are adapted for use with children, and can be varied according to the child's age, background, and temperament. The exercises in the book are intended for adults and are much more complete. You may wish to try them out.

☆ Get very relaxed and then imagine a moment of joy—a joyful experience you've had. Try to see it as clearly as if you were going through it for the first time. Include all the details. After you've felt the joy of that experience, go on and relive another and another. If this is done in a group setting, turn to a partner and share a joyous experience. Include enough detail to help your partner feel some of the joy you felt.

☆ Think of all the people who need joy and send them joy like a beam of light. Send joy to sick people, sad people, people in nursing homes and hospitals, classmates, teachers, friends, parents, brothers and sisters. You can send to people who are no longer on Earth. Send your beam of joy to troubled spots in the world and to the ocean waters.

☆ Send joy to every part of your body. Send it as a beam of violet light into your head, your stomach, your throat, your legs, your arms, etc. See your whole body covered with joyous violet light. Feel joy throughout your body.

☆ Remember watching someone else who was filled with joy. Try to observe how they were joyful physically, mentally, and emotionally. Remember their voice, looks, words, and actions. Recall it so thoroughly that you can share in their joy. It might be someone who was sharing your joy. What was it that triggered their joy?

☆ Get in touch with your gratitude. Make a list of all you have to be grateful for. Gratitude releases much joy. Poet Don Blanding says joy is a "thanks beyond words for inner delight, for well-being and being well."[20]

☆ Practice charging everything you use with joy. Remember, it's a perceptible energy. Send a beam of joy into your food, your water, your paper and pencil, your book, your clothing, etc. Our vibration accumulates on everything we touch. This is how cats and dogs can find us. Advanced teachings tell us that the physical things we handle are but condensed energy and we can place whatever quality we desire upon them. Let's make a game of infusing all we touch with joy.

A Joy Face-Lift. This exercise from Blanding's *Joy Is An Inside Job* could be easily adapted for your children:

Go to the mirror.
Let your features hang down like wet wash on a rainy day.
Wipe your face clean of expression.
Become receptive, acquiescent, responsive, expectant.
Begin thinking of Joy . . . 20 feet in every direction.
Open your heart and let Spring blow through you like a fresh breeze.
Form the word "joy" with your lips but do not speak it yet.
Watch the animation spread over your features.
Watch your eyes begin to light up like fireflies at dusk.

Watch the smile-lines spread, lifting, lifting the features.
Now say the word "Joy" softly.
Then say it with increasing zest.
Joy. Joy. JOY! . . .

The word "Joy" is a pump-primer to persuade Joy to come forth. The artesian well of Joy never runs dry. We clog it with our thoughts. The word "Joy" is the drill to penetrate to the artesian flow.[21]

A Group Exercise. Display on a table a number of your favorite objects. If your group is small, have about twice as many as the number in the group. Encourage children to touch them and to choose one that they like best. (By our choices we discover who we are.)

Each child takes a turn at telling the group what he likes about the object he chose and how it could help him or someone else get in touch with joy. Empathy is built because the children begin to see the world as someone else sees it.

As a writing activity, have the children choose three different objects and write about the joy each could trigger and how it could be a token of joy for someone. They might write an ode to the object they like best.

The Ideal Day Exercise. Each day that we do this exercise we release more joy-fulness, says Arnold Patent. We focus on the joyfulness within before we get out of bed, and project that feeling into all our activities for the day. The details of the day will be in accordance with the energy we are emitting. Joyfulness will attract joyful people and events.

Happy Buttons

Here is a challenge for you. Create a Happy Button or Joy Button game appropriate to the age group of your children. When they push the Happy Button they are to tune into their joy.

Maybe you'll want to pass out gummed-back stickers that the children can put on their foreheads. Throughout the day there could be time-out periods, when each one is encouraged to press her Happy Button. Or the Happy Button might be a creative bedside device that they can push each morning to fill themselves up with joy before getting up.

Or maybe the Joy Button is something that you yourself wear and when your children want to see you smile they get to push it. Consider wearing a Hug Button, a Kiss Button, a Listen To Me Button. Whenever your children have one of those needs, they get to push the appropriate button. Wouldn't it be more joyful to have children push these kinds of buttons than the ones they so often push to get our attention?

Use your imagination and create a Happy Button game that is uniquely yours. Consider a Happy Button song or chant.

Nature Activities

Deviation from Nature
is deviation from happiness.
SAMUEL JOHNSON

Being with nature and discovering its natural order awakens us to the joy and serenity that lie within us. Spending time, quietly, in the outdoors allows us to experience the world of nature firsthand.

Bonding with nature gives us comfort, security, and a safe place from which to explore our world. If allowed to happen, this occurs naturally around age seven. Unfortunately, what more commonly occurs is a bonding to our man-made environment. Even when they spend time outdoors, many take the "comforts of home" to entertain them—TV, radio, stereo, dirt bike, and so forth.

Being with nature—listening and observing—is a wonderful way to directly experience the naturalness, the balance, the orderliness, the resourcefulness, and the serenity of the Universe. As we look deeply into the patterns of nature, we discover an incredible order that awakens a sense of joy. We sense something that is infinitely greater than we are and yet part of us.

Let's give our children the freedom to explore nature, but let's also teach them to honor its process—to observe without interference. Nature offers us comfort. It is nurturing. Have you noticed how much being outdoors restores us? Encourage your children when they are unhappy or just need a change of pace to go outside and watch the clouds or ants or stars—or just to go walking. Their perspective will change.

Heart Walk. Suggest that your children take a heart walk, where they focus on admiring nature—the flowers, leaves, plants, birds and their songs, mountains, clouds. A great teacher says that admiration can release many fountains of joy within us. It can also bring peace and health. Cultivate in children an admiration for beauty in whatever form it takes. "It is possible," says Saraydarian, "to change many negative things in children just by creating the opportunity for them to admire."[22] Admiration can make us whole and balance us because it releases joy-energy. Sometimes this feeling of admiration can be heightened by using a mantra such as "Oh God, You are so magnificent!" Younger children might prefer "How beautiful is everything!" Such techniques can focus the wandering mind that gets sidetracked.

You can help children focus their attention on small sights of beauty by giving them each a paper tube from a roll of toilet tissue. Seeing nature through a small field of vision can enhance the beauty of little things that might otherwise be overlooked.

Blind Walk. "Blindfolded activities dislodge our thoughts from self-preoccupation, and free our awareness to embrace more of the world around us."[23] In this activity being blindfolded helps to develop an awareness of nature through touch, smell, and sound. A feeling of trust is also fostered, since the children work in pairs, taking turns being blindfolded.

Make the boundaries clear before beginning the exercise and switch roles after about 10 minutes. The leader guides his partner's hands to interesting objects and brings her up close to intriguing sounds and smells. Caution the leader to watch out for logs, low branches, and such. It's nice to end the walk by having the children sit with their eyes closed and share the sounds, smells, and textures that they experienced. You can read about a really delightful blind walk on pages 17–19 of *Sharing Nature With Children*.[24] A most worthwhile book!

Finding Your Tree. I have heard of two variations of this blindfold activity:

1. The children work in pairs. The blindfolded partner is led to a tree in the woods and is encouraged to explore the tree and feel its uniqueness. The seeing partner may suggest touching the leaves, hugging the tree, feeling for plants or lichens growing on it, etc. Then the blindfolded child is led back to the starting place by an indirect route. The blindfold is removed, and the child is instructed to go find her tree.
2. In this version, the sequence is just the opposite. The children pair up and one child in the pair selects a tree and, with no blindfold, becomes familiar with it. Then they go back to the starting place and that child is blindfolded and turned around a few times by his partner. The blindfolded child then tries to find his tree accompanied by the seeing partner, who keeps him on course.

In both versions, roles are switched when the tree is found. The children may enjoy painting or sketching their tree friend as a reminder of the experience. This experience is almost sure to change the way they feel about trees.

The Rock Game. This blindfold game is appropriate for preschoolers. The blindfolded children sit in a circle and each is given a rock that is distinctly different in size and shape from the others. After the child has gotten to know her rock by carefully feeling it, it's placed in the center of the circle. The blindfolds are removed and each child is instructed to find her rock. This can be done with leaves, flowers, shells, oranges, etc.

The Eyres, authors of *Teaching Children Joy*, use this activity to teach that everything in nature is unique and that the same is true with people. Everyone is special. If you have preschoolers, you may wish to read their chapter, "Teaching the Joy of the Earth."[25]

Barefoot Walks. Take your children on barefoot walks in nature. Recently, I talked with a woman who extolled the virtues of going barefoot outdoors as much as possible. Since she lives at the Reeves Mountain Nature School in Arizona, she is able to go barefoot most of the time. Here are some of the reasons she and others find it such a worthwhile activity:

> ✩ Walking barefoot puts us in touch with the Earth's vibration: there is nothing between our feet and the Earth to block the flow of its energy.
>
> ✩ Through walking directly on the ground, we absorb from the minerals in the Earth their purifying life-giving essence.
>
> ✩ As the science of Reflexology has shown, the sole of the foot has points related to all of our organs and these get a good massage when we walk barefooted.
>
> ✩ Walking barefooted keeps us very conscious, because we'll get hurt if we're not wide awake. It keeps us in the "here and now."
>
> ✩ Barefoot walks develop patience, because on most terrains it's difficult to travel fast.

Silent Walks. A nice addition to the barefoot walk is the silent nature walk. When shared with like-minded others, it can be an especially rewarding experience. It enables us to become harmoniously attuned with both nature and our walking companions. "Through watching nature in silence, we discover within ourselves feelings of relatedness with whatever we see—plants, animals, stones, earth and sky," states Cornell. "As above, so below. As within, so without." For his moving description of a silent sharing walk, I again recommend *Sharing Nature With Children*.

Cloud Watching. To encourage cloud awareness with preschoolers, I like taking off from *It Looked Like Spilt Milk*.[26] Cut out clouds of different shapes from white paper, and put these on the flannel board to discuss before going outside to watch the real ones. Older children and child-like adults enjoy poofing clouds away, the way Richard Bach describes in *Illusions*.[27]

Starlight Activation. Have the children go out under the stars at night and visualize pulling the starlight down into their bodies in order to clear and reactivate their energy systems. When a child has a particular question of concern, encourage him to meditate upon it in the starlight. The extra energy activation can bring clarity to the mind. Allow children time simply to star gaze and become familiar with the canopy above.

Nature's Six Inches. Let each child choose a six-inch plot of ground and study it thoroughly. A simple microscope or magnifier makes the exploration especially joyous when children discover whole new worlds.

The microscope can also stimulate children to make drawings that provide an interesting record of their discoveries. Studying pond water with a microscope is another fun experience.

Natural Aquarium. A friend shared with me how, as a teenager, she got hours of joy from an aquarium that was completely self-sustaining. She filled it with life from a pond—minnows, snails, plants, hydras—and watched while it brought itself into perfect balance. She covered the aquarium with glass so it never lost its water but rained inside itself. The snails kept the glass crystal clear, and the plants would bubble and oxygenate the water. She didn't need to feed the fish for well over a year. It was a joyful way to learn about the balance in nature.

Being One With Nature. Indoors or out, have the children sit quietly, and closely observe a plant. It could be a potted cactus, a rose, a large tree—anything. Lead them in some form of deep relaxation, such as a breathing exercise. Next ask them to extend their awareness into the plant. They might make themselves very small and go up the stem or trunk. Ask what they see and what it feels like to them. There are even adult classes that are teaching this kind of awareness, and it is very natural to children. You can do the same thing with any life-form, such as a mushroom, an insect, or a small animal. The identification some people make is truly amazing.

Gardening. Having their own garden can be a joyful and valuable learning experience for children. There is real pleasure in watching seedlings emerge, finding the first flower bud, and eating the first pea from one's own garden. Children often find vegetables they've grown themselves taste a lot better than those they get from the store.

Gardening can teach patience, but choose plants with a good potential for growth. The child's interest is maintained by seeing change. Sow a few feet of several vegetables. For quicker results you might have the child transplant some vegetables or flowers. The choices should be the child's. While transplanting, it is an appropriate time to explain the root system of a plant and the need to be careful handling plants. The responsibility for weed control is best worked out ahead of time and might be a cooperative effort.

Place the child's garden plot in a fairly sunny area, where it can be easily watered. Keep the plot small enough so that the child can enjoy maintaining it on his own— about 30 square feet or less, depending on the child's age. For younger children, the parent may need to prepare the soil and shape the beds with furrows. Since there is so much to this subject of gardening, I suggest you go to a local nursery to get some pointers.

In a relaxed state, go within and recall some of the joyous experiences you've had with Nature. Share these with your children to awaken their desire to know more about their Mother Nature. Try out the activities in *Naturewatch: Exploring Nature with Your Children*.[28]

NATURE

I like the warmth of the sun,
The breeze of the wind,
And the squirrel runs up a tree.

The ants hurry to get food for winter,
I sit on a stump and a chipmunk runs by.
As I sit on the stump,
A tree gives me shade.
NATALIE COLLINS, 2ND GRADE

PART III

Putting It All Together

The Sculptor

I took a piece of plastic clay
And idly fashioned it, one day,
And as my fingers pressed it, still,
It moved and yielded to my will.

I came again, when days were passed,
That bit of clay, was hard at last,
The form I gave it, still it bore,
And I could change that form no more.

Then I took a piece of living clay
And gently formed it, day by day,
And molded with my power and art,
A young child's soft and yielding heart.

I came again when years were gone,
It was a man I looked upon,
He still that early impress bore,
And I could change it, nevermore.

AUTHOR UNKNOWN

Creating A Lesson Plan

The teacher especially, and even the parent, may want to think in terms of a lesson plan. A concept or principle is more likely to be remembered if it is approached in several ways. Ideally, according to the Education in Human Values Program, a lesson in human values is best centered around a story and includes a related quotation for memory work, a song to touch the feeling nature, a silent-sitting time either to prepare for the lesson or to contemplate the ideas learned, and related activities to apply those ideas. The following sample lessons contain these five elements, but please feel free to use just what appeals to you and use it in your own creative way.

Lesson 1: The Judgment Trap

QUOTE: "Judgment always involves rejection." *A Course In Miracles*, Text, 42

SONG: "Judgment, Judgment Go Away" (See Chapter 7.)

STORY: "The Whole Picture"

Everyone turned toward the door as Jill opened it for another guest.

"Happy Birthday, Jill," Sally said as she laid her package on the table with the other gifts. She joined the group seated in the family room.

"Everyone's here now." Jill called to her mother, "Tell us about that new game you fixed for us."

One of the girls reminded Jill, "Marita isn't here yet."

"Oh, I didn't invite her." Jill turned, and quickly asked her mother, "Shall I pass out these pictures for you?"

When she had given each girl one of the odd-shaped pieces, there was one left. Jill knew her mother had cut one for Marita. Hoping no one would notice, she handed it to her mother, saying, "I guess you are playing, too, huh?"

Everyone was busy looking at what they had. Becky held hers up for everyone to see. "I got Mickey Mouse."

"This isn't show-and-tell. Not yet, anyhow." Jill's mother explained that each piece had been cut from a large picture. "The point of the game is to guess what the whole picture might be. If you tell what you have, the others might easily guess." She explained that each one would look at their picture, then write down what the big picture could be. "We'll see who's the best guesser."

Becky wrote something quickly, then tapped her foot impatiently.

Sally was thoughtful a moment, then wrote and wrote until Becky wanted to know if she were writing a whole story.

Andrea was last to finish, but first to tell what she had guessed. "I have a boy with a camera, so I think he is making a movie of Becky's Mickey Mouse."

Sally had a picture of a fairy castle. "I am sure a princess must be in the big picture."

"And I am sure it is a carnival," Becky told them. "My picture shows a carousel."

When all the pieces were fitted together and the extra piece added, Becky squealed, "Disneyland! It's Disneyland!"

Sally stood by the table as the others went back to their chairs. She said, thoughtful, "It's hard to see the whole picture when you have just one little piece."

Jill noticed that Andrea whispered something to Becky. Becky looked at Jill and nodded. What were they saying? Were they wondering why she had not invited Marita? She felt her face get warm, but she didn't care. She blurted out, "She didn't invite me to her party. That's why."

"What party? Marita hasn't had any party." Becky looked at the others. "She didn't, did she?"

All the girls shook their heads.

"I came by her house the other day," Jill defended herself. "A lot of kids were playing in her yard. It looked like a party to me. They even had balloons."

Andrea had an explanation. "She was excited about her cousins from Colorado coming to visit her. I bet those were her cousins you saw."

Sally said, "You saw just one piece of the picture."

Jill felt ashamed. "What shall I do? I wasn't having much fun without Marita here. I've spoiled everything." She ran out of the room.

In a few minutes she was back, wiping her eyes, but with a question. "If I went after her now, do you suppose she would come?"

"I'll go with you," offered Sally.

"Let's all go!" shouted Becky.

Jill apologized. Sally assured Marita that it was all a misunderstanding. Andrea and Becky talked at the same time, begging Marita to come.

"But I have no gift for you," explained Marita.

"Just having you there is good enough for me," Jill said.

"Okay, just a minute." Marita was gone even less than a minute when she came back with a paper sack. "I didn't have any wrapping paper, but I did remember having something I think you will like."

After a game of ring-toss and a treasure hunt, there was birthday cake. Then it was time to open the gifts. Curious about the bag, Jill opened it first.

Was this some sort of joke? Or was Marita trying to get even? A plain old rock was all that was in the bag.

"What is it? We want to see it." Becky was impatient as usual. "Pass it around."

Jill reached in. What shall I do? she wondered. What will the girls say? I guess I deserve it, judging as I did.

When she pulled her hand out of the bag, the other side of the rock caught sunlight from the window. "How beautiful!" she exclaimed, seeing a cave of tiny purple crystals inside the rock. "What is it?"

"It is called a geode," Marita explained. "I hope you like it."

"Oh, I do." Jill opened the other gifts and thanked each giver, then went back to the geode. "No one would ever guess that a plain gray rock could be so pretty inside."

As the girls passed the geode around with exclamations of "Gorgeous!" "Lovely!" and "Awesome!," Jill thought about what had happened today. I certainly learned not to judge by what can be seen on the outside. And I'll always remember that one piece does not show the whole picture.

SILENT SITTING/TUNING IN: Suggested Focus—How am I judging people or situations without having the whole picture?

DISCUSSION:

1. Share an experience in life when someone judged something before they had the whole picture.

2. Is there a situation in your life now where a part of the picture is missing? What more would you like to know?

3. Think of a time when someone saw something as:

     unlovely that was really lovely
     wrong   "   "   "   right
     awful   "   "   "   wonderful

RELATED ACTIVITIES:

1. TV Viewing Blindfolded:

This activity could be useful for children who tend to judge others by physical appearance. Blindfold the children and turn the TV on to an unfamiliar station. Let them listen awhile and guess what the people might look like. Explain that if they were blind there would be no ugly people. They would be seeing with their heart instead of their eyes and the heart can see the inner being, which is always beautiful. You could also discuss how what is considered beautiful in one culture or period of history may not be in another.

2. Peephole Vision:

Hand each child a paper towel tube or a toilet paper tube, or as an alternative, have them poke a hole with their pencil through a sheet of paper. Ask them to look through the tube or hole and describe how much of the room they can see that way. Have them note how much their vision is limited by the perimeter of what they're looking through. Explain that just as they're getting only a peephole vision of the room, their vision of other people is a peephole vision. Suggest that they get up close and look at each other, noting that they can see only a fragment of the person. We can't rightfully judge anyone or anything because our awareness is always limited. Only Universal Mind has unlimited awareness.

Lesson 2: Focus on What You Want, Not on What You Don't Want

QUOTE: "Thoughts held in mind produce after their kind."

SONG: "What You Focus On Expands" (See Chapter 7.)

STORY: "Life of Enchantment"

Ker-plunk! Out of the sky dropped a little fairy right into the crowded dark chrysalis of a former caterpillar. She called, "Hi! I'm Airey." The former caterpillar (soon-to-be-butterfly) couldn't do a very good job of hiding his irritation toward his uninvited guest, since there was hardly any room, even for him.

He creaked his head against the wall of his home and glanced at her. "I'm Flutter-coon."

Airey squashed into a corner to look into his eyes. "I was just flying by and noticed you bulging out of your cocoon. I popped in to give you a hand if you want to get out of here."

The tiny space shuddered with Fluttercoon's explosion. "Out of here?! I am so sick and tired of sitting here curled up day after day. I keep growing and have a constant headache and a crick in my neck and my legs are so numb I don't feel them anymore. It's dark and depressing in here . . ."

"Excuse me," Airey interrupted gently. Fluttercoon's mouth clamped shut. "You are only telling me what you don't want. You can do that if you want, and I still love you. Yet you seem so unhappy, I'd like to assist you. There is another way of looking at things and living a life of enchantment."

She stopped. Fluttercoon sensed she was waiting for him. It all seemed like fairy-talk, yet she had come from the sky and she could fly and she looked safe. Maybe it was possible . . .

"Go on," he prodded.

Airey smiled. "God's only answer is Yes. Every thought you focus on, God says Yes. He doesn't hear "not" or "don't" or "can't." When you say you don't want to be in this cocoon, the "don't" disappears and God hears that you *want* to be here. To that he says Yes!"

Fluttercoon cocked his head in concentration as Airey jumped out of the way.

"Tell me what you really want, Fluttercoon. Say it out loud and God will say Yes."

What *did* he really want? His thoughts slammed to a stop in his aching head, slowly creaking in another direction. Uncharted, untraveled. It proved difficult at first.

"What do I want? Umm. It would be nice to see the outside again. Get out of here. Maybe I could try my wings in flight. What do you think?"

Airey stayed very still. "What do you want?"

"Oh," as he blinked his eyes, "I know a lot of what I don't want. Okay. I want to let go of this home. I do want to test my wings."

"What do you want?" Airey prompted again.

(*Stronger*) "I want to be outside of this chrysalis. I want to fly!"

"How do you intend to do that?"

Fluttercoon took a deep breath. "I am going to kick my way out of this thing!"

Airey grabbed his hand and said, "Yes, I really hear you. Let's go!" A numb leg and a tiny fairy leg both pulled back and, with the force of heaven, kicked out the walls of the cocoon.

Then all was space, light, brilliance, colors.

Airey and Fluttercoon landed on a leaf as they watched the remains of his old home drift to the ground. Flutter used one damp wing to shield his eyes from the nearly blinding sunlight, and the other to cradle his friend.

"Thanks for giving me a hand, Airey!" he said to the fairy, and to the sky, "Thank you God, for saying Yes! It was so easy! What was I afraid of? It was nothing!" Flutter sang with tears of sunlight, of happiness.

Airey beamed at him. "Yes, it was fun."

"Hop on my back and I'll take you for a ride. I WANT TO FLY!" Flutter shouted.

Trusting, she climbed on his back. He flapped his wings a few times, drying them. Then away they flew, forgetting what they didn't want. They were too busy living enchanted lives, celebrating and playing in the sky.

Copyright © 1986, Cindy L. Thomas[1]

SILENT SITTING/TUNING IN: Suggested Focus—Picture yourself seeing things and saying things in a way that you will get what you want.

DISCUSSION:

1. What have you been focusing on today? In the last hour?

2. What do you want in your life?

3. What can you do so that you might receive that?

4. What don't you want in your life?

5. Considering the principle in the story and song, how might that come, or have already come, into your life?

RELATED ACTIVITIES:

1. Song Reminder Activity:

Younger children particularly like this activity, and you might sing the song to them ("What You Focus On Expands") while they're doing it. Have a large bowl about half full of water with some liquid detergent in it. Let the children take turns at blowing through straws into the water. Bubbles will form and expand as more and more air is focused through the straws. As the bubbles get bigger and fall over the sides of the bowl, help the children see that it is the focused air that is causing the expansion. Relate this to the song.

2. "What Gets My Attention Gets Me":

This activity could reinforce the story for older children. In the middle of a large piece of construction paper have them draw a stick figure labeled "Me." All around it they can sketch symbols or write words of things, people, ideas, and situations that they put their attention on, the positive and negative. Give them pieces of string to tape between the stick figure and the symbols. The string can be labeled "Attention." Since "What gets their attention gets them," they should sever the cord of attention if it is coming to something they don't want. Explain that they can mentally cut that cord whenever they find they're focusing on what they really *wouldn't* want any more of in their life.

VISUALIZATION EXERCISE: Have all involved focus on an event or activity that is unquestionably for the highest good, and together visualize what they want, not what they don't want. It could be anything from a successful family outing to world peace.

Lesson 3: An Attitude of Gratitude

QUOTE: "Gratitude is not only the greatest virtue, but the parent of all the others." Cicero

SONG: "I Am Grateful" (a variation of "I Am Happy"—see Chapter 7.)

STORY: "A Gift to One Is a Gift to All"

(This puppet skit emphasizes our unity with all people everywhere and proposes a new way of looking at giving and receiving. It is written for an inexperienced adult puppeteer to perform with two hand puppets. Feel free to alter it to suit your audience.)

CHARACTERS: Herman (a puppet with movable mouth), Katie (a puppet with either movable mouth or hands).

PROPERTIES: A beautifully gift-wrapped box, which should be about the size of the puppets.

At rise Herman is standing next to the gift box and looking it over.

HERMAN: Oh Goody! Goody! Maybe it's a gift for me. Wonder what it is. Do you know? (*He leans toward the audience.*)

KATIE: (*entering*) No, Herman, that isn't a gift for you. It's just an empty box—a symbol of the gifts you receive every day.

HERMAN: What do you mean, Katie? I don't get a gift each day. Do you? (*He looks at audience.*)

KATIE: Does something have to be bought at the store or gift-wrapped for it to be a gift?

HERMAN: Well, no, I guess not.

KATIE: Think of some gifts that you like to receive—something not bought or gift-wrapped.

HERMAN: Oh, let me see . . . I like it when someone does me a special favor, when I get a party invitation, when somebody takes me somewhere special like the movies or skating.

KATIE: Those don't happen every day, though, do they? Think of some gifts you might receive almost every day—like a big hug, a pat on the back, or maybe a compliment.

HERMAN: Sure. Let me think. Help me, boys and girls. (*Leans toward audience. If audience doesn't offer these answers, he responds with: a smile; someone who listens to me; help with a problem; a prayer; something to eat.*)

KATIE: See—you receive a lot of gifts each day. Right?

HERMAN: Right. I hadn't thought of those things as gifts.

KATIE: Well, I have a big surprise for you, Herman. You receive hundreds and thousands and thousands of gifts every day. You don't really know about these gifts, but a part of your mind does.

HERMAN: Well, what do you mean?

KATIE: This is a really big secret. Few people know about it. We're connected at some level with everyone on the planet.

HERMAN: Wow!

KATIE: Each day thousands of people are giving gifts to each other. These gifts are blessings for you and me. The more joy and happiness in the world, the happier we feel.

HERMAN: Does that mean that when I help someone at school, other children around the world will feel a little bit happier?

KATIE: Yes, every time you act loving to someone, you are blessing multitudes of others.

HERMAN: What great news! Wow! Now I see what is meant by the "Brotherhood of Man." We're all brothers because we're all part of God.

KATIE: You've got it, Herman. Here's a statement I use to remind myself of this connection. "Today I give thanks for the many gifts I'm giving and receiving." This really makes me feel good.

HERMAN: Thanks for the idea. That's like another gift, isn't it? I'm going to put it on my mirror so I'll remember, too. "Today I give thanks for the many gifts I'm giving and receiving."

KATIE: Boys and girls, will you say it with me? (*Looks at the audience and repeats the statement.*) Thank you!

HERMAN: Say it with me, too. "Today I give thanks for the many gifts I'm giving and receiving." Thanks! Bye now. (*Turns to exit.*)

KATIE: Hey, wait Herman! I want to give you this box as a symbol of the gifts you're receiving. (*Pushes box off stage towards Herman.*) Bye, boys and girls! (*Both exit.*)

SILENT SITTING/TUNING IN: Suggested Focus—Something the child is especially grateful about, or a personal prayer of gratitude.

RELATED ACTIVITIES:

1. Gratitude Awareness:

There is a French proverb that says, "Gratitude is the heart's memory." Ask the children to remember whatever they are grateful for and make a list. If appropriate, have them share in small groups or in the group as a whole.

For older children, suggest that they start a gratitude diary. Any kind of empty book can be used and at any time. I prefer to use mine in the evening just before bedtime so that I end my day focusing on the positive and not the negative.

2. Visual Analogies:

Gratitude magnifies. Have the children write very small on little slips of paper some of the blessings in their lives. Then let them look at the slips of paper through a magnifying glass. Explain that an attitude of gratitude magnifies or increases our good. (What we focus on expands.)

A related analogy is to use a saucer of sand to represent our day, the iron particles in the sand to represent our blessings, and a magnet to represent an attitude of gratitude. If one has an attitude of gratitude, one can scan one's day and pick out many blessings, just as the magnet picks out the iron particles. An ungrateful heart is like fingers that search through the sand without finding iron particles.

3. Thank-You Notes:

Older children might be encouraged to write thank-you notes. Familiar and unique reasons to send thank-you notes can be discussed. They might make a list of people they want to send a note to and set dates for doing so.

4. The Gift Box:

Let each child decorate a gift box to be kept in his bedroom as a reminder of the gifts he is giving and receiving each day. Have each write on separate slips of paper all the ways that he can give a gift to others; then have him put the papers inside the box. Suggest that he draw out, at random, one slip each day and do it. Examples might include: kind, loving thoughts . . . a ticket to be exchanged for a helping hand . . . a sincere compliment . . . volunteering to do an unpleasant chore . . . ignoring a rude remark . . . doing a kind deed anonymously . . . cleaning a room . . . a prayer . . .

dropping a coin for someone to find . . . sharing a dream . . . smiles . . . a thank-you note . . . a funny card . . . saying Yes . . . hugs . . . taking a dog for a walk . . . sharing a funny joke . . . singing or whistling . . . keeping a secret . . . talking to a plant . . . playing soothing music.

5. A Bulletin Board or Table Display:

In the center, place a gift box with lines of yarn extending from the box to words and objects which symbolize the many gifts the children are giving and receiving.

Lesson 4: The Value of Prayer

QUOTES: 1. "A day hemmed in by prayer is not likely to unravel."
2. "Make prayer the bookends of your day."

SONG: "Talk to God" (Tune: "This Old Man")
When I play, when I sing
When I do most anything
I can talk to God in my own way
And feel Love's light throughout the day.

I say thanks, sometimes please
On my bed or on my knees
I breathe in feelings of peace, joy, and love
And pray for guidance from above.

STORY: "Jodie and Her Secret"

(This puppet skit points out the value of starting each day with prayer. It can be performed by either two adult puppeteers or one puppeteer working three puppets. The latter is possible by shaking one puppet off and slipping the next one on with one hand or using an assistant.)

CHARACTERS: Jodie (a girl puppet with hands), Billy (a boy puppet with hands), Ernie (a boy puppet with hands).

PROPERTIES: Rock large enough for puppet to sit on; a loosely woven piece of fabric with one end hemmed and the other fringed; a pair of bookends (use your imagination— colored paper can cover most anything).

SETTING: Outdoors

At rise Jodie is sitting on the rock holding the fabric and singing to herself.

JODIE: I'm so happy, happy, happy! What a wonderful day this is going to be! (*In a sing-song voice*)

BILLY: (*Entering*) Hello Jodie! Why are you so happy this early in the day?

JODIE: (*Jumps up and goes to Billy*) Because only good is going to happen to me today, Billy. It's going to be a happy day!

BILLY: How do you know that?

JODIE: Mom told me a very special secret, but it's the kind I can share. She said a day hemmed by prayer is not likely to unravel. She read it somewhere.

BILLY: I don't understand.

JODIE: I didn't either until she gave me this cloth. (*Waves the fabric.*) See this cloth? It represents my day. (*Holds it close to Billy.*) See this hem I made here? If I put a hem all around the fabric it won't come apart.

BILLY: And what if you don't hem it?

JODIE: It will come apart or unravel, like it's starting to do here.

BILLY: Oh, I see! (*Reaches over and pulls a loose thread.*)

JODIE: The cloth is like my day. It might fall apart too if I don't use prayer to hem it. Prayer helps my day to go smoothly and peacefully without a lot of problems. (*Add specifics if you wish to.*)

BILLY: How do you pray, Jodie? I'm not sure how.

JODIE: Well, I hold my special cloth and then I ask God to guide my day. I ask to be a help to others and to stay peaceful and loving, no matter what. (*Insert own thoughts on prayer, but keep it simple.*)

BILLY: Gosh, thanks! That seems easy enough. I've got to run home and I'll try out your idea.

(*If just one puppeteer, shake off Billy and slip on Ernie while Jodie is speaking.*)

JODIE: (*Waves*) Bye! Remember, you can share our secret. (*Sits on rock and chants.*) Thank you God for this fine day; Guide me to live it just your way.

ERNIE: (*Entering*) Oh, look at Jodie with a piece of blankie. (*Taunting*). Baby! You don't need your blankie. (*Grabs it and runs.*)

JODIE: (*Jumping up*) Hey, stop that you bully. Give that back!

ERNIE: Try and catch me. Ha, ha, ha! (*Runs off stage.*)

JODIE: (*Returns to rock and sits down*) I guess I really didn't need that fabric to remind me to pray. I'll always remember that a day hemmed with prayer won't unravel. There's no magic in the piece of cloth. It just helped me to remember. And I forgive Ernie—that was the best he could do at the moment.

ERNIE: (*Quickly entering*) Here, baby, I decided to give you your old rag back. (*Drops it and makes a fast exit.*)

JODIE: (*Picks up cloth.*) Gee, I wonder if he felt some of the prayers I said? (*Sits on rock and chants.*) Thank you, God, for this fine day; guide me to live it just your way.

(*If one puppeteer, shake off Ernie and slip on Billy while Jodie is speaking.*)

BILLY: (*Enters carrying the bookends*) Hi, Jodie. I've got something to show you.

JODIE: What are those?

BILLY: These are bookends. You put books between them so the books stand up. You know.

JODIE: Yes, but why are you carrying them around?

BILLY: Well, I liked your idea, Jodie, of having something to remind you to pray, so when Mom told me that prayer makes wonderful bookends for our day, I thought I would use bookends, instead of a piece of cloth.

JODIE: Oh, I get it. The bookends remind you to start and end the day with prayer. What a neat idea!

BILLY: I'm going to put them by my bed to help me remember to pray as I wake up and as I fall asleep. I want to remember to thank God for all the good in my life.

JODIE: Fantastic, Billy! I'm going to thank God for this wonderful idea you shared with me.

BILLY: Well you gave me an idea first, Jodie. It's fun to exchange ideas.

JODIE: Say, that gives me an idea. (*Leans toward Billy and whispers in his ear.*)

BILLY: Sure. That's a good suggestion, Jodie. Boys and girls, Jodie wants me to ask you if you have any ideas about prayer that you would like to share with us— prayers you know, or how or when you pray. I want to learn as much about prayer as I can.

NOTE: If no ideas are forthcoming, reword the request so as to draw out questions and ideas about prayer. If appropriate, end the skit with Jodie leading the group in a prayer. It may be a prayer of thanksgiving or an affirmative prayer regarding world peace or something closer to the child's life.

SILENT SITTING/TUNING IN: Suggested Focus—"Every thought is a prayer." (Based on the idea that energy is directed by thought.)

DISCUSSION:

1. What are the different purposes of prayer that they know of? (e.g., blessing, thanksgiving, protection, gratitude, praise, guidance, support, etc.)

2. When might it be inappropriate to pray? (e.g., to beat another person or team, to get things, to win a war, etc.)

3. How do they honor a person's free will when praying for others? (Add some form of "God's will be done"; surround person with light unless specific changes have been requested.)

4. How is prayer different from meditation? (e.g., talking vs. listening).

5. How do they put "feet under their prayers" (take action)? Offer examples.

6. Do they have a bedtime prayer they've been taught, such as the following, or do they make up their own bedtime prayers?

> Now I lay me down to sleep,
> I know the Lord my soul will keep;
> And I shall wake to see the light,
> For God is with me all the night.

RELATED ACTIVITIES:

1. Create a prayer:
   As a group, or individually, encourage the children to create some special prayers

of their own—e.g., a meal time blessing, a prayer of protection, a bedtime prayer, etc. They might enjoy writing prayers for younger children.

For example: I sleep in peace
>> And without care,
>> Knowing Love is always there.

"Lord, lead my steps to where I am needed" is a prayer for being of service. Encourage the children to create their own prayer for being of help to others.

2. The power of praise:

This demonstration of the effect of praise on plants can easily be adapted to the classroom. Take your child to the store and let her pick out two identical plants. Suggest she give them the same amount of light and water, but that one of the plants she will praise, talk to, and send love. For this experiment, she will ignore the other plant. Experiments show that plants have the same emotional response as humans. Help the child draw conclusions as to the value of affirmative prayer.

3. Daily spiritual check list:

Individually or as a group, have the youngsters work on a list of spiritual activities they want to include in their day. Here is one to trigger their thinking:

Today have I:

>> spent some time alone in prayer?
>>
>> spent some time listening for answers or guidance?
>>
>> acted upon intuition when it followed my prayer and listening time?
>>
>> sent prayer statements to special needs as they arose?
>>
>> said a silent "thank you, God" when some good has happened?
>>
>> said a "thank you" to what didn't appear good, knowing it contains a lesson?
>>
>> forgiven myself for anything I feel wrong about?
>>
>> released any grudge or grievance against others?
>>
>> tried to see the Light in all other people?
>>
>> found a way to help somebody outside of my family? In my family?

4. Cross-cultural prayers:

Have children bring in examples of prayers from various religions and cultures— e.g., Jewish, Catholic, American Indian, Sufi, etc. Look for similarities in purpose or objectives. Elaborate on the "Brotherhood of Man" through the avenue of prayer. A bulletin board or wall display might be appropriate. In the center could be the word CREATOR and yarn strings could extend out to pictures of different peoples and places. Prayers symbolic of that culture or religion could be next to the pictures.

Lesson 5: The Joy of Serving

QUOTE: "The only ones around you who will be really happy are those who will have sought and found how to serve."—Albert Schweitzer.

SONG: "Oh, I Love to Be a Blessing" (third stanza of "The More We Get Together"—see Chapter 7.)

STORY: "Helping in Distress"

One evening a certain blind man was walking along a road singing a song to the accompaniment of a harp he held in his hand. He had once been a very good singer and player of the harp, but now he had become old and blind. He could hardly earn money enough to buy one meal a day. Suddenly he slipped and fell down on the road. Three boys passing by rushed toward him, and lifted up him and his harp. One of the boys said, "Let us take this old man home."

The second one said, "It won't solve the problem, though it's the easiest thing to do."

The third boy said, "We must do some real service to the old man."

The first boy said, "Please cheer up—we will try to help you."

The second boy took up the harp and tuned it up.

The third boy began to sing a song to the accompaniment of the harp.

Soon people began to gather round them. The boys sang so sweetly and movingly that everyone threw a coin into the hat of the first boy, who was walking round. After an hour, when the crowd had dispersed, the boys counted the money and gave it to the old man.

The old man felt so happy that he shed tears of joy and said, "Oh, my dear ones, how can I ever thank you? Will you not tell me your names?"

"My name is Faith."

"My name is Hope."

"My name is Love," cried out the boys. "Grandpa, may we take leave of you now?"

The old man could well understand the situation. He realized his mistake. Had he not lost faith, hope, and love in himself and in others? How nicely these lads had taught him a lesson. (From *Stories for Children*[2].)

SILENT SITTING/TUNING IN: Suggested focus—Picture yourself being of service in new ways (to family, friends, strangers).

RELATED ACTIVITIES:

"If we want children to love, we must teach them to serve," say the Eyres. They have a wonderful chapter on teaching the joy of sharing and service in their book, *Teaching Children Joy*.[3] Here are three of their suggestions:

> 1. Build a family reputation for service and helping:
>   Always stop to help people in distress—those out of gas,

needing directions, etc. Let your children see that helping other people is the thing to do.

2. Sponsor a child:

There are many "sponsoring" organizations that give opportunities, at a moderate cost, to feel the joy of sharing with others who are in real need. Let your child miss a meal once a month and send the money to a sponsored child.

3. Do "secret good turns":

Watch for people in need, and plan for ways to make them happier. One way is to help a needy family anonymously. Have each child give a toy.

The *Education in Human Values Lesson Plan Book*[4] has an extensive list of service projects that youngsters can do—some of the suggestions to the children follow:

1. Remember the birthdays of children who live in institutions. Have a monthly party and honor the children whose birthdays fall within the month.

2. Entertain nursing home patients. As their birthdays are often forgotten, the above idea would be appropriate for them, too. Even a short skit and a few songs will bring cheer to these people.

3. Help hospitalized children. Children with serious ailments are confined to hospitals for long periods of time. Collect storybooks, coloring books, games, puzzles, and arts and crafts supplies, and give them to the hospital. Send them cards on their birthday, or during the holidays.

4. Make friends with children who are severely handicapped. Play games with them, work on arts and crafts together, read to them, and just be a friend. These children usually do not have the chance to make friends with other children.

5. Feed the birds in your neighborhood during the winter months.

6. Get training for emergencies. Learn how to call the police, fire department, or doctor. Learn first aid.

7. Recycle newspapers, glass bottles, aluminum cans, and plastic containers. Collect these materials and bring them to centers for recycling. Or you can start a recycling center yourselves.

8. Invite a child from an institution to be a guest of your family for a day or weekend.

9. Donate equipment to children's institutions. Very often they do not have the money to provide games, sports equipment, or even clothing for their children. Organize a drive to

collect these things, put them in good condition, and donate them to the ones that need them.

10. Collect or make toys and give them to schools for the mentally retarded. They should be simple and safe.

11. Help an elderly or handicapped neighbor by shoveling the snow in front of their home. Clear snow from the fire hydrants on your block.

12. Contact an organization that aids the elderly and offer to help. The elderly who live alone have difficulty in doing things we take for granted. You can visit them regularly, shop, run errands, write letters, or read aloud from books or newspapers.

13. Select a clean-up project. Pick an area in your town that is littered with garbage and clean it up. Not only will you be getting rid of an eyesore, but you will also help to reduce a health hazard.

14. Collect food for the poor people who depend upon charitable organizations for their food. Collect canned or dried food and toiletries and give them to these service organizations.

Ask the children to come up with other service projects they could add to the list. Maybe there's some valuable service that could be done right within their family, church, or neighborhood.

Food for Thought. The Indian Avatar Sai Baba says we should not think of the gift of food as charity—that we do not have the authority to give, in charity, what has been given by God or to feel proud of ourselves for doing so. It was God that gave the rains and ripened the grain. Our giving should be an offering of gratitude to God by giving to God in human form.

Lifting Others. There is another form of service that should not be neglected: helping people that are really "down in the dumps." Telling them uplifting true stories or sharing joyful moments from one's own life is often the needed lift. Sometimes it can be as simple as passing on some good news. Or it might be reminding them of something they're truly grateful for but have forgotten to think about. Letters of appreciation can offer a needed lift. Sometimes just one's silent presence is the most helpful gift. When I am feeling down, my son has an uncanny way of putting on just the right music to lift or soothe my spirit.

Invisible Help. All of the above suggestions are visible forms of help—outer-plane work. Children can be taught to think in terms of invisible, or inner-plane, help also. Invisible help is offered through the mind and heart, through our thoughts and our love. Children are capable of shining light into darkness, of radiating love to those in need. They are usually vivid visualizers: they can beam pink love rays to Grandma Jane, or they can see Uncle Bob looking happy again.

Invisible help can also include using affirmative prayer or symbols, holding ideas, and sending light. Encourage the children to think up ways to be "invisible helpers." They might think of sending light and love to animals or to Mother Earth herself.

The Daily Deed. Talk about developing the habit of doing some visible and invisible good deeds each day. Depending on the children's age, they might want to experiment with this for a week or a month and notice how it releases their joy.

> *Trouble makes us one with every human*
> *being in the world and unless we touch*
> *others we're out of touch with life.*
> OLIVER WENDELL HOLMES

> *As you give more love you have more joy.*

The Joy of Change

GUIDING CHILDREN THROUGH TIMES OF CHANGE

> . . . *change is our greatest source of happiness,*
> *stimulation and continual growth. It has the power to*
> *uplift, to heal, to stimulate, surprise, open new doors,*
> *bring fresh experiences, and create excitement in life.*
> *It elevates us from mediocrity and saves us from false*
> *security.*
>
> LEO BUSCAGLIA, *Bus 9 To Paradise*

Change is a basic law of nature. To resist change is to resist nature. Since change is inevitable, preparing our children for change is one of our most important responsibilities. What do we need to consider if we want to prepare them both for the normal changes one can expect in growing up and for those unexpected changes that can upset a whole way of life?

First, we need to remember the importance of high self-esteem. Children who have been made to feel valuable and important and who are secure in their relationship with their parents can usually handle anything that comes along; for them, *Magical Child* tells us, anxiety over survival never becomes an issue.

Since our children imprint to our consciousness in their early years, it is important that we hold the thought in our consciousness that they are born complete with all they need to fulfill their plan and purpose in life. They were designed for survival. It is imprinting the limiting beliefs of parents and society that gets in the way.

Our beliefs about change are one such area that can be limiting. Since our consciousness is transmitted to the child, we want to fill it with a philosophy of hope and expectancy that welcomes change. We want to hold thoughts of everything working together for the good and to know that nothing is ever taken away unless something better is coming. We want to develop an attitude of gratitude that believes there is a potential blessing in everything—not just in the obvious good. It is the unpleasant changes that help us to grow more quickly.

Modeling such an attitude toward change is the indirect approach. I feel the direct approach is also called for. Let's set out to give our children a philosophy of change. Let's help them see change as part of the Universe's unfolding pattern of good for them. Newness is where the joy of life comes from, says an ancient teacher. Teach children to have positive responses to whatever happens in the world. Make it a family activity to look for the good in all the supposedly negative happenings, be it a war, an airline crash, an illness, or a burnt piece of toast. This doesn't mean we have no compassion. "Nothing deepens joy like compassion."[1] It means we stretch our imaginations to see what good may come from the situation.

I once read a tract that suggested we pronounce everything and every situation "good" because that is righteous judgment. We are not to judge by appearances, which are likely to be misleading. When we pronounce an unhappy situation good, we're not saying that negativity is good. We're looking right *through* the appearance and recognizing the presence of Spirit, of Perfection. It's a beautiful way of eliminating good/bad, right/wrong thinking, since we choose to see good in everything. We choose joy. We align ourselves with the true nature of the Universe. Our deep joy will reduce suffering because of our oneness with all others.

Even though we choose to see everything as good, it's important that we not withhold facts from our children. Don't try to hide the death, the serious illness, the divorce, the bankruptcy, the danger in your life—and theirs. Children can cope with life the way it is, if they know *what* it is. They always know when you are hiding something from them. It only makes it harder on them when they don't know what it is.

Change and Behavior Style

Observe how each of your children responds to change. Whether the required change is a minor adjustment or a major shift, it helps to know how the different behavior styles feel about change. The temperament of your child will influence how you will support him, and how much the stress of change will affect him.

As explained in Chapter 4, your children chose to be in a certain body and in a certain personality or temperament for the work they're here to do—the lessons they wish to learn. They are not their body or temperament. These are only the tools that they have chosen.

Whatever a child's behavior style, it is important to see each child as creative and resourceful, and to know that all styles are capable of coping with change. They just approach it differently, depending upon their needs.

Here's a brief review of the **D**, **I**, **S**, and **C** styles in regard to their flexibility for change.

The **D** style seeks dominance or control. This style not only welcomes change, but actively brings it about. The **D** feels any change is better than none. He doesn't like to stay in any one place too long. The **D** is a risk-taker, a challenge-seeker, and performs well in a crisis. **D** children will flow easily with any changes that come and may take the lead in coping with them.

Just the opposite of the **D** style is the **S**. The **S** is steadfast, supportive, stable, security-minded, slower-paced, and definitely resistant to change. Because **S** children fear loss of security, change can be threatening to them. They require planned change. You need to give them plenty of warning if the routine they've adjusted to is going to be different.

Arnold Patent says: "Security is a feeling that comes from trusting the Universe, believing that it functions in a way that is naturally supportive of everyone and everything in it."[2]

My own two children are perfect examples of these two behavior styles. My high **D** daughter came home one day and announced that she had just gone parachute jumping for the first time. She explained that she just *had* to have a new challenge. Because of this need for change and challenge, by the age of twenty-three, she managed to live in a foreign country for three extended periods of time.

My son, a high **S**, likes a structured routine, with no sudden surprises. I used to have to let him know several days in advance if we were considering going out to dinner. He tends to say no to anything unless he's been given time to think it over. D and I styles say yes and count the cost later.

Next comes the **I** style. **I** people are influencers, people-oriented, and very optimistic. They love variety and spontaneity. They go with the flow and readily accept change, but unlike the **D**'s, they do not instigate it.

The fourth style is the **C**. **C**'s are conscientious and cautious. They're the thinkers, the analyzers, the quality-control people. It is important for them to know the reasons behind a change. They want to make sure the change is thought through and done in the right way. Because of their need for control and order, **C** children are disturbed by unexpected change.

You'll recall that none of us is a pure style. We're each a blend of the four, with one or two styles being most dominant.

The more unlike you and your child are, the more helpful behavior style information will be. For instance: are you holding your child back from challenges because of your own security needs? It is said that many souls now coming to Earth want a challenge and so have chosen this challenging time in Earth's evolution. Many will comfort and guide their parents when the changes start.

If you have **S** or **C** children who don't readily accept change, consider giving them practice in facing unplanned change. Help them become more flexible and adaptable, while still honoring their basic temperament. An example might be postponing dinner while you all go to visit a friend in the hospital, or having your child stay with a neighbor because you have to leave town for the day. Consider switching routines. Remind your children that the only constant thing is change. Make up songs that help them embrace change without fear. "Changes Don't Bother Me" in Chapter 7 is one I made up for this purpose.

Use a visual analogy to explain that change is needed for growth, e.g., show them a small houseplant that has gotten root-bound and needs transplanting if it is to keep on growing. Or use an artificial plant in a pot, with a tangled mass of string for the roots. Explain to the child that roots need a lot of soil to grow in, but these have grown so much that there is hardly any soil left for them in the pot. The plant now needs to be taken out of its old pot and put in a larger one, or it will stop growing. People are just like the plant, and at times they need more room to grow. Compare the flowerpot to the child's old ways of thinking about herself. Those ways can feel really comfortable, but unless she pushes out of her comfort zone, her growth will be stunted, just as the plant's growth is stunted when it outgrows its container. This is a useful lesson for children who need to take a risk, such as joining the Scouts, going away to camp, or moving to a new school or community.

Whenever an uncomfortable change *is* called for, the more quickly it takes place, the easier it will be. You can demonstrate this by having the child put on a couple of Band-Aids. Have her pull one off slowly and the other one off quickly. Let her feel how much less painful it is to remove a Band-Aid quickly. Apply this, not only to uncomfortable changes in the child's life, but to other areas where the child resists (e.g., chores) or procrastinates (e.g., homework). The Band-Aid example can help her learn to do what must be done without fussing about it or trying to avoid it.

Stress

Stress comes from resisting what *is*. It's important during times of change to become aware of the stress signals of the different styles. Each style changes its pattern when tension becomes stress. A tense **D** style is bossy, but under stress, the **D** will avoid or withdraw. Under tension, the **I** style tends to attack, but as the pressure becomes stressful, this style will comply or go along with demands. Tense **S**'s usually give in or submit, but when stressed, they attack. The **C** style reverses the **D** behavior: first avoiding or withdrawing and then becoming bossy or dictatorial.

The Stress-Proof Child[3] has a list of stress symptoms that parents and teachers need to be aware of. Examples are:

Unexplained aching muscles	Frequent headaches
Impulsive, uncontrolled eating	Restlessness
Difficulty staying awake	Difficulty concentrating

Lack of naturalness and spontaneity	Pounding heart
Habitual picking at sores and scabs	Difficulty sleeping
	Neck or backaches
Nail biting, hair pulling, other nervous habits	Chronic irritability
	Unexplained tiredness

When these signs of stress are in evidence, the authors suggest helping your child learn relaxation techniques. These vary from exercise to conscious breathing or listening to music. I particularly like their suggestion called "Quick Relax." It's so valuable for youngsters to have at their command a quick method of centering—of regaining their equilibrium.

The Quick Relax, which takes only seconds, has three basic steps and a fourth optional one. In abbreviated form, here they are:

1. Become aware that you are upset. This means learning to recognize "body signals."
2. Smile inwardly and tell yourself that you can calm yourself down. (This step takes the child out of the victim role and puts him in control.)
3. Breathe slowly and easily through imaginary holes in your feet. The child is to imagine cool air flowing up through holes in the bottom of his feet, up through his legs and into his stomach. He is to hold the air for a few seconds and then push the "stressful air" back down his body and out through the holes in his feet.
4. Go in your mind to a place where you are fully relaxed and happy. The more details the child can imagine, the more effective this step will be. Ask her to notice smells, sounds, the air, her clothing, the people around her.

Most children have stress-reduction techniques of their own. Notice them and honor them. Asking about them helps children be more aware of them.

Music and Stress

Consider how music in your environment can affect tension and stress. We naturally respond to the rhythms around us. To show how our heart responds, musician Steve Halpern beats out a slow rhythm and has people check their pulse, followed by a fast beat and another pulse check. He suggests muscle testing to music to determine what is healthy for you.

Beautiful music, appropriately chosen, can relieve stress. The rock beat, however, creates it. Dr. John Diamond, in his book *Your Body Doesn't Lie*, says that the rock beat causes the entire body to be thrown into a state of alarm.[4] This can lead to decreased performance in school, hyperactivity, and restlessness. The rock beat seriously hampers children's energy flow, distorting their senses and mental abilities.

Harmonious music, however, helps bring our physical, emotional, mental, and etheric bodies into alignment. It assists in rearranging the portion of our body that has been distorted through negative thoughts, words, feelings, and emotions.

As harmonious music is played, the constructive tonal qualities reverberate out into the atmosphere and bathe all discordant bodies with a healing energy. I once knew a wise old woman who had been a concert pianist. She made it her planetary service to sit down each evening at her grand piano and for two hours send healing music out to all those in hospitals and nursing homes.

So in times of stress, let's make it a practice to play healing and harmonizing music, not only for our family but for our neighborhood, our community, our planet. To cultivate stability and joy, Hal Lingerman offers a lovely list of classical pieces, beginning with Pachelbel's Canon in D.[5] There is also a lot of New Age music available to help us bring peace and harmony into our homes, but much that is called New Age music on the radio really isn't. *Music Power* has extensive lists of music for every occasion—from the Montavani Strings for relaxation to Ron Dexter's *Golden Voyage* for meditation.[6] Another good source for obtaining New Age music, via mail order, is the Miracles Contact Center.[7] Those seriously interested in healing music can write for the "New Dimensions in Sound" catalog, which lists a number of cassettes to reduce stress, as well as educational tapes about music, and which even offers tapes for the birthing process.[8] (One tape combines heartbeat sounds from within the womb with light lullabies to relieve the stress of newborns.)

Fear

One of the greatest enemies of our joy is fear. Much of our stress is rooted in fear. Fear has been defined as an emotional response to doubt. It is what we doubt that creates fear, not what we know. Our knowing will tell us that the Universe is benevolent and on our side. Some consider fear to be the signal disease of the 20th century. Its most prevalent aspect is "victimitis"—something we can eliminate from our thinking.

If we remember the universal principles in our life, we know that ours is an orderly universe, governed at all times by immutable laws. If we take responsibility for our life, we can agree with Dr. Ron Smotherman that we are none of us victims, but the authors of *all* our experiences, even of those we dislike.[9]

One approach that could help your child understand that she is not a victim is through creative problem solving. Ask her to picture a relationship she has with another person about her own age and then to describe that relationship to you. If she expresses any blame or feelings of frustration, ask her to define the problem. Then ask whose problem it is. If she tends to blame the other person, ask her who is being most bothered by it, who really wants to have things changed. Once a child begins to own a problem, she is no longer a "victim." She is ready to find a solution. This is when knowing the steps in creative problem solving can be especially valuable.

Creative Problem Solving

Whether catastrophic or mundane, problems are something none of us can escape. All of us respond to problems in one of three ways: (1) we do nothing, (2) we react, that is, we act without thinking, or (3) we problem solve. Avoidance and reaction block joy, whereas solving problems creatively enhances joy.

Here is a simple problem-solving procedure you can teach your children by sitting down with them from time to time and applying it to their challenges. It always helps to remember that every problem has a solution.

1. *Relax.* Use the Quick Relax or a deep relaxation method suggested in Chapter 5. Relaxation clears your mind and lessens the tendency to react or act impulsively. If you truly relax and open your mind, an intuitive solution might pop in at this stage.

2. *Choose your self-talk.* When you choose your self-talk, you are really choosing your attitude. You can shift gears mentally so that you approach problem solving with a positive, expectant attitude. Tell yourself, "I can do it. I can handle it." Calling the situation a challenge or an opportunity for growth instead of a problem releases more energy because of the mind-pictures it creates. Here we acknowledge that we, at some level and at some time, chose this challenge for the growth it would bring us. We might shift our focus so much at this step that what seemed like a problem is no longer a problem.

3. *Define the problem/challenge.* It has been said that a problem well-defined is a problem half-solved. Many times we have not recognized the real problem underneath the one we are trying to solve. Through the process of questioning, adults can help children become clearer about their problem and can lead them to the broadest possible statement of it. The more broadly stated, the more room there is for new ideas. It is here that we can ask ourselves, "How would we really like it to be?" Encourage the children, at each step, to listen to their inner teacher. Not only will this help identify the problem—what they really want, but it may give them an intuitive solution that much sooner, so they can skip the remaining steps.

4. *Gather data.* For this step you collect facts and the opinions of others. Teach your children to ask, "Am I sure I have all the facts?" "Have I observed the situation correctly, or would someone else's opinion help?" The "Whole Picture" story in the previous chapter is a good example of insufficient data, as is the story of the seven blind men and the elephant.

It is important to realize at this stage that there are no real problems: what we see as a problem is only a situation with some important facts missing from our view. Somebody with the "Whole Picture" or a more expanded consciousness would see the solution right away. Again, during this step, we want to listen within to learn what facts to gather. One additional fact might solve the problem. Or we could get an intuitive solution—knowing without knowing *how* we know.

5. *List all options or solutions.* This step is often called imagination storming or brainstorming. It is the idea-gathering stage, as compared to the data-gathering stage. Here it is important to list all options, even those that obviously won't work. The principle involved is that of deferred judgment. The creative side of the brain does not work well when the analytical side is in operation. If we turn on hot and cold water at the same time we get only tepid water. You might demonstrate this to the child, and compare hot and cold water to the faculties of imagination and evaluation.

Many studies have shown that the greater the number of ideas, the greater the likelihood of solutions, so it is important to come up with as many alternatives as possible. Very often, "quantity breeds quality." In the *Children's Problem Solving* series, Elizabeth Crary has written stories that introduce a variety of alternatives and give young children the chance to decide for themselves what the character in each story will do. The reader goes to the appropriate page to see how that decision turns out.[10]

Listening within is again called for. The inner teacher can help us come up with many possible solutions to later weigh or it might tell us intuitively what we *know* is the right answer. For instance, the child might know that she should call her friend right now and apologize. That may be all she needs to do to solve that particular problem.

6. *Let go and put subconscious to work.* This step is especially important for complex problems. It's aptly called the "do nothing" stage. During this stage, we let the facts and ideas simmer in our mind but do not consciously think about the problem. The creative power of the subconscious mind won't start to work on a task until the conscious mind stops wrestling with it. Some think of this as getting ourselves out of the way of Divine illumination. Whether from the subconscious or from a higher source, the perfect solution often presents itself during this stage.

7. *Select the best solution.* This can be done by measuring all possible outcomes against the universal principles and the five values of Love, Truth, Peace, Right Action, and Nonviolence. For example, is the means toward the solution consistent with the outcome you want?

Another way of arriving at the best solution is to ask for guidance and go within and listen. Then measure any answer against the above criteria.

Once a child has the seven steps clearly in mind and understands the reasons for each of them, he has a valuable tool for meeting future challenges. Even when he can't recall the steps consciously, his subconscious can tune into them in times of need. For additional information on problem solving with children, see *Kids Can Cooperate: A Practical Guide to Teaching Problem Solving* by Elizabeth Crary.[11]

Such an approach to problems can serve the children well during these times of planetary change. Help them understand that these changes are necessary, good, and in no way punitive. Such changes will be challenging, but with a shift in perception, our children will be able to avoid the contagion of fear.

Energy

Since we choose our thoughts, we'll be less likely to succumb to thoughts of fear if we're aware of what it does to our energy. Think of energy as being on a vibrational scale. At the top of the scale is the high joy vibration, where we feel oneness with everyone: we express and draw to us total, unconditional love. Through the power of unconditional love, we see that there is nothing to fear. At the bottom of the scale are low vibrations of fear, doubt, and the like, where we feel separate—apart—from others. Since, through the Law of Magnetism, like attracts like, when we choose these low vibration emotions, we attract other things that are also at a low vibration, such as troubles, mishaps, or accidents.

Stuart Wilde says, "Your life unfolds to the dictates of energy. Nothing less, nothing more."[12] As we grow in love of self and others, we raise our vibrations and so are led away from negative events.

As Wilde explains it, there are millions and millions of probability patterns or events that have the same vibrational frequency. Positive events have a higher frequency than negative ones, and we are constantly moving up and down within a wave band of these vibrations. He gives the example of a family picnic that starts out in a joyous high vibration and ends up in quarreling. If the family drives home in that low vibration, they might attract a car accident or other mishap, because the two energies would be compatible. I remember many years ago having an emotional outburst and then a few minutes later falling down a flight of stairs and breaking my wrist. Here was a clear case of compatible negative energies.

Protection

"Once you let your energy drop, your chance of misfortune rises dramatically," observes Wilde. This is why fear has been called our worst enemy and why we want to offer our children some means of protection from it. On the highest level, we do this by knowing that there is nothing in the Universe to fear. We don't acknowledge evil or duality or separation from others.

When we know we are one with everyone and everything, what is there to protect against. What is there to fear?

Since many of us or our children may not yet be at that level, we may want to consider the following ideas. Having a prayer statement to use whenever we get into a situation can help us function on the inner levels while we deal with outer activity. "There is only God" is often used in this way, as is "I am Light." In my son's younger days, I often sent him out the door each morning by reminding him to say, "Only good goes from me, only good comes to me," on his way to school. I loved it when one morning he popped his head back in the door and said, "I'm changing it to 'Only God goes from me, and only God comes to me.'" Some Bible verses, such as the Twenty-third Psalm, are used in this way. A popular prayer for protection is based on a poem by James Dillet Freeman:

> The light of God surrounds me;
> The love of God enfolds me;
> The power of God protects me;
> The presence of God watches over us;
> Wherever I am, God is!

Many parents teach their children to protect themselves with white light. Youngsters wrap it around themselves in spirals or put themselves in a tube of white light that connects them to the Source. They may also see themselves as centers of white light, radiating light to all those around them.

A most valuable form of protection is "the call," a request or a command directly between a person and a higher source, often used in emergencies. "The call compels the answer." Children need to know that they can call upon the Source in many forms and names: their guardian angel, a spirit guide, Holy Spirit, Jesus, the Divine Mother, and the saints and masters they know. Young children usually want the Creator in form, and they especially relate to a guardian angel. Let them know that their guardian angel is with them at all times and can be called upon.

Remind children often that their real parent is Mother-Father God. It is a source of comfort and joy for children to know that they have a Divine Parent to call upon when their earthly parents are not available. They need to know that their earthly family is not their only source of love, that God is the primary source of love, and that they are loved deeply by aspects of God's Love as well, such as angels, spirit guides, and many others. Help them to realize that they are not just a small, isolated person but a part of Oneness. They need to know that help is always there.

Joyce Vissell, co-author of *Models of Love*,[13] has many inspiring things to say on this subject. She relates her own amazing story of protection as a young college student; she also tells of two instances when her young daughter was lost (in a department store and in the woods) and received immediate Divine help—when she remembered to ask for it. There are many such true stories. If you share them with children, they will surely come to mind when your children most need them.

Polly Berends, who speaks so clearly on the subject, says the conviction we seek to reinforce in the child is that "she is a fully equipped consciousness, not dependent upon us—that she can and will be able to see her way through anything because God will always be with her to give her the needed idea at the needed moment."[14]

So let's assure our children that they'll know what they need to know, when they need to know it.

Manifestation

In times of change, loss, or scarcity, inner joy would surely be released if children knew they can create—and are now creating—by their thoughts and feelings, by their picturing, and by their words. This is happening all the time. If we can convince the young child of the power of words combined with feeling, we will see amazing instant manifestations. A dramatic example of this is quoted from *Magical Child*.

> A man came to a magical child seminar as the result of an experience that had unnerved him and threatened his academic and rational world view. His eight-year-old son was whittling with a knife, slipped and severed the arteries of his left wrist. Following an instant's panic at the sight of the spurting blood, the father, as if in a dream, seized his screaming son's face, looked into his eyes, and commanded, "Son, let's stop that blood." The screaming stopped, the boy beamed back, said, "Okay," and together they stared at the gushing blood and shouted, "Blood, you stop that." And the blood stopped. In a short time, the wound healed . . . . [15]

As the vibration on the planet accelerates, we'll see that manifestation is speeding up, also. It is our fear and doubts that limit our ability to manifest deliberately. Those children who are encouraged to love themselves and to believe in themselves will become one with the manifestation process. Since what they focus on will expand, we can encourage them to focus daily on Joy.

Serving

Give children constructive activities that they can do to help this world. Individuals, countries, and Mother Earth need healing and uplifting. Children are natural healers and peacemakers. For an interesting perspective on this, see the chapter, "The Child As Healer," in *The Radiant Child*.[16]

Selfless service is definitely a path to joy. During times of change, or any time, children can be given many important ways of serving. Let them know that when they feel depressed they can release energies of joy by performing a good deed with no expectation of return. A list of suggested ways to serve is given in Chapter 12 of this book ("The Joy of Serving"). Children can render valuable service anytime and anywhere by "holding an idea in mind." They can understand that it is ideas that run the world. They can learn that "thoughts held in mind produce after their kind." Holding ideas of the best possible outcome is really important work for youngsters—for *all* of us. The thoughts we want to hold are, of course, those that are in alignment with universal principles. These principles must be anchored in our thinking so that the gales of mass thinking do not blow them out of our awareness.

A visual analogy can illustrate this for youngsters: a fan represents gusts of mass-consciousness thinking; small pieces of paper represent our thoughts or ideas; rocks are used to represent the convictions we have. Get the child to offer some ideas she firmly knows are true about herself and the way the world works. Put rocks on these and turn on the fan to represent the gales of mass thinking that are constantly sweeping through our thought atmosphere. Point out that those universal principles that are anchored in their belief system will stay with them and help them through troubled times.

You and the children could offer many examples of mass-consciousness ideas—and the ideas the children might want to hold in mind to counteract them. Older children might want to make a list of these. A common example is that mass-consciousness believes there is a flu season. Children can hold in mind that there is no such thing—that in reality sickness and disease do not exist. Help them to apply this principle to all suggestions of scarcity, lack, and limitation. Anything temporal or impermanent is not of the Source, and therefore, not real.

As Patent says, "Our function is to keep reminding ourselves of the difference between what is real in our lives and what is an illusion. . . . The only *real* feeling we ever have is joy."[17]

"Joy is Changelessness—in Change"[18]

Probably the most important lesson we can offer our children is an awareness of the unchangeable—the permanent. We won't get so caught up in the changes of the appearance world if we know that *it* is not reality. To quote Saraydarian: "The awareness of permanency is a great source of joy. It is the impermanence of things that makes our joy disappear. Impermanent life, impermanent body and health, impermanent conditions, possessions, money, friends, wife and husband. Once the Permanent One is found through expansion of consciousness, joy replaces fear."[19]

Our children need to know that there are some things they can count on not changing: the power of Love, the universal laws or principles, the center of Peace and Joy within, and the security that is found only in the Spirit and not from anything in the outer world.

When children are in touch with the changeless, they can become that "center of peace within chaos." They can be the eye of the hurricane, no matter how much confusion is going on around them. Bartholomew tells us that this kind of peace needs to be built daily. It just doesn't come on command. He would have us practice feeling peace in our heart because "the heart center is where all fear fades."[20]

There is an influx of information coming to the planet at this time to help humanity with the changes it will likely face. I have read much about it and there seems to be one common message throughout: keep tuned in daily to your higher self. I quote one representative source:

> Since the only survival skill you can count on is trust in God and in the mighty realms of light that are a part of God's helping team at this time, use it! "Tune in" each day, through inner quietude or meditation. . . . Who but this omnipotent source and its creations can broadcast helpful information or advice to you on the planet? Who else knows the path and soul contract of each being on earth?[21]

Another book sums up the message to parents and teachers in this way:

> Teach your children to love and trust God . . . and not to judge themselves and others. Then they will be safe during whatever experience arises, as will you. Loving, focused thoughts will carry you through any difficulty.[22]

It seems that with this kind of Divine Help, change should not create resistance or fear in us. If we're living according to principle, we can relax and choose joy, our natural state. In fact, the wisdom teachings tell us that "as difficulties increase, joy supplies more energy to overcome them. You even digest your food better when you are joyful."[23] It seems that the energy of the higher spheres cannot be assimilated without joy.

I find it expands my joy to read what many great spiritual leaders say the Earth will be like after the expected changes. Can you picture the joy that is being projected for our new radiant earth:

> In this upcoming, radiant time, existence will be harmonious. All lifeforms of mineral, plant, animal, and human will be cooperating with each other. There will be a complete absence of destructiveness in nature and human relationships, resulting in a blissful existence.
>
> The quality of life will increase as peace reigns at the focal point for all that occurs. Truly, the human spirit will soar to the highest level possible while still living in a physical body, and creativity will peak higher than ever.
>
> You will still have free will about everything except violence and negative actions. Harmfulness in thought will end

and caring will take its place. Count upon this change for that is why the Time of Awakening, followed by the Time of Survival, and then the Time of Radiance, is here.[24]

Just imagine living in this Golden Age on Earth! Let's accept the New with Joy and Wonder and Trust and allow our children to lead us. Many of them have come in for this time of transition and transformation. They are our teachers of joy!

A Reminder

Life as it is, is perfect.
Children as they are, are perfect,
and we are all children for all time.
RON SMOTHERMAN, *Play Ball*

And what is perfection? It is the joy that is the most fundamental reality of the Universe, and of ourselves as parts of it. This joy recognizes our wholeness, our completeness, our unity with the Source.

There is an analogy that I love from Robert Ellwood.[1] Real joy is like the sun, which shines powerfully all the time, and our other feelings—even happiness—are like clouds that may obscure it. Although clouds can hide the sun, they are hardly its equal. Like our ordinary feelings, they are fleeting mists, they come and go.

Remember that to release children's joy is more important than anything you do in the world, because joy will determine their success in life, their state of health, and their relationships with others. It will open their hearts and minds and will serve as a protection for them. Releasing joy will increase their vibration, thus raising them into the higher dimensions. They will help usher in the Age of Joy, the Golden Age.

Appendix

Because the joyful child is a global child, indeed, a cosmic child, his awareness must go beyond national boundaries to encompass our planet and even our universe. He needs to know how he is interconnected with everyone and everything. Dr. Robert Muller's curriculum directly addresses that need and is intended to underlie all grades, levels, and forms of education—including adult education. The following copyright-free material has been extracted from a paper by Dr. Muller:

A WORLD CORE CURRICULUM

by Dr. Robert Muller
Chancellor of University of Peace – Costa Rica
Former Assistant Secretary-General, United Nations

As I do in the United Nations, where all human knowledge, concerns, efforts, and aspirations converge, I would organize the fundamental lifelong objectives of education around four categories:

     I.   Our planetary home and place in the Universe
     II. The human family
     III. Our place in time
     IV. The miracle of individual human life

    All existing humanistic, religious, national, ideological or other educational systems can be adapted to this core curriculum. At the end of each section, education experts could ask themselves the question: "How can my philosophy, nation, religion, ideology, or educational system contribute to the attainment and perfection of this world curriculum?" and write the answers.

Summary of the World Core Curriculum

I.   OUR PLANETARY HOME AND PLACE IN THE UNIVERSE
     The infinitely large: the universe, the stars, and outer space

Our relations with the sun
The Earth's climate
The atmosphere
The biosphere
The seas and oceans
The polar caps
The Earth's land masses
The Earth's arable lands
The deserts
The mountains
The Earth's water
Plant life
Animal life
Human life
The Earth's energy
The Earth's crust and depths
The Earth's minerals
The infinitely small: microbiology, genetics, chemistry and nuclear physics

II. OUR HUMAN FAMILY
  A. Quantitative characteristics
    1. The total world population and its changes
    2. Human geography and migrations
    3. Human longevity
    4. Races
    5. Sexes
    6. Children
    7. Youth
    8. Adults
    9. The elderly
    10. The handicapped
  B. Qualitative characteristics
    1. Our levels of nutrition
    2. Our levels of health
    3. Our standards of life (rich and poor)
    4. Our skills and employment
    5. Our levels of education
    6. Our moral levels
    7. Our spiritual levels
  C. Human groupings
    1. The family
    2. Human settlements
    3. Professions
    4. Corporations
    5. Institutions
    6. Nations
    7. Federations, regional organizations
    8. Religions
    9. Transnational networks
    10. World organizations

III. OUR PLACE IN TIME

The universe:	past	present	future
Our sun	"	"	"
Our globe	"	"	"
Our climate	"	"	"
Our biosphere, down to the cell, genes, and the atom	"	"	"
The human family	"	"	"
Our age composition	"	"	"
Levels of health	"	"	"
Standards of living	"	"	"
Nations, religions, world organizations, etc., down to individual	"	"	"

IV. THE MIRACLE OF INDIVIDUAL LIFE

A. Good physical lives
   1. Knowledge and care of the body
   2. Teaching to see, to hear, to observe, to create, to do, to use well all our senses and physical capacities
B. Good mental lives
   1. Knowledge
   2. Teaching to question, to think, to analyze, to synthesize, to conclude, to communicate
   3. Teaching to focus from the infinitely large to the infinitely small, from the distant past to the present and future
C. Good moral lives
   1. Teaching to love
   2. Teaching truth, understanding, humility, liberty, reverence for life, compassion, altruism
D. Good spiritual lives
   1. Spiritual exercises of interiority, meditation, prayer, and communion with the universe and eternity or God

In his New Genesis: Shaping a Global Spirituality, *Dr. Muller comments at length on the four categories of his curriculum. Here is much of what he has to say about Category IV:*

IV. THE MIRACLE OF INDIVIDUAL LIFE

It is becoming increasingly clear that in this vast evolutionary quantum change the individual remains the alpha and the omega of all our efforts. Individual human life is the highest form of universal consciousness on our planet. Institutions, concepts, factories, systems, states, ideologies, theories have no consciousness. They are all servants, instruments, means for better lives and the increase of individual human consciousness. We are faced today with the full-fledged centrality, dignity, miracle, sanctity, or divinity of individual human life, irrespective of race, sex, status, age, nation, physical or mental capacity. . . .

An immense task and responsibility thus behooves all teachers and educators of this planet: it is no less than to contribute to the survival and good management of our planetary home and species, to our further common ascent into a universal, interdependent, peaceful civilization, while ensuring the knowledge, skills and fulfillment of the flow of humans going through the Earth's schools. The pressures for a proper universal, global education are being felt everywhere, from the United Nations and multinational business to the local communities and individuals. It is a potent, invaluable trend of cardinal importance to our survival and future evolution. A world core curriculum might seem utopian today. By the end of the year 2000 it will be a down-to-earth, daily reality in all the schools of the world.

Elsewhere, Dr. Muller explains this "task and responsibility":

Education of the newcomers is basically the teaching of the art of living and of human fulfillment within the immense knowledge of space and time acquired by humanity. It is to make each child feel like a king in the universe, an expanded being aggrandized by the vastness of our knowledge, which now reaches far into the infinitely large and the infinitely small, the distant past and the future. It is to make him feel proud to be a member of a transformed species whose eyesight, hearing, hands, legs, brain and heart have been multiplied a thousand times. Like the early Christians, the task is to help to maturity beings who exude a resplendent joy of living, who are witnesses to the beauty and majesty of creation. Knowledge, peace, happiness, goodness, love and meaningful lives—these must be the objectives of education. . . .

Global education must prepare our children for the coming of an interdependent, safe, prosperous, friendly, loving, happy planetary age as has been heralded by all great prophets. The real, the great period of human fulfillment on planet Earth is only now to begin.

"The World Core Curriculum in the Robert Muller School" and autographed copies of Dr. Muller's books are available from World Happiness and Cooperation, P.O. Box 7170, Ardsley-on-Hudson, NY 10503.

References and Resources

Reference notes and bibliography are combined below. Included, as well, are addresses not easily accessible elsewhere. When a reference says see Chapter——, no.——, it refers to a chapter and number in this section.

About the Book

1. Schuller, Robert H. *Daily Power Thoughts*. (Eugene, OR: Harvest House, 1975.)

Chapter 1: A Look at Joy

1. Saraydarian, Torkom. *Joy and Healing*. (Sedona, AZ: The Aquarian Educational Group, 1987.) He has a great many unique books. Obtain order form/price list by writing: P.O. Box 267, Sedona, AZ 86336; or calling: (602) 282-2655.
2. Ibid.
3. Ibid.
4. Buscaglia, Leo. *Bus 9 to Paradise: A Loving Voyage*. (Thorofare, NJ: Slack, 1986.)
5. Porter, Grady C. *Conversations with JC*. (Piermont, NY: High View Publishing, 1985.)
6. Saraydarian. *Joy and Healing*. See no. 1 above.
7. Blanding, Don. *Joy Is an Inside Job*. (New York: Dodd, Mead, 1953.)
8. Patent, Arnold M. *You Can Have It All*. (1991.) Celebration Publishing, Sylva, NC. His seminar tapes are also available from this source.

Chapter 2: Foundations of Joy

1. Barksdale, Lilburn. *Building Self-Esteem*. (1974.) The Barksdale Foundation, P.O. Box 187, Idyllwild, CA 92349. (Write for free catalogue.)

2. Ganz and Harmon. *Feeling Good* and *A Program in Stress Management*. (Two cassettes and workbook, 1986.) 2675 W. Hwy 89A, Ste. 1098, Sedona, AZ 86336.
3. Barksdale. *Building Self-Esteem*. See no. 1 above.
4. *The Spiritual Hunger of the Modern Child*. (Charles Town, WV: Claymont Publications, 1984.)
5. Sai Baba, Sathya. *Sathya Sai Speaks*. Vol 7. 153. (Santa Ana, CA: Sri Sathya Sai Education Foundation.) Available from Sathya Sai Book Center, P.O. Box 278, Tustin, CA 92681; (714) 669-0522.
6. Bennett, William. Speech given at forum on values in education. (New York: Manhattan Institute.)
7. Education in Human Values Foundation. Direct inquiries to: Michael Goldstein, M.D., Chairman, 3070 Roycove, Covina, CA 91724.
8. Berends, Polly Berrien. *Whole Child–Whole Parent*. (New York: Harper & Row, 1975.)
9. Pearce, Joseph. *Magical Child*. (New York: Bantam Books, 1980.)
10. Boone, J. Allen. *Kinship with All Life*. (New York: Harper & Row, 1954.)
11. Jenkins, Peggy D. *A Child of God: Activities for Teaching Spiritual Values to Children of All Ages*. (Englewood Cliffs, NJ: Prentice-Hall, 1984.)
12. Vissell, Barry and Joyce. *Models of Love: The Parent-Child Journey*. (Aptos, CA: Ramira Publishing, 1986.)
13. Patent, Arnold. *You Can Have It All*. See Chapter 1, no. 8.
14. Berends. *Whole Child–Whole Parent*. See no. 8 above.
15. Bartholomew. *I Come as a Brother*. (Taos, NM: High Mesa Press, 1986.)
16. Roman, Sanaya. *Living With Joy*. (Tiburon, CA: H.J. Kramer, Publishers, 1986.)
17. Foundation for Inner Peace. *A Course in Miracles*. (1975.) Foundation address: P.O. Box 635, Tiburon, CA 94920.
18. Bartholomew. *I Come as a Brother*. See no. 15 above.
19. Dyer, Dr. Wayne W. *What Do You Really Want for Your Children?* (New York: Avon Books and William Morrow, 1985.)
20. Vivekananda, Swami. *Education*. (Coimbatore, India: Sri Ramakrishna Mission Vidyalaya, 1967.)
21. Berends. *Whole Child–Whole Parent*. See no. 8 above.
22. Jampolsky, Gerald G., M.D. *Love Is Letting Go of Fear*. (Berkeley, CA: Celestial Arts, 1979.)
23. Berkus, Rusty. *Life is a Gift*. (Encino, CA: Red Rose Press, 1982.)

OTHER RESOURCES

Armstrong, Thomas, Ph.D. *Awakening Your Child's Natural Genius* and *In Their Own Way: Discovering and Encouraging Your Child's Personal Learning Style*. (Los Angeles: Jeremy P. Tarcher, Inc., 1991.)

Branden, Nathaniel. *How to Raise Your Self-Esteem*. (New York: Bantam Books, 1987.) Also: *Experience High Self-Esteem*. (New York: Simon & Schuster, 1988.)

Briggs, Dorothy Corkille. *Your Child's Self-Esteem: The Key To His Life*. (Garden City, NY: Doubleday, 1970.) Also: *Celebrate Yourself: Making Life Work For You*.

Canfield, Jack, and Wells, Harold C. *100 Ways to Enhance Self-Concept in the Classroom: A Handbook for Teachers and Parents*. (Englewood Cliffs, NJ: Prentice-Hall, 1976.)

Chinmoy, Sri. *A Child's Heart and a Child's Dreams: A Guide for Parents and Children*. (Jamaica, NY: AVM Publishing Co., 1986.)

Clarke, Jean Illsley. *Self-Esteem: A Family Affair*. (Minneapolis, MN: Winston Press, 1978.) Also: *Self-Esteem: A Family Affair Leader Guide*. (New York: Harper & Row, 1981.)

Clarke has also coauthored a *Help! For Parents* series and an affirmations workbook. Order from Daisy Press, 16535 9th Avenue N., Plymouth, MN 55447.

Crary, Elizabeth. *Kids Can Cooperate: A Practical Guide to Teaching Problem Solving.* (Seattle, WA: Parenting Press, 1979.) For order form write: P.O. Box 15163, Seattle, WA 98115.

Harmon, Ed, and Jarmin, Marge. *Taking Active Charge of Your Life.* (Barksdale Foundation, 1985.) For further information on this unique program, see Chapter 9, no. 1.

Johnson, Spencer, M.D. *The One-Minute Mother: The Quickest Way for You to Help Your Children Learn to Like Themselves and Want to Behave Themselves.* (New York: William Morrow, 1983.) Also recommended: *The One-Minute Father.* (New York: William Morrow, 1983.)

Shiff, Eileen, ed. *Experts Advise Parents: A Guide to Raising Loving Responsible Children.* (New York: Delacorte Press, 1987.)

Chapter 3: Who is Teaching Whom and How?

1. Pearce, J.C. A 1986 talk in Los Angeles to the Council for Excellence Through Self-Esteem. Pearce is author of two recommended books: *Magical Child,* and *Magical Child Matures.* (Both published by Bantam Books.)
2. Berends. *Whole Child–Whole Parent.* See Chapter 2, no. 8.
3. Partlow, Frances. *Training of Children in the New Thought.* (New York: Sydney Flower, 1903.)
4. Pearce. *Magical Child.* See no. 2 above.
5. Keyes, Ken, Jr. *The Hundredth Monkey.* (Coos Bay, OR: Vision Books, 1983.)
6. Smotherman, Dr. Ron. *Play Ball: The Miracle of Children.* (1983). Context Publishers, P.O. Box 2909, Rohnert Park, CA 94928.
7. Martin, Bette. *The Children's Material* (1978). Miracle Experiences and You Publishing, P.O. Box 64146, Tucson, AZ 85740–1146.
8. Gibran, Kahlil. *The Prophet.* (New York: Alfred A. Knopf, 1968.)
9. Welter, Paul, Ed.D. *Learning from Children.* P.O. Box 235, Kearney, NE 68848.
10. Vivekananda. *Education.* See Chapter 2, no. 20.
11. Martin. *The Children's Material.* See no. 7 above.
12. Deranja, Michael Nitai. *The Art of Joyful Education.* (Nevada City, CA: Ananda Schools, 1980.)
13. Moorman, Chick. *Talk Sense to Yourself: The Language of Personal Power.* (Portage, MI: Personal Power Press, 1985.)
14. Quoted in Vissell. *Models of Love.* See Chapter 2, no. 12.
15. Dyer. *What Do You Really Want for Your Children?* See Chapter 2, no. 19.
16. Mander, Jerry. *Four Arguments for the Elimination of Television.* (New York: William Morrow, 1978.)
17. Vissell. *Models of Love.* See Chapter 2, no. 12.
18. *Spirit Speaks.* "Kids 'n Karma." (Issue 8.) P.O. Box 84304, Los Angeles, CA 90073. Good treatment of heavy subjects such as defective children, incest, child abuse, drugs, addictions.
19. Essene, Virginia. *New Teachings for an Awakening Humanity.* (1986.) S.E.E. Publishing Company, 1556 Halford Ave. #288, Santa Clara, CA 95051.
20. Chinmoy. *A Guide for Parents and Children.* See Chapter 2, Other Resources.
21. Hart, Dr. Louise. *The Winning Family: Increasing Self-Esteem in Your Children and Yourself.* (New York: Dodd, Mead, 1987.) See especially her chapters on creativity and games.

OTHER RESOURCES

Armstrong, Thomas. *The Radiant Child.* (Wheaton, IL: Theosophical Publishing House, 1985.) Appendix B has an annotated bibliography of books concerning the child's higher nature; Appendix C, an annotated list of transpersonal child studies.

Carey, Ken. *Notes to My Children: A Simplified Metaphysics.* (Kansas City, MO: Uni-Sun, 1984.)

Carrairo, Mary E. *Modern Education: One Size Fits All.* (South Hadley, MA: Bergin & Garvey Publishers, 1988.)

Cook, M.B./Hilarion. *Child Light: Parenting for the New Age.* (Ontario, Canada: Marcus Books, 1987.)

Diamond, Carlin. *Love It, Don't Label It!* (1985.) Fifth Wave Press, 22 Salvador Way, San Rafael, CA 94903.

Eyre, Linda and Richard. *Teaching Children Joy.* (Salt Lake City, UT: Shadow Mountain, 1984.) Practical suggestions and activities for preschoolers.

Jafolla, Mary-Alice. *The Simple Truth.* (Unity Village, MO: Unity School of Christianity, 1982.)

Milicevic, Barbara. *Your Spiritual Child.* (Marina del Rey, CA: DeVorss, 1984.)

Nelson, Jane. *Positive Discipline.* (New York: Ballantine Books, 1981.) She has also co-authored two wonderful books with H. Stephen Glenn: *Raising Children for Success* and *Raising Self-Reliant Children in a Self-Indulgent World.* (Both published by Sunrise Press, Fair Oaks, CA.) For order form write: Sunrise Press, 4984 Arboleda Dr., Fair Oaks, CA 95628.

Richards, M.C. *Toward Wholeness: Rudolf Steiner Education in America.* (Middletown, CT: Wesleyan University Press, 1980.)

Winn, Marie. *Unplugging the Plug-in Drug.* (New York: Penguin Books, 1987.)

Chapter 4: Why They Do What They Do

1. Keirsey, David, and Bates, Marilyn. *Please Understand Me: Character and Temperament Types.* (Del Mar, CA: Prometheus Nemesis Books, 1978.)
2. Butler, Kathleen A., Ph.D. *Learning and Teaching Style in Theory and Practice.* (Maynard, MA: Gabriel Systems, 1986.)
3. Geier, Dr. John and Downey, Dorothy E. The Child's Profile and *The Child's Library of Classical Profile Patterns,* the set of interpretation guides for the 15 Profile Patterns. I highly recommend that parents or teachers administer the Personal Profile system on themselves before administering the Child's Profile, so as to understand their own style in relation to the child's style. These materials can be ordered through Joyful Child Inc., P.O. Box 5506, Scottsdale, AZ, 85261; (602) 951-4111.
4. Butler, Kathleen A. "Stressing Style." In *Challenge: Reaching and Teaching the Gifted Child.* (Carthage, IL: Good Apple, 1984.)
5. Ibid.
6. Keirsey and Bates. *Please Understand Me.* See no. 1 above.
7. Butler. "Stressing Style." See no. 4 above.
8. Cathcart, Jim, C.S.P. and Alessandra, Anthony, Ph.D. *Relationship Strategies: How to Deal*

with the Differences in People. An educational kit containing six audio cassettes and a workbook. A valuable tool for understanding behavior styles. Can be obtained from Abbott International. See address in no. 2 above.

OTHER RESOURCES

The first five books are based on the work of Rudolf Steiner.

Davy, Gudrun, and Voors, Bons. *Lifeways: Working with Family Questions.* (Gloucestershire, U.K.: Hawthorn Press, 1983.)

Lissau, Magda. *The Temperaments and the Arts.* (Chicago, IL: Private Publication, 1983.)

Steiner, Rudolf. *The Four Temperaments.* (New York: Anthroposophic Press, 1971.)

Spock, Marjorie. *Teaching as a Lively Art.* (Spring Valley, NY: Anthroposophic Press, 1978.) One chapter on temperaments.

Querido, Rene M. *Creativity in Education: The Waldorf Approach.* (San Francisco, CA: H.S. Dakin, 1984.) One chapter on temperaments.

La Haye, Beverly. *How to Develop Your Child's Temperament.* (Eugene, OR: Harvest House, 1977.)

Littauer, Florence. *Personality Plus: How to Understand Yourself.* (Old Tappan, NJ: Fleming H. Revell, 1983.)

Chapter 5: The Joy of Listening Within

1. Ellwood, Robert. *Finding Deep Joy.* (Wheaton, IL: Theosophical Publishing House, 1984.)
2. Goldsmith, Joel S. *The Art of Meditation.* (New York: Harper & Row, 1956.)
3. Partlow. *Training of Children in the New Thought.* See Chapter 3, no. 3.
4. Chinmoy. See Chapter 2, Other Resources.
5. Rozman, Deborah, Ph.D. *Meditating with Children.* (Boulder Creek, CA: University of the Trees Press, 1983.) Also: *Meditation for Children.* (Milbrae, CA: Celestial Arts, 1976.)
6. Hendricks, Gay, and Roberts, Thomas B. *The Second Centering Book.* (Englewood Cliffs, NJ: Prentice-Hall, 1977.) Also: *The Family Centering Book.* (Prentice-Hall, 1979.)
7. Burleigh, Walter and Marta. *Balancing Program.* P.O. Box 421, Cortaro, AZ 85652.
8. Ouseley, S.G.J. *Color Meditations; with Guide to Color-Healing.* (Portsmouth, England: Grosvenor Press, 1981.)
9. Anderson, Mary. *Colour Healing.* (Wellingborough, U.K.: The Aquarian Press, 1979.)
10. Foundation for Inner Peace. *A Course in Miracles.* See Chapter 2, no. 17.
11. Coit, Lee. *Listening: How to Increase Awareness of Your Inner Guide.* (Wildomar, CA: The Breezes of Joy Foundation, 1985.)
12. Thurston, Mark. *The Inner Power of Silence.* (Virginia Beach, VA: Inner Vision, 1986.)
13. Scarantino, Barbara Anne. *Music Power: Creative Living Through the Joys of Music.* (New York: Dodd, Mead, 1987.)
14. Herzog, Stephanie. *Joy in the Classroom.* (Boulder Creek, CA: University of the Trees Press, 1982.)
15. Goelitz, Jeffrey. *The Ultimate Kid.* (Boulder Creek, CA: University of the Trees Press, 1986.)
16. Hill, Christopher, Ph.D., and Rozman, Deborah, Ph.D. *Exploring Inner Space.* (Boulder Creek, CA: University of The Trees Press, 1978.) Games—preschool through adult.
17. Diamond. *Love It, Don't Label It!* See Chapter 3, Other Resources. I particularly recom-

mend her twelve steps for weekly family meetings and the philosophy that makes them work.
18. Addington, Jack and Cornelia. *The Joy of Meditation.* (Marina del Rey, CA: De Vorss & Co., 1979.)

Chapter 6: Joyous Self-Talk

1. Helmstetter, Shad, Ph.D. *What to Say When You Talk to Yourself.* (New York: Pocket Books, by arrangement with Grindle Press, 1986.)
2. Moorman. *Talk Sense to Yourself: The Language of Personal Power.* See Chapter 3, no. 13.
3. Ganz and Harmon. *Feeling Good: A Program in Stress Management.* See Chapter 2, no. 2.
4. Ibid.
5. Ibid.
6. Ibid.
7. Moorman. *Talk Sense to Yourself.* See no. 2 above.
8. Helmstetter. *What to Say When You Talk to Yourself.* See no. 1 above. See also Helmstetter. *Predictive Parenting: What to Say When You Talk to Your Kids.* (New York: Pocket Books, 1989.)

Chapter 7: The Power of Songs and Quotes

1. Jenkins. *A Child of God.* See Chapter 2, no. 1.
2. Moshier, Carmen. *Say and Sing Your Way to Successful Living! TODAY.* (Dallas, TX: The Today Church, 1974.)
3. King, Charles. *The Charles King Songbook.* Available from Charles E. King, Rt. 3, Box 600, Walla Walla, WA 99362; (509) 525-3555.
4. Moshier, Carmen. Cassettes: *Jump For Joy!, Red Carpet World,* etc. To order or obtain price list write to: Carmen's Music, 3709 W. Washington Street, Las Vegas, NV 89107; (702) 878-9265.
5. Meyer, Warren. *Sing—Be Happy.* (1976.) Order from Warren Meyer, Unity Church, 351 38th St., Richmond, CA 94804; (415) 235-0336.
6. Berends. *Whole Child–Whole Parent.* See Chapter 2, no. 8.
7. Scarantino. *Music Power.* See Chapter 5, no. 13.
8. Lovejoy, Rosie. Angelight Music, P.O. Box 420, Mt. Shasta, CA 96067; (916) 926-2937.
9. Timmaris and Diane. *For a Child's Heart.* Mirabi Music, P.O. Box 1013, Encinitas, CA 92024.
10. *The Joy of Music: A Collection of New Children's Music.* From Joy Sounds, P.O. Box 271585, Houston, TX 77277-1585.
11. Lovable Creature Music, 105 King St. Ithaca, NY 14850 (607) 273-4175.
12. Angel Cards from Findhorn. May be ordered through Miracles Contact Center, 3124 Gurney Avenue, St. Louis, MO 63116.
13. Saraydarian. *Joy and Healing.* See Chapter 1, no. 1.
14. Foundation For Inner Peace. *A Course in Miracles.* See Chapter 2, no. 17.
15. Roman. *Living with Joy.* See Chapter 2, no. 16.
16. Patent. *You Can Have It All.* See Chapter 1, no. 8.

Chapter 8: The Joy of Stories and Storytelling

1. Geisler, Harlynne, Storyteller. 4182-J, Mount Alifan Place, San Diego, CA 92111. Send $3.00 to receive Information Packet that includes 51 storytelling activities and 8 bibliography sheets.
2. Brown, Jeanette Perkins. *The Storyteller in Religious Education.* (Boston, MA: The Pilgrim Press, 1951.)
3. Davy, Gudrun, and Voors, Bons. *Lifeways: Working with Family Questions.* (Gloucestershire, U.K.: Hawthorn Press, 1983.) From Section III: "Children's Ways: A Key to the Images in Fairy Tales," by Almut Bockemuhl.
4. Bennett. New York speech. See Chapter 2, no. 6.
5. Bettelheim, Bruno. *The Uses of Enchantment.* (New York: Random House, 1976.)
6. Armstrong. *The Radiant Child.* See Chapter 3, Other Resources.
7. The Sathya Sai Book Center of America. For address, see Chapter 2, no. 5.
8. Ananda School. Box 103-B, 14618 Tyler Foote Rd., Nevada City, CA 95959.
9. Vedanta Society Bookshop. 2323 Vallejo St., San Francisco, CA 94123.
10. Eyre. *Teaching Children Joy.* See Chapter 3, Other Resources.
11. Berends. *Whole Child–Whole Parent.* See Chapter 2, no. 8.
12. Weiner, Elizabeth. *Unfinished Stories: Facilitating Decision Making in the Elementary Classroom.* (Washington, D.C.: National Education Association, 1980.) Available for $7.95 from NEA Professional Library, P.O. Box 509, West Haven, CT 06516; (202) 822-7200.
13. Auromere. 1291 Weber St., Pomona, CA 91768. Catalog available.
14. Rosicrucian Fellowship. 2222 Mission Ave., P.O. Box 713, Oceanside, CA 92054.
15. Saunders, Antoinette, Ph.D., and Remsberg, Bonnie. *The Stress-Proof Child: A Loving Parent's Guide.* (New York: Holt, Rinehart and Winston, 1984.)
16. Geisler. See no. 1 above.
17. National Association for the Preservation and Perpetuation of Storytelling (NAPPS). P.O. Box 309, Jonesborough, TN 37659; (615) 753-2171.
18. Freeman, Dennis. P.O. Box 1153, Chino Valley, AZ 86323; Burdulis, Cat. 111 W. Glenrusa Ave., Phoenix, AZ 85015.
19. Wellner, Cathryn. "But the Storyteller Knows Me." *Puget Soundings.* December, 1984, p. 26.
20. Parnes, Sidney J. *Creative Behavior Workbook.* (New York: Charles Scribner's Sons, 1967.)
21. Gilbert, Michael William, Storymaker. P.O. Box 63, Indian Hills, CO 80454.
22. Creative Concepts. P.O. Box 8697, Scottsdale, AZ 85252.
23. Kids On The Block, Inc. 822 Fairfax St., Alexandria, VA 22314; 1-800-836-KIDS. (In VA: (703) 836-0550.)
24. National Association for the Preservation and Perpetuation of Storytelling. See no. 17 above.

Chapter 9: "What's That For?"

1. Harmon, Ed, and Jarmin, Marge. *Taking Active Charge of Your Life.* (Barksdale Foundation, 1985.) A self-esteem course for teens and preteens consisting of a comprehensive Facilitator's Manual and either filmstrips or a video. Also available is a paperback book for youngsters of cartoons and captions from the filmstrips, along with an activity page. For further information, write or call the Barksdale Foundation, P.O. Box 187, Idyllwild, CA 92349; (714) 659-4676.
2. Jenkins. *A Child of God.* See Chapter 2, no. 11.

Chapter 10: The Joy of Creating

1. Torrance, E. Paul. *Guiding Creative Talent*. (Englewood Cliffs, NJ: Prentice-Hall, 1962.)
2. Dyer. *What Do You Really Want for Your Children?* See Chapter 2, no. 19.
3. Patent. *You Can Have It All*. See Chapter 1, no. 8.
4. Dyer. *What Do You Really Want for Your Children?* See Chapter 2, no. 19.
5. Ibid.
6. Torrance, Paul E. *Encouraging Creativity in the Classroom*. (Dubuque, IA: W.C. Brown, 1970.)
7. Jenkins, Peggy D. *Art for the Fun of It*. (New York: Prentice-Hall Press, 1980.)
8. De Mille, Richard. *Put Your Mother on the Ceiling: Children's Imagination Games*. (New York: Viking Press, 1976.)
9. Synectics, Inc. *Making It Strange*. 4 booklets and a teacher's manual. (New York: Harper & Row, 1968.)
10. Turner, Thomas N. *Creative Activities Resource Book for Elementary School Teachers*. (Reston, VA: Reston Publishing Company, 1978.)
11. Jenkins, Peggy Davison. *The Magic of Puppetry: A Guide for Those Working with Young Children*. (Englewood Cliffs, NJ: Prentice-Hall, 1980.)
12. Jenkins. *Art for the Fun of It*. See no. 7 above.
13. Pearce. Los Angeles speech. See Chapter 3, no. 1.
14. Turner. *Creative Activities Resource Book*. See no. 10 above.
15. Ibid.
16. Scarantino. *Music Power*. See Chapter 5, no. 13.
17. Ostrander, Sheila, and Schroeder, Lynn. *Super-Learning*. (New York: Delacorte Press, 1979.)
18. Lingerman, Hal A. *The Healing Energies of Music*. (Wheaton, IL: Theosophical Publishing House, 1983.)
19. Ibid.
20. Lissau. *The Temperaments and the Arts*. (Written for teachers in Waldorf Schools.) See Chapter 4, Other Resources.
21. *Scarf Juggling* comes with three brightly colored scarves. Available from Juggle Boy, Inc., 7506-J Olympic View Dr., Edmonds, WA 98020.
22. Peck, Judith. *Leap to the Sun: Learning Through Dynamic Play*. (Englewood Cliffs, NJ: Prentice-Hall, 1979.)
23. Dr. Marjorie L. Timms is a teacher of drama in nontraditional environments—prison theater, drama and theater for parents of children with disabilities and for deaf students, and Shakespeare in the Park. She is currently Director of Theater Arts for Phoenix Day School for the Deaf. The drama books listed below are a few of the many recommended by Dr. Timms.
24. Spolin, V. *Improvisations for the Theater*. (Evanston, IL: Northwestern University Press, 1972.)
25. Heathcote, D. "Drama as Education." In N. McCaslin, *Children and Drama*. 2nd ed. (New York: Longman, 1975.)
26. Shaftel, F.R., and Shaftel, G. *Role-Playing for Social Values: Decision-Making in the Social Studies*. (Englewood Cliffs, NJ: Prentice-Hall, 1967.)
27. Fox, Jonathan. "Playback Theatre: The Community Sees Itself." In G. Schattner and R. Courtney, eds., *Drama in Therapy*. Vol.II. (New York: Drama Book Specialists, 1981.)

Chapter 11: Fun and Games

1. Buscaglia. *Bus 9 to Paradise: A Loving Voyage*. See Chapter 1, no. 4.
2. Weinstein, Matt, and Goodman, Joel. *Playfair: Everybody's Guide to Noncompetitive Play*. (San Luis Obispo, CA: Impact Publishers, 1980.)
3. Kohn, Alfie. *No Contest: The Case Against Competition*. (Boston, MA: Houghton Mifflin, 1986.)
4. Orlick, Terry. *The Cooperative Sports and Games Book*. (New York: Pantheon Books, 1978.) See also: *The Second Cooperative Sports and Games Book*. (New York: Pantheon Books, 1982.)
5. Weinstein and Goodman. *Playfair*. See no. 2 above.
6. Sobel, Jeff. *Everybody Wins: 393 Noncompetitive Games for Young Children*. (New York: Walker, 1983.)
7. Weinstein and Goodman. *Playfair*. See no. 2 above.
8. Ibid.
9. Orlick. *The Cooperative Sports and Games Book*. See no. 4 above.
10. *Animal Town Game Co. Catalog*. P.O. Box 2002, Santa Barbara, CA 93120; (805) 682-7343.
11. Dyer. *What Do You Really Want for Your Children?* See Chapter 2, no. 19.
12. Herzog. *Joy in the Classroom*. See Chapter 5, no. 14.
13. Rozman. *Meditation for Children*. See Chapter 5, no. 5.
14. Goelitz. *The Ultimate Kid*. See Chapter 5, no. 15.
15. Herzog. *Joy in the Classroom*. See Chapter 5, no. 14.
16. Boone. *Kinship with All Life*. See Chapter 2, no. 10.
17. Eberle, Robert F. *Scamper*. (Buffalo, NY: D.O.K. Publishers, 1971.)
18. Rice, Alice N. 10055 E. Cactus Road, Scottsdale, AZ 85260; (602) 391-2315.
19. Saraydarian. *Joy and Healing*. See Chapter 1, no. 1.
20. Blanding. *Joy Is an Inside Job*. See Chapter 1, no. 7.
21. Ibid.
22. Saraydarian. *Joy and Healing*. See Chapter 1, no. 1.
23. Cornell, Joseph Bharat. *Sharing Nature with Children*. (Nevada City, CA: Ananda Publications, 1979.) Ananda School, P.O. Box 103–B, Nevada City, CA 95959.
24. Ibid.
25. Eyre. *Teaching Children Joy*. See Chapter 3, Other Resources.
26. Shaw, Charles G. *It Looked Like Spilt Milk*. (New York: Harper & Row, 1947.)
27. Bach, Richard. *Illusions*. (New York: Delacorte Press, 1977.)
28. Katz, Adrienna. *Naturewatch: Exploring Nature with Your Children*. (Reading, MA: Addison-Wesley, 1986.)

Chapter 12: Creating A Lesson Plan

1. Thomas, Cindy L. "Life of Enchantment" A story. (1986.) 555 North May, #2, Mesa, AZ 85201.
2. Education in Human Values Program. *Stories for Children—Part II*. See Chapter 2, no. 7.
3. Eyre. *Teaching Children Joy*. See Chapter 3, Other Resources.
4. Education in Human Values Foundation. *Lesson Plans for Education in Human Values, International Edition*. See Chapter 2, no. 7.

Chapter 13: The Joy of Change

1. Saraydarian. *Joy and Healing*. See Chapter 1, no. 1.
2. Patent. *You Can Have It All*. See Chapter 1, no. 8.
3. Saunders and Remsberg. *The Stress-Proof Child: A Loving Parent's Guide*. See Chapter 8, no. 15.
4. Diamond, John. *Your Body Doesn't Lie*. (New York: Warner Brothers, 1980.)
5. Lingerman. *The Healing Energies of Music*. See Chapter 10, no. 18.
6. Scarantino. *Music Power*. See Chapter 5, no. 13.
7. Miracles Contact Center. See Chapter 7, no. 12.
8. "New Dimensions in Sound" catalog. Sounds of Light, Box 835704, Richardson, TX 75083.
9. Smotherman, Ron. *Winning Through Enlightenment*. (1980.) Available from Context Publications, P.O. Box 2909, Rohnert Park, CA 94928-6506; (707) 576-1700. Also available is Smotherman's delightful *Playball! The Miracle of Children*.
10. Crary, Elizabeth. *Children's Problem Solving Series*. (Seattle, WA: Parenting Press, 1983.) See Chapter 2, Other Resources.
11. Crary. *Kids Can Cooperate*. See Chapter 2, Other Resources.
12. Wilde, Stuart. *The Force*. (Taos, NM: Wisdom Books, 1984.)
13. Vissell. *Models of Love: The Parent-Child Journey*. See Chapter 2, no. 12.
14. Berends. *Whole Child–Whole Parent*. See Chapter 2, no. 8.
15. Pearce. *Magical Child*. See Chapter 2, no. 9.
16. Armstrong. *The Radiant Child*. See Chapter 3, Other Resources.
17. Patent. *You Can Have It All*. See Chapter 1, no. 8.
18. Saraydarian. *Joy and Healing*. See Chapter 1, no. 1.
19. Ibid.
20. Bartholomew. *I Come as a Brother*. See Chapter 2, no. 15.
21. Essene, Virginia. *Secret Truths for Teens and Twenties*. (Santa Clara, CA: Spiritual Education Endeavors Publishing Company, 1986.)
22. Essene. *New Teachings for an Awakening Humanity*. See Chapter 3, no. 19.
23. Saraydarian. *Joy and Healing*. See Chapter 1, no. 1.
24. Essene. *Secret Truths for Teens and Twenties*. See Chapter 3, no. 19.

A Reminder

1. Ellwood, Robert. *Finding Deep Joy*. (Wheaton, IL: Theosophical Publishing House, 1984.)

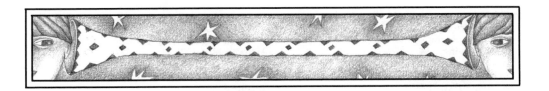

Index

reminders about, 47–48
and self-worth, 44
and stress, 49, 222
summary chart of, 59
Supportive, 45, 46–47, 50, 51, 57–58, 167, 221–22
and tasks versus relationships, 49
teaching children according to, 44
treating others according to, 48–49
Body
control of, in meditation, 68
and self, 11
Boomerang Law. *See* Cause and Effect, Law of
Breathing
and control of emotions, in meditation, 69
and color centering, 73

Cause and Effect, Law of, 17, 19–20, 139
C children. *See* Conscientious behavior style
Centering, 35, 64, 73–74
benefits of, for teachers, 35
color, 73–74
"entering the silence," 64
Change, 219–32
and behavior styles, 220–22
and changelessness, 230–32
modeling gratitude toward, 220
nature of, 219
preparing children for, 219–20
seeing through appearance of, 220
sharing with children, 220
and universal principles, 230
Character, shaping, through stories and storytelling, 126–27
Character education. *See* Values education
Color centering, 73–74
Colors
attributes and powers of, 73–74
guided imagery meditations with, 74
healing and energizing with, 73–74
Concentration, and control of thoughts, in meditation, 69–70
Confidence, language of, 85
Conscientious behavior style, 45, 47, 50, 51, 58, 89, 167, 221–22
basic goal of, 50
and contribution to group, 50
favorite questions of, 47, 56
and influence over others, 50
needs and preferences, 45, 47, 58, 167, 221
and self-criticism, 89
overused behavior of, 51
ways to motivate, 51
Conscientious learning style, 47, 55, 56
favorite questions of, 47, 56
needs and preferences of, 55
Consciousness
benefits of aligning, with universal principles, 17

changing, through affirmations, 86
learning below level of, 28
Consciousness, mass, 38, 230
Consciousness, transmission of, 10, 28–32
in parenting, 10, 28, 32
in meditation, 67
and self-esteem, 10
in teaching, 10, 32, 67
Cooperative games, 179–84
Creative climate, 148–50
nature and benefits of, 148–50
and psychological freedom, 148
and quiet time, 149
and risk-taking, 149
and self-esteem, 149–50
and sensory awareness, 150
Creative drama, 170–75
and "acting," 171
exercises, 174–75
nature and value of, 171
preparing for, and responding to, 172–73
and rehearsing for life, 170
sample activity: The Beautiful Duckling, 173–74
Creative drama exercises, 174–75
in and out of costume, 174–75
"living statues," 174
trading places, 174
Creative imagination, 148, 150
Creative problem solving, 224–27
overcoming fear through, 224–25
overview, 225, 227
steps for, 225–26
Creative writing, activities, 162–65
Creativity, 147–75
aids to, 148
and art, 159
and creative climate, 148–50
and creative drama, 170–73
and creative movement, 169
and music, 166
nature and importance of, 147–48
society and children's, 147

D children. *See* Dominant behavior style
Denial, language of, 85
DISC children. *See* Behavior styles
Doing Kits, 191–93
activities with, 192–93
description of, 191–92
Dominant behavior style, 45–46, 48, 49, 50, 51, 57, 167, 221, 222
basic goal of, 49
contribution to group, 50
favorite questions of, 56
and influence over others, 50
needs and preferences of, 45–46, 48, 49, 57, 167, 221

ABOUT THE AUTHOR

Peggy Joy Jenkins, Ph.D. was the recipient of a 1990 Golden Balloon Award from World Children's Day Foundation, a branch of UNICEF, for the outstanding contribution of this book to the well-being of children. She is the author of *Nurturing Spirituality In Children, A Child of God, The Magic of Puppetry,* and *Art for the Fun of It*—parent/teacher education books highly praised for the quality and variety of the educational activities they describe. *Art for the Fun of It*, a book that encourages creative thinking, has been adopted as a text by many schools and colleges and has over 50,000 copies in print.

Dr. Jenkins is the founder and director of a nonprofit educational service organization called JOYFUL CHILD INC. Its purpose is to offer easy-to-use models that honor and awaken the natural joy, the inner essence, of children and adults. To this end, JOYFUL CHILD INC. offers a quarterly national magazine, *Joyful Child Journal*, symposiums, facilitator training seminars, and parenting classes.

In 1996, the first Joyful Child Family Center, a preschool and training facility opened in Scottsdale, Arizona. Facilitators from around the country are trained and licensed to offer Joyful Child classes to parents, teachers, and caregivers in their home states. This book is the main textbook for these trainings and seminars.

Peggy Joy Jenkins is also a seminar leader in parent/teacher education, and a consultant in the area of behavior/learning styles. Her formal education includes a M.Ed. in Early Childhood Education and a Ph.D. in Adult Education. The mother of two grown children, Dr. Jenkins currently resides in Scottsdale.

For further information you may contact the publisher or:
JOYFUL CHILD, INC.
4920 E. Altadena Avenue
Scottsdale, AZ 85254-4627
TEL (602) 494-3383 • FAX (602) 953-3453
Journal TEL: (602) 953-7567